The Pagan Book of Living and Dying

The Pagan Book of Living and Dying

◆

Practical Rituals, Prayers, Blessings,
and Meditations on Crossing Over

Starhawk, M. Macha NightMare, and The Reclaiming Collective

HarperSanFrancisco
An Imprint of HarperCollinsPublishers

HarperCollins Web Site: http://www.harpercollins.com

HarperCollins,® 🔥 ®, and HarperSanFrancisco™ are trademarks of HarperCollins Publishers Inc.

FIRST EDITION

Designed by Nancy Singer

Library of Congress Cataloging-in-Publication Data
Starhawk.
  The pagan book of living and dying : practical rituals, prayers, blessings, and meditations on crossing over / Starhawk, M. Macha Nightmare, and the Reclaiming Collective. — 1st ed.
    p.   cm.
  Includes bibliographical references.
  ISBN 0–06–251516–0 (pbk.)
  1. Death — Religious aspects — Goddess religion. 2. Death — Religious aspects — Neopaganism. 3. Witchcraft. I. M. Macha Nightmare. II. Reclaiming Collective (San Francisco, Calif.) III. Title.
  BF152.D43S73   1997
  299'.93 — dc21   97–26317
  ISBN 0–06–251516–0   CIP

97 98 99 00 01 ❖/RRD 10 9 8 7 6 5 4 3 2 1

To the memory of Bertha Goldfarb Simos
and Nicholas Pappas

Charge of the Goddess

TRADITIONAL BY DOREEN VALIENTE,
AS ADAPTED BY STARHAWK

Listen to the words of the Great Mother, Who of old was called Artemis, Astarte, Dione, Melusine, Aphrodite, Cerridwen, Diana, Arionrhod, Brigid, and by many other names:

Whenever you have need of anything, once a month, and better it be when the moon is full, you shall assemble in some secret place and adore the spirit of Me Who is Queen of all the Wise.

You shall be free from slavery, and as a sign that you be free you shall be naked in your rites.

Sing, feast, dance, make music and love, all in My presence, for Mine is the ecstasy of the spirit and Mine also is joy on earth.

For My law is love unto all beings. Mine is the secret that opens the door of youth, and Mine is the cup of wine of life that is the cauldron of Cerridwen, that is the holy grail of immortality.

I give the knowledge of the spirit eternal, and beyond death I give peace and freedom and reunion with those that have gone before.

Nor do I demand aught of sacrifice, for behold, I am the Mother of all things and My love is poured out upon the earth.

Hear the words of the Star Goddess, the dust of Whose feet are the hosts of Heaven, Whose body encircles the universe:

I Who am the beauty of the green earth and the white moon among the stars and the mysteries of the waters,

I call upon your soul to arise and come unto me.

For I am the soul of nature that gives life to the universe.

From Me all things proceed and unto Me they must return.

Let My worship be in the heart that rejoices, for behold, all acts of love and pleasure are My rituals.

Let there be beauty and strength, power and compassion, honor and humility, mirth and reverence within you.

And you who seek to know Me, know that the seeking and yearning will avail you not, unless you know the Mystery: for if that which you seek, you find not within yourself, you will never find it without.

For behold, I have been with you from the beginning, and I am That which is attained at the end of desire.

Contents

List of Rituals, Prayers, Songs, Chants, Poems, and Meditations

(Material not otherwise attributed was created by Starhawk.)

Acknowledgments

This book could not have become manifest but for the hard work and dedication of many people, in greater ways and in smaller ways.

I especially thank Starhawk, whose inspiration this book was. Several members of the Reclaiming Collective contributed their writing to the book, but others did less glamorous, lower-profile work that was just as important. Chief among these people is Patti Martin, who transported people and material to and from printers, issued checks, distributed books (the original edition), staffed sales tables, filled mail orders, and generally kept track of all monies. To Patti I extend a sweeping curtsy.

Thanks to Anne Hill for annotating the music and providing camera-ready copy of all the songs and chants on her handy-dandy Finale program.

We—the Collective and I—thank Leah Samul, who researched printing techniques, printings costs, and legal matters, input material, edited text, tracked down biographies, and offered valuable suggestions on many of the pieces that appear in both editions of this book.

We thank Lisa Bach, our original editor on this book, for all her work in shaping its direction and structure. We also thank Caroline Pincus who guided it to completion; Sally Kim who cheerfully lead us through the maze; managing editor Terri Leonard; Kathy Reigstad, with her gemcutter's eye; and everyone else we encountered at HarperSanFrancisco. They all made every visit to the office pleasurable, even in the midst of moving.

Thanks to Sam Webster for Mac help; to Rowan Fairgrove for last-minute library help; to Panthera.

Thanks to Tove Beatty of Maitri Hospice; Clare Prout and the Voyager Trust (formerly the Pagan Hospice and Funeral Trust) and the Soul Midwives in England for sending out connecting threads and broadening our perspectives; to Megory Anderson and the Sacred Dying Foundation, for support and general webweaving.

We thank all the contributors who so generously shared their experiences and wisdom.

My special thanks go to two of our number who have crossed over since we first began this project—Raven Moonshadow and John Patrick McClimans. These two splendid men offered us the opportunity to learn valuable lessons, and to heal ourselves and our communities, by inviting us to share in the intimacy of their dying process. I thank the many people who were touched by Raven's teaching, especially Vibra Willow and M. A. Bovis, for sharing the vigil during Raven's last week of life. I also thank John's widow, Shirin Morton, and his life companion, Linda Frankel, for tolerating the disruption to their household, and Joi Wolfwomyn and Orion Stormcrow for sharing the vigil of John's passing.

To my daughter Deirdre Blessing, thanks for your unwavering confidence.

To my beloved Corby, thanks for meals, quiet, walks, massages, and general all-around support (not to mention putting up with my crankiness).

Love and blessings,

M. Macha NightMare
San Rafael, California
Spring 1997

How This Book Came to Be

Reflections on My Mother's Death

On August of 1992, my (Starhawk's) mother died. My brother and I were fortunate to be with her during the last days of her life, to sit vigil at her bedside and help midwife her crossing.

My mother came from that generation of Jews who rebelled against the Orthodoxy of their parents. She was an educated woman with a doctorate in social work, a psychotherapist whose belief systems were centered more on post-Freudian theory than Mosaic law. But she had a strong attachment to Judaism as her connection with her family, her identity, her roots.

While she was still conscious, I asked her if she wanted to say the Shemah with me, the traditional prayer the dying say, the prayer that is believed to express in a few lines the core truth of Judaism. She said yes. I asked her if she wanted to say the usual version or one of the new feminist versions, and she answered that she preferred the old one. Together we repeated these words:

Shemah Yisroel Adonai Elohenu Adonai ehud.
Hear, O Israel, the Lord Our God, the Lord is one.

As we recited the words together, I felt a profound sense of grief. Here was the prayer that, as a child, I had said every night before I went to sleep, the prayer that was on the lips of martyrs as they died, the prayer that the victims of the Holocaust murmured as they went to the gas chambers, the prayer said by all of my ancestors back for thousands of years. In saying it together with my mother as she died, I felt connected to all of them.

And yet it was not a prayer that I could believe in.

My discomfort began with the obvious language of patriarchy, hierarchy, and exclusivity, and I began reflecting on how the prayer might change if those elements were stripped away. I knew that "Adonai," which literally means "My Lord," was not actually the God-word written in the prayer, but a verbal substitute for the name too holy to be spoken, JHWH. "Hashem," which means "the name," could easily be used instead. For "Israel," the people to whom proclamation was directed, we could substitute "people." For masculine language I could substitute the feminine. "Listen, people, She Whose name cannot be spoken, Whom we call Goddess, She Who is the great mystery, is one."

But saying the Goddess is one is only half of the truth, for she is also many, She of a thousand names and infinite aspects, some of them male.

"Listen, people, She Whose name cannot be spoken, Whom we call Goddess/God of mystery, is one in many, many in one."

I started to wonder what prayer might serve as a core statement of Pagan belief—should a tradition as anarchic as ours ever want one. Perhaps we do not; our tradition strongly resists any centralization of creed or imposition of authority. We encourage creativity and spontaneity.

But dying changes everything. When you are dying, you do not have the energy to create. When you are grieving, you are already overwhelmed, faced with decisions and demands at a time when coping is extraordinarily difficult. You are in no position to design new rituals or to write new liturgies.

As my brother and I negotiated the difficult days following my mother's death, we found ourselves taking a great deal of comfort in the body of Jewish tradition that was long established. Jews have a set ritual for washing the body—and a group of community volunteers who do it. There are rules for when the funeral must be carried out (bodies must be buried within twenty-four hours, unless the Sabbath day intervenes), how the coffin should be built (of plain wood, with no metal used in its construction), and what prayers should be said.

At one time, every Pagan tradition had a similar body of custom and tradition. Now much of this has been lost. We do not know what words were on the lips of the Witches who burned. We do not know what whispered prayers were said under the breath of those who watched.

But we do know how Pagans viewed death—from our oral tradition, from the evidence of burials and artifacts, from folktales and myths, and from our own experience. The core teaching in the Pagan tradition is that birth and death are one. We pass through the same gateway coming into life and going out again, and on the other side is a realm of change and renewal. Death will bring us to rebirth. And our encounters with the gates and the passages, the choices we make and the dilemmas we face, are our most profound encounters with what we call "Goddess."

My mother was a psychotherapist, an expert in loss and grief who worked daily with the bereaved. Over many years of discussion and advice, her understanding of grief as a healing process became part of me. This book began as a tribute to her. After accompanying her through the process of her dying, I vowed to create Pagan liturgy for death. I began very slowly writing some of the prayers and chants found here, collecting others that were already in use.

Months passed, and then years, and the book was still progressing at a slow pace. Meanwhile the need for it was becoming more and more evident: I continually found myself photocopying portions and faxing them to friends who were in need of this material. Finally I realized that this project was not one I could or should do alone. Macha has always had a special understanding of death—as well as experience in editing and publishing. So I turned my material over to her, and she greatly expanded it, organized it, and recruited others to fill in the gaps.

The first edition of this work, entitled *Crossing Over,* was published by the Reclaiming Collective in 1995. With this expanded edition, we offer this work to the broader community. We feel that the Pagan tradition has insights into death that can be helpful to people of many faiths. Whether or not you identify as Pagan, you are welcome to use the material presented here and to adapt it to your own needs, values, and beliefs. For this book is not just about dying; it is also about living fully and joyfully every station on the wheel of birth, growth, death, and rebirth.

Starhawk, 1995
Cazadero, CA

How to Use This Book

This book is a collection of resources for those who are assisting a dying person, grieving a beloved, or planning a funeral or memorial service. It can certainly also be useful to someone who is dying, but it is not primarily written as a guide for how to die.

The material we present here is for you to use in creating the rituals that you need. Everything we say here is a suggestion only. We know that your experience, your beliefs, and your approach to spirituality may differ from ours. All the rituals, invocations, chants, songs, and liturgy can be adapted so that they feel right to you. This is a blanket permission that extends throughout the book. For the sake of brevity, we will not constantly repeat it, but know that we encourage you to make use of this material in the way that best fits your own needs.

We have attempted to use nongendered language wherever possible. To avoid the awkward construction of he/she within chants and prayers, we have alternated genders, placing parentheses around gender-specific words that may need to be changed. We have also used parentheses around content that may need to be changed—for example, references to wombs or breasts—and to indicate alternate choices of phrasing. Because constantly repeating "the dying person" or "the dead person" is irritating, we have sometimes substituted "your friend"—although of course the person in question may be your partner, lover, mother, father, child, and so on.

Part One of this book presents an overview of Pagan thealogy and practice and an introduction to the Reclaiming tradition. If you are already familiar with much of this material, you are certainly free to skip over it. You can also use the rituals and prayers in later sections of the book without the background presented here; however, your experience will be enriched if you do take the time to read it. For ease of reference, we have included a glossary.

Part Two describes the Pagan understanding of death, reincarnation, the afterlife, and karma. It includes many meditations and visualizations that can be helpful in working with issues surrounding death.

Part Three takes us through the dying process, from preparing for death, to sitting vigil with the dying, to the moment of death itself (with suggestions for funerals and memorials), to a description of a home cremation. Prayers, songs, and chants are included for you to use or adapt. If someone close to you is dying or has just died and you need to know what to do, this is the section to turn to.

Part Four explores many of the special circumstances and issues around death; it includes sections on AIDS, children, violence, sudden death and organ donation, and choice.

Part Five is about what happens afterward: grieving, cleaning the rooms of the dead, creating and working in community, and living through the first year of bereavement. We end with an essay on practical, legal, and financial preparations for death.

Feel free to reproduce sections of this book for use in ritual. However, because the material is copyrighted, please do not reprint it without permission from HarperSanFrancisco.

This book has now been expanded and has become a labor of love, with contributions from a far-flung community. Most of our contributors are part of the widespread Reclaiming community, but others represent some of the rich variations among different Pagan traditions. We offer these pages to you in the hope that they will be of help and comfort when the wheel turns for you or those you love.

Introduction

Several of us Pagans and Witches, as we have aged, have had considerable firsthand (or hands-on, if you will) experience with death and dying. We have been challenged as to how to deal with it — intellectually, energetically, emotionally, physically, and spiritually — and have found no resource at hand to help us through these crises. As Carol Christ has said,

> Symbol systems cannot simply be rejected, they must be replaced. Where there is no replacement, the mind will revert to familiar structures at times of crisis, bafflement or defeat.

In 1988, when my former husband, a Witch, was dying, in his great pain he called for "the Witches." We came, and we did everything we could to draw off pain, to ease his transition, but we had no written resources within our own spiritual tradition. We found comfort in reading from Francesca Fremantle's translation of *The Tibetan Book of the Dead*, and I believe Rod took comfort from our oral readings. We chanted "Set Sail" and "Gone Beyond," chants we use at Samhain (and that you will find elsewhere in this book). We cleared the way to the West. We hung an image of the Tibetan Goddess Kurukulia on the West wall. We laid on hands to comfort and ease pain. We purified the air with salt water. (Incense and candles were not an option in a hospital room with oxygen equipment.) We did everything we could think of, or were inspired to do, and we did it with love. We drew from every source we knew, however eclectic. It was a great privilege to be present at his crossing over. Yet we did not have our own Craft material.

A few days after Rod's passing, we took his ashes out into the ocean beyond the Golden Gate and performed a short service there. We again used the chants and songs we had used before his spirit left his body. Starhawk said inspired and eloquent things at the ceremony. But still, we had no resource of Craft liturgy, prayers, and songs.

In 1992, Starhawk's mother declined in health and left this existence. Since then, Starhawk has worked on creating liturgy for death.

This book began with Starhawk's vision. Fortunately for me, (Macha) she saw this work as a place where I could explore and expand my understanding of death and dying. And fortunately for all of us, she also saw this book as a place where we could display, in the best setting possible, the vast talents, insights, spiritual depth, and richness of present-day Pagans and Witches.

The Reclaiming Collective (of which both Starhawk and I are members), based in the San Francisco Bay Area, heartily supported our first effort at making much of this material more widely available. Reclaiming paid for the production of the original edition, called *Crossing Over: A Pagan Manual on Death and Dying,* published at Samhain 1995. We created that book for our co-religionists, to help them move through times of challenge and pain.

I wrote in the Introduction to that 1995 precursor of the present volume, "We — Reclaiming Collective and Friends — offer this book as a point of beginning as we as a Pagan community create and define our approach to death, and our working with death. . . . We consider this to be open-ended, a work in process, as we all continue to define our Craft and Pagan tribes. So we ask you to contribute your feedback for possible future expansion and refinement."

This request produced many of the wonderful contributions that have found their way into this current work. In all, forty Witches and Pagans — not only from California but also from New England, New York, Florida, Iowa, Illinois, and Texas, as well as from British Columbia and Alberta to the North, Britain to the East, and El Salvador to the South — have shared their experiences and contributed meaningful liturgy.

Not everyone who contributed writings and songs to this book is in our small Reclaiming Collective, or even in our larger community.

But all have graciously shared their work with us because we asked. We thank them.

All prayers, chants, and songs not specifically identified as being written by someone else were written by Starhawk. Prayers and chants within a specific essay are the work of the writer of that essay. Transitional material was written by Starhawk and Macha.

Part One

Pagan Tradition

1

The Sacred Cycle

Go into a forest, a meadow, or a garden—anywhere plants grow and die and insects, birds, and animals forage. In any natural environment, death is constantly occurring. Leaves drop to the ground; plants end their lifespan. A butterfly ceases its fluttering and falls. A rabbit lies dead behind a bush.

Instantly the processes of decay begin. Subtle cues of scent or some unknown sixth sense alerts all the families of creatures that feed on death, from the tiny one-celled bacteria and fungi, to the beetles and termites, and on up to the vultures and coyotes. The earth takes in the dead through a thousand mouths that reduce each body to its most basic elements, and those elements, in turn, feed the living, nourish the roots of the great trees, and send the vultures winging aloft. As any good gardener knows, it is the processes of decay that sustain the fertility of the soil. All growth arises from death.

This cycle of birth, growth, death, decay, and regeneration is the basic life-sustaining process on this planet. From the time of the emergence of human beings as a thinking, conscious species, people who have lived embedded in nature have observed these processes in action and have acknowledged our dependence upon them by naming them *sacred*. They have understood death as a natural part of the cycle of life, and have known, not through faith but through direct observation, that death is the matrix in which new life is born.

For human beings, the death of a leaf at the end of summer, the culling of seedlings, or the salmon's end after spawning is easy to accept as part of the natural cycle. But our own death, or the death of those we love, is not. We feel fear, pain, and grief at the thought of our own consciousness coming to an end.

Religions, theologies, and mystical traditions worldwide have attempted to reconcile us to death. Perhaps the major impulse toward a religion, for most people, comes from the recognition of our own mortality, from the deep desire to believe in an afterlife and the wish for comfort for our losses.

This book describes the understandings and practices of one of those traditions, the Goddess tradition as it has evolved over the last twenty-five years in the extended community that has grown up around the Reclaiming Collective of the San Francisco Bay Area. Our traditions around death arise from our deepest core values and beliefs about life, so we begin this book with some background in our history, practices, and thealogy. We cannot talk about death without delving into the mystical, entering the realm of spirits, voyaging through the otherworld, examining the nature of the soul. But even confirmed skeptics and atheists can take comfort from the roots of our tradition in the observed processes of nature. You do not have to believe in the cycle of birth, growth, death, and rebirth, or take it on faith as revealed truth, or accept it as dogma. You are not asked to accept truths mediated through someone else's experience, even the experience of a great teacher or mystic. You can simply walk out into a forest and observe the cycle in process.

Pagans—another name we use for ourselves—have preserved understandings of death that can be helpful to Pagans and non-Pagans alike. Because our spirituality is rooted in the earth, we honor and embrace the natural cycles of birth and death. We are taught no distaste for bodily reality, no sense of corporeal life as somehow unclean or of matter as inferior to spirit. Our worldview includes layers of reality that go beyond the visible and quantifiable, and we do believe our connection to those we love extends beyond death. But we have no desire to make our view a dogma. We offer our insights with respect for intellectual freedom and in the hope that they can be helpful personally and collectively in our encounters with death.

Acceptance of death as part of the natural cycle can be a healthy counterbalance to our present-day combination of denial and obsession.

Modern Western culture hides death away in hospital rooms, isolating the dying. We undertake tortuous and heroic measures to prolong the last physical signs of life, without considering the whole well-being of the dying person. Although recent years have made us more conscious of the rights of the dying to refuse painful, last-ditch interventions, heroic measures are still the norm. Helping the terminally ill to consciously end their lives is a crime, while denying health care to the living is seen as sound fiscal practice.

At the same time as we fear and deny death, we are obsessed with violence. Who could begin to compile the body count from our movies and television shows? Daily we watch people stabbed, shot, blown up, and burned—often at the hands of those who claim to love them—or vaporized by space aliens. The children who grow up watching this fare fear that their schoolfellows are packing weapons in their book bags. Our young men, and even our young women, can be shipped off to fight electronic wars that seem like video games as long as the blood and stench and suffering are far away.

Our disconnection from the cycles of birth, death, decay, and regeneration runs through every aspect of our society. We have forgotten the connection between decay and fertility. Our agriculture substitutes quick-fix fertilizers for compost, mulch, and manure, thereby impoverishing the soil and polluting our waters. Our technology creates products with no thought of how they will end their useful life and be returned to the cycle of the elements. We make plastic bags of a nearly eternal substance in order to carry a lettuce on a twenty-minute trip from the grocery store to home. We create a whole nuclear industry before we have solved the problem of what to do with its wastes. Our landfills are overflowing and toxic-waste sites dot the land, because we behave as if death and decay were anomalies instead of integral parts of every activity.

Acceptance of death as part of the cycle of life has both personal and social implications. Imagine if we truly understood that decay is the matrix of fertility, if we designed our products with that truth in mind, as nature does, if everything we manufactured were recyclable or could, in its breakdown, feed something else. Our landfills would empty and our true collective wealth would increase. Our cemeteries might become orchards. We might view our own aging with less fear and distaste, and greet death with sadness, certainly, but without terror.

The cycle of birth, growth, death, decay, and regeneration is the core of Pagan thealogy—from *Thea*, Goddess, rather than *Theo*, God. "Pagan," a word that comes from the Latin root *Paganus*, means "country dweller." Pagans, who lived close to the land, held on to their ancient understandings of life and death long after Christianity had seemingly converted all of Europe. "Pagan" has been used as a pejorative term for centuries, but today throughout the Americas and Europe many people are proudly reclaiming the term as we both reclaim the insights and understandings of our ancestors and adapt them to a new time.

To Pagans, as to indigenous cultures worldwide, nature is sacred—that is, from nature we draw our inspiration, our teachings, and our deepest sense of connection. Nature has an inherent value that supersedes human convenience or profit, and the balance of nature cannot be ethically sacrificed to human ends. Our Goddesses and Gods are immanent: embodied in the living processes of nature and human culture. Or perhaps we might more accurately say that our deities are themselves embodiments of the complex interrelationships and cycles of the natural world.

Today scientists such as James Lovelock propose what they call "the Gaia Hypothesis"—the theory that the earth functions like a living, self-regulating organism. This theory is not news to Pagans (or to any other indigenous culture on the planet). We see the earth as a living being, and all of life as interconnected. The networks of microscopic fungi that inhabit the roots of the great redwoods feed those giants. The great forests of the West Coast create the rains that fall inland. The pollution of a small stream in the Rockies eventually flows into the ocean and then circles the globe.

To Pagans, all life is imbued with consciousness and all living beings are constantly communicating. The consciousness of a tree may be different from yours or mine; indeed, unless it is a very large and old tree, it may be less the consciousness of "this individual seedling oak" and more the consciousness of "oakness"—a group or collective sense of being. But awareness, presence, is still there—in a tree, even in a rock or a mountain. When birds sing and dogs bark, we can hear their communication. Although trees communicate less perceptibly—perhaps chemically or energetically, certainly in ways that are harder to define—we can train our ears to hear and learn ways to speak back.

Indeed, Pagans know that conversation is not only possible but necessary and desirable. We see human beings as part of nature, with our own tasks to perform and role to play in the balance. We need to talk to trees for our own health and connection and well-being; and trees likewise need and want to talk to us, just as they need to communicate with insects, birds, mycorrhizal fungi, and soil bacteria. Humans are not the pinnacle and ultimate justification for the universe, nor are we doomed to be a blight on the planet, inevitably destroying what we touch. The terrible imbalances of present-day culture are an anomaly in the million-year human heritage, and we have both the capability and the moral responsibility to bring our way of life back into balance. Only by understanding the cycles of birth, growth, death, and rebirth can that balance be achieved.

Pagan spirituality is centered in community. While many of our practices further personal growth and healing, our goals are centered not so much on individual salvation or enlightenment as on communal health and balance. Individuals need the love, support, and challenge offered by a strong community in order to survive and thrive. We meet for ritual in small groups, circles, or covens, the members of which develop intimate bonds and deep connections with each other. Today we also often gather in larger groups for seasonal rituals or festivals. Our definition of "community" includes the animals, plants, rocks, trees, and waters that surround us, the broader human community around the globe, those who have come before us, and those who will come after us. Death does not sever community.

We hope this book will help to strengthen and empower our communities. Hillary Rodham Clinton popularized the African proverb "It takes a village to raise a child." We might paraphrase that to "It takes a whole community to get through a death." Only the love and support of those around us can help us let go of life when our time comes, or weather the pain of bereavement when someone we love dies.

However we define our thealogy and whatever images we use to clothe the Sacred, we recognize that the ultimate heart of the world is mystery. The great powers of life and death can never be wholly known, defined, or controlled. We can approach them with awe and wonder, we can increase our own knowledge and wisdom without limits, but we will never know all. Acknowledging the mystery lets us approach the world with wonder and humility, with caution to limit our errors, and with a sense of joy and liberation.

"Goddess" and "Goddess Tradition"

"Goddess" is the word we use as shorthand for "the great cycles of birth, growth, death, and rebirth" or "the heart of mystery." When we speak of "the Goddess," we often mean "that life, that consciousness, which underlies the living being which is the earth, and who is herself a cell in that great living being who is the cosmos."

We also use the word "Goddess," however, to refer to various aspects of that life-force that have taken on particular attributes, faces, and personalities: Demeter, the Greek Goddess of grain and agriculture, for example, or Kali, the Hindu Great Goddess of birth, life, and death. There are thousands of Goddesses from cultures all over the world, as well as thousands of Gods—male deities who also embody the cycles of life, death, and regeneration.

"Goddess tradition" refers to the many branches of Paganism that hold as central a focus on the Goddess as the embodiment of the cycles of birth, growth, death, and rebirth. Goddess-based spirituality includes men, although some groups and some traditions within the larger movement may be for women only or focus exclusively on female deities. Men, too, may choose to create ritual with other men, and great power and healing can come from women's and men's mysteries.

We of the Reclaiming tradition honor many Gods, many male images of deity. But our emphasis is on the imagery of the female, the life-bearer, because we value life itself as the domain of the sacred. We do not elevate spirit above matter; we hold that spirit is immanent in matter, in the physical, material world. This emphasis on the world itself as the body of the divine affects our view of death, karma, and rebirth, as you will see.

We also feel that at this time in history an emphasis on the female is necessary to counterbalance millennia of male domination in the spiritual as well as the material realm. "Don't we need balance?" people sometimes ask. "Why not a neutral term rather than either 'God' or 'Goddess'?"

Our imaginations are conditioned to read "neutral" as "male." In theory God is a neutral term—yet how many of us can use it without subconsciously thinking of a man with a long white beard? Perhaps our children, or their children, will not suffer the same constraints of the imagination, but that transformation lies in the future.

Balance is not stasis, but movement. Think of a seesaw. If one end is down on the ground, you cannot bring it into balance by standing in the center. You must put a weight on the opposite side. The term "Goddess" does this. In time, when the arms of the seesaw are truly balanced, neutral language may work well, but twenty-five years of a feminist spirituality movement cannot counterbalance many ages of patriarchy, especially when male domination is still the rule globally.

In compiling the chants and prayers in this book, we have tried to strike a balance between female and male imagery. We encourage you to rework the material here, if necessary, so that its imagery fits your own beliefs.

"Witch" and "Witchcraft" are misunderstood terms that we proudly reclaim, both in these pages and in the Pagan community. While the popular understanding of "Witchcraft" often includes either devil worship or the wielding of supernatural powers, we know that the term has a more ancient and honorable history. It derives from the Anglo-Saxon root *wic,* meaning "to bend or twist"; it is related to "willow," a sacred tree much used for its flexible withes in basketry and building. Witches were those who could bend or twist fate, who could weave new possibilities, who used willow bark (from which aspirin is now derived) and other herbs in healing, who preserved the communal knowledge of the properties and uses of plants, who kept the old earth-based way long after most of European culture was at least nominally Christian.

Today the word "Witch" is generally used for a woman or man who follows an initiatory Pagan tradition with the Goddess at center, for a priestess or priest who has made a deep personal commitment to their earth-based spiritual path. We have no separate word for male Witches.

Throughout this book, we will use the terms "Goddess tradition" and "Paganism" roughly interchangeably. When we describe our thealogy, practices, and beliefs, readers should be aware that nobody can speak for the entire Pagan community. We interpret the Goddess tradition through the lens of Reclaiming's perspective, and further, through our own individual insights and intuitions. We encourage everyone who uses this book to adapt and change its elements as needed to fit your own values.

This book is not the place for a full history of the Goddess tradition or for a comprehensive survey of its current revival, but a little background information may prove helpful.

A Short History of the Goddess Tradition

While earth-based spirituality lies at the root of religions and cultures worldwide, most people who identify as contemporary Pagans trace their roots back to the indigenous earth-based traditions of Europe and the Middle East. The earliest images of Goddesses—indeed, the earliest artwork of any kind, are found in the Paleolithic big-bellied, full-breasted, wide-hipped figures found from the Ukraine to the caves of southern France and dating back more than twenty-five thousand years. Iconographically, they are closely related to the many thousands of Goddess figures found in the sites of what archaeologist Marija Gimbutas terms Old Europe, an area encompassing Anatolia (Turkey), Greece, the Balkans, and westward to Iberia (Spain and Portugal) and the British Isles; stretching eastward and south into Egypt, ancient Canaan and Mesopotamia; and extending in time from the seventh through (in places) the third millennium before the common era. This ancient civilization was a mosaic of village cultures that were roughly egalitarian, peaceable, and creative. Agriculture, pottery-making, architecture, writing, and mathematics all were born in this time. Religious imagery focused on the cycles of life and death, on food, fertility, and sexuality as images of the sacred.

Archaeologists may argue about this picture, but for contemporary Goddess worshipers what is important is that it presents a model of a cooperative, peaceful, and innovative society lying hidden at the roots of European culture. Knowing that such societies are possible, we need not accept war and domination as inevitable. To identify with the Goddess is to consciously choose cooperation over domination, peace over war, freedom over systems of control.

Goddess traditions today do not claim an unbroken lineage going back to the Stone Age. Rather, we say that the same symbols that moved people then speak to us today, that the same cycle of birth, growth, and death honored in Old Europe and among indigenous cultures worldwide can inspire us today to create, to change, to face life's powerful moments of challenge and transformation, and at the end of life, to accept and honor death.

Beginning in roughly the fourth millennium and continuing over a period of several thousand years, Old Europe was challenged by the emergence of a new, warlike culture characterized by reverence for male gods, mythologies of conquest and domination, fascination with weaponry and battle, and hierarchies of power—in particular, male domination over women. Most historic religious traditions of Europe, the Middle East, and India date from this period of transition or later and contain within them a mixture of elements, strands of the older tradition that reverenced the cycles of life interwoven with myths of battle and domination.

In Europe, the old ways lingered on as folktales and customs, traditions of healing and magic, the domain of the Witches. When Christianity began to spread, it at first coexisted with the Old Religion, much as in Latin America today the church is often the site of processions and celebrations that remain from precolonial times. Every village had its Witch—its herb woman or cunning man—who served the ordinary people who had no access to doctors. In fact, the herbal healing techniques were probably preferable to the medical science of the time, which depended heavily on astrology, bleeding, and reference to Greek philosophers rather than empirical science.

But beginning with the Crusades against heretics and peaking in the sixteenth and seventeenth centuries C.E. (common era), the institutional church, under a variety of pressures and challenges to its power and authority, unleashed a persecution directed at traditional healers and all the remnants of the Old Religion. Women, primarily but not exclusively, were its victims. Estimates range from hundreds of thousands to millions who lost their lives over the roughly four hundred years of the Burning Times. Anyone could be accused of Witchcraft, and once someone *was* accused, the victim's denial of wrongdoing was read as refusal to repent. People were tortured into false confessions and forced to name others as accomplices, and so the accusations spread.

This period left a legacy of fear and horror around the word "Witch" and the dynamic, evolving worldview held by the traditional healers. The Old Religion was forced into a period of secrecy, which also contributed to people's false ideas about what Witchcraft represents. Only in this century have Witches felt safe enough to "come out of the broom closet" and resume the open practice and development of our tradition.

In the 1940s, a retired British civil servant named Gerald Broussard Gardner discovered a coven of Witches in the New Forest area of England, and he began practicing and later writing about and teaching the tradition. The Craft grew in a small way throughout the sixties, when many people were searching for nontraditional spiritual forms. Beginning in the seventies, many women were drawn to Paganism as an alternative to the male domination in the "major" religions as well as many of their wilder offshoots. The eighties saw a new influx of both women and men involved in environmental and peace issues who were drawn to a spirituality that puts the earth at the center. Today, in the nineties, the Goddess tradition is continuing to grow organically and widely, and Pagans are increasingly open and vocal about who we are and what we stand for.

The Reclaiming Tradition

This book on death and dying has emerged from a community that practices the Reclaiming tradition of the Craft. The Reclaiming tradition began in the San Francisco Bay Area in the late 1970s and early 1980s, as a small collective teaching the Goddess tradition and creating public rituals that linked our spirituality with our political awareness. Today we have grown into a distinct tradition of the Craft with sister communities throughout the United States, Canada, Europe, and El Salvador. Our Wiccan roots are in the Feri tradition as taught by Victor and Cora Anderson, but our practice encompasses many, many sources, including direct inspiration. Our political roots are in feminism, nonviolence, peace, justice, and environmental and gay rights activism. Starhawk has been one of the major voices of our tradition, and many people have been attracted to that tradition through her writings. But she is not the "author" of the tradition; rather, her work emerges from a living, evolving community of many creative minds and visions.

The Reclaiming tradition resists the tendency of our culture to elevate gurus and create spiritual celebrities. One of our core values is that each individual is her or his own spiritual authority. That authority extends to the most basic and intimate decisions about our bodies, about our own unique encounters with the forces of life and death. As friends, as lovers, as partners, as family, as community, we have the right, the ability, and the responsibility to help one another through the dying process, to care for our own dead, to comfort and support the bereaved. This book can be a guide, but we fully hope and expect that every suggestion, every prayer, and every instruction will be weighed by each reader against an internal sense of what is right for that individual.

In a book about death, questions of ancestry are necessarily relevant. Reclaiming's tradition draws particularly from the ancient Goddess traditions of Europe and the Middle East, especially the pre-Celtic peoples of the British Isles.

Reclaiming's style of ritual has also been strongly influenced by the vibrant diversity of the San Francisco Bay Area, by the wealth of spiritual traditions in which we were raised or which we have studied, and by the land itself and the living wisdom of its first peoples. We would be arrogant and stupid not to learn from the wealth of spiritual traditions that surround us—but we would be liars if we set ourselves up as authorities on any of them.

Because of the legacy of the Witch persecutions, people of European ancestry are often unaware of the rich tradition of earth-honoring spirituality in that heritage. The hungry take food where they find it, and often that has meant drawing on cultures and traditions that are not one's own, that seem more earthy, more whole, or more exotic.

Indigenous people are raising the issue of cultural appropriation, and rightfully do not want to see their spiritual teachings mined for nuggets of salable insights or misrepresented for profit by those who have no true authority. Too often spiritual teachers and traditions are unclear about the origins of their ceremonies and the source of their authority. Cultural traditions are often taken out of context and stripped of their meaning, or used to make profits for those who are not part of the culture the traditions come from. European religions and culture have dominated and suppressed many indigenous traditions. Can we wonder that there is resistance to the wholesale use of native imagery, symbols, mythologies, and ceremonies? It is as if the invaders had confiscated the house, wrecked it as fast as they could, and then demanded to be freely given all of Grandmother's finest jewelry.

To approach another tradition with integrity, we need a sense of our own roots and a willingness to become involved in the real-life struggles of people for land, for the preservation of culture, sometimes even for simple human survival. When we can meet other traditions not with romanticism or patronizing charity but with the friendship of equals, the possibility of fruitful interchange exists.

As a Euro-based tradition, we must own both sides of our inheritance. We, too, were suppressed by the Europeans—but we *are* them!

And whatever ancestry we claim, all of us are the descendants of both victims and victimizers. We cannot redress all the injustice of the past, but we do offer the material in this book, and we do so to all people regardless of your roots, your background, your gender identification or sexual orientation, and your beliefs about Paganism. In addition, we encourage you also to seek out and incorporate the traditions of your people, to find the prayers, the songs, the food, and the offerings that will make your ancestors feel at home.

Whatever our roots, we recognize that our era is one of great cultural contact and interchange. The Reclaiming community includes ancestors from Mexico, Central and South America, Africa, Asia, and the native peoples of this continent—in short, from around the globe—as well as from all the varying cultures associated with differences of class, religion, sexual orientation, and place. Any real spirituality must take root in the place in which it is practiced, and it is inevitably influenced by the traditions around it.

With other traditions of the Craft, Reclaiming shares a focus on the Goddess as the wheel of birth, growth, death, and regeneration. Life and the elements that sustain it—air, fire, water, and earth—are sacred, along with human creativity and sexuality in its diverse expressions, passion, and freedom. Because what is sacred must not be exploited or despoiled, the Reclaiming tradition sees action in the world in the service of the earth as one of the core expressions of our spirituality. But that action comes out of a deep understanding and disciplined practice of magic—in Dion Fortune's terms, "the art of changing consciousness at will," a definition that might also serve for a politics that aims at transforming the power relations of both individuals and society. Perhaps what most defines our tradition is that we see magical practice, social action, and personal healing as three legs of a tripod that must each be strong for the community to be in balance.

Death is a highly political subject, and certainly this book reflects our views, both directly and in our choice of material. You will notice, for example, that we do not have rituals for the military and we do include rituals for abortion. Nevertheless, we would rejoice if opponents of abortion drew comfort from this book when faced with death, and would heartily bless any person in the military who drew on this material to create her or his own rituals.

Our tradition highly values egalitarianism. Each individual is a living embodiment of the sacred. We work in nonhierarchical structures, and our rituals are usually designed for maximum participation. The rituals in this book are written with the underlying assumption that we are each the ultimate expert on our own death, and we are all capable of healing, comforting, guiding, and blessing one another, of creating our own rituals and being our own priestesses and priests. At times of grief and crisis, however, we need to be taken care of, to have others create and lead ritual for us.

Because freedom of thought is important to us, we accept no dogmas and implement no required beliefs. We do, however, have a working model of the universe that includes interconnected realms of matter and spirit. This worldview underlies all we say and do about death. But we offer it to you in the spirit of an evolving hypothesis. Test it against your own experience, and change or revise the material here as you see fit. At the heart of the cosmos is mystery, that which can never be defined or controlled. Any images we place around that mystery are only tools to help us more deeply encounter the sacred.

Reclaiming's approach to magic and ritual is experimental: we are constantly learning, growing, trying new techniques, and critiquing the results. Our practice is alive and growing, something to be constantly extended, refined, renewed, and changed as the spirit moves us and need arises, rather than a tradition to be learned and repeated in a formulaic manner.

2

Current Practice

Our approach to death is shaped by the ways we experience the sacred in life. A spiritual tradition provides a framework for our encounters with the great forces of birth and death. Through ritual, ceremony, personal meditation, and spiritual practice we make room in our lives for moments of wonder and connection. Our sacred calendar of holy days brings alive the mythology of birth, death, and rebirth and allows us to experience the mystery of regeneration in the turning of the wheel of the year.

In the following section, Reclaiming and Feri priestess T. Thorn Coyle introduces us to the celebrations that mark the seasonal cycle as followed by Reclaiming. She outlines the basic ritual form we use with groups and outlines a variety of approaches to personal practice.

Wheel of the Year

T. THORN COYLE

Pagans celebrate the Solstices and Equinoxes and what we call the Cross-Quarters: Samhain, Imbolc, Beltane, and Lughnasad. These holidays are tied to a Celtic agricultural calendar of plantings and harvest. We look at what we sow and reap in our daily lives and chart our internal and community progress in these ways. The wheel of the year is the cycle of nature and the cycle of the soul. Will the harvest be good this year? We can only wait and see.

Samhain Eve: Also known as Halloween or All Souls, Samhain is the Witches' New Year. This is the season when the veils between this earthly world and the worlds of spirits, ancestors, and the Fey are thin—hence the idea that ghosts and goblins walk about on this night in particular, needing "treats" as bribes to keep them from mischief.

Witches honor their ancestors at this time more than any other. We use this time to commune with our beloved dead and to grieve for what has recently passed from us. It is the time in which we travel to the crossroads where all possibilities meet. From there we venture to the Isle of Apples, land of eternal twilight, crossing the sunless sea made of our tears. Those who have passed on and those who are yet to come meet us in this place; together we wander the groves of fragrant trees that live in bud, fruit, and blossom.

We hold our rituals to mark the ending of the year and the beginning of the heart of the dark time. Gazing into the cauldron of the Dark Goddess, we seek Her wisdom. Building altars for our dead and cooking their favorite foods, we begin the time of stories. The stories start with our memories and their gifts, as we eat the fruits of the final harvest.

Winter Solstice Eve: Midwinter, the longest night, falls at the time when the sun is farthest from the earth. We light fires on this night and vigil with the Great Laboring Mother, awaiting the birth of the sun. Like many winter festivals, it is a time of lights and candles, of bread-baking and gift-giving. We rise before dawn on Solstice day to sing up the sun and welcome the new light.

Imbolc: Also known as Oimelc, Candlemas, and Brigid, Imbolc is that time of still-winter when the trees begin to give blossom in warmer climes and the first flowers poke up shoots. The days grow visibly longer in colder places. This time is sacred to Brigid, the Goddess of poetry, healing, and smith craft. We gather at Her holy well and sacred flame to be renewed and to pledge our work in the community for the coming year as we stand between the fallow time and the time of planting.

Spring Equinox: Also known as Eostre or Oester, this festival celebrates spring's arrival and the balance of day and night. This is the time when day and night are equal, and the lambs frisk about on green hills. Traditionally, this is a time for egg hunts and other celebrations of fertility, both our own and that of the earth. A good time for all creative projects and new ventures. Stop, take a deep breath, and feel the momentary order of the universe.

Beltane Eve: Also known as May Eve, this is the traditional time for dancing around the May pole, weaving the magic of love and community into the bright ribbons. On this night, great fires were traditionally lit from dead, fallen wood in the forests. People made love all night by the bonfires and gathered flowers for garlands in morning. This is the time at which we honor our sacred bodies through joy and pleasure, and in so doing honor the body of the earth. We also jump the Beltane fire or flaming cauldron to cleanse ourselves from winter's sickness. Friends and partners jump together to cleanse relationships from old misunderstandings and hurts.

The veils are thin here too, making this the time of birth, the waxing of the year, just as Samhain is the time of death, the waning of the year. The Fey and otherworldly presence is particularly strong in this time of flowers. Set out a bowl of cream, a piece of cake, or a glass of good whiskey as an offering to the Faery folk.

Summer Solstice: Midsummer, also known as Litha, gives us the longest day and the zenith of the sun's power. Brother Lugh is at the height of his beauty and must fall. This is the day when light both triumphs and fails, for though the sun blazes, the days grow shorter after this time. On Solstice Eve we cleanse ourselves in the ocean and build a Wicker Man, hanging offerings from his branches and throwing onto that kindling anything that needs to be let go—old spells or old habits. We light his pyre as the sun sets and sing him on his way. Then we look through the garland of the Goddess and ask for clear sight as we gaze toward harvest time. The Wicker

Man falls, traveling into the shortest night, carrying both wishes and failed dreams.

Lughnasad: Also known as Lammas ("loaf mass"), on this holiday we celebrate the wake of Lugh, our fallen God, the sacrifice that dies and rises, like the sun and the grain. This is the first harvest, the time of the Reaper, the time to look at what we have sown and wonder, Will it bear healthy fruit? There is uncertainty here, and patience is needed. We eat the sweet and burn the bitter, separating hope from fear.

Autumn Equinox: At the Autumn Equinox, or Mabon, we witness another harvest, another day of balance. Day and night are of equal length, looking toward the shortening of the days. We gather around the table together to eat fresh-baked bread, crack nuts, and drink the juice of pressed apples. We meditate on what we need to prepare ourselves for winter's coming. The yield of our planting apparent, now is the time to look at how we have done in our year's work and consider what still needs to be done before the year's close.

Ritual Basics

T. THORN COYLE

Many Pagans use ritual as a focusing tool, a way of acknowledging the Sacred and gathering energy for whatever workings need to be done. Rituals, like ritual objects, access our Younger Self, the part of us that responds to things viscerally rather than intellectually. These rituals vary according to tradition. Here I outline a basic ritual stemming from the Reclaiming tradition.

In the following descriptions, I use the word "priestess" to mean any person, male or female, performing the task or rite. While there may be a single priestess, there may also be several priestesses taking on the different roles. I give examples of invocations and meditations, but in reality the words used may be changed.

Pagans love altars. Generally, for ritual, there will be at least one altar with objects representing the four directions, the center, Goddess, and God. In other cases, such as large public rituals, each quarter will have its own altar with the appropriate colors and tools (see "Personal Practices of Pagans," on page 22).

Rituals generally begin with the cleansing of participants. This can be done by bathing, aspurging (sprinkling) with water and herbs, or using incense, salt water, or a dish of earth. Salt water represents the womb, the ocean, the Mother to whom we all return. It can take in all that needs cleansing and transform it. The dish of earth, representing the body of the Mother, can also be used, as can incense, to clear away that which keeps us from the work at hand.

The priestess pours the water into a bowl, saying, "Blessed be thou, creature of water." She then adds salt to the bowl, saying, "Blessed be thou, creature of earth." Using her athame, or ritual blade, or her fingers, she blends the two together: "Inner and outer, above and below, may all that needs changing be transformed; may all that needs healing find rest here." Then all in the room are invited to breathe, speak, shout, or shake off anything they are carrying that hinders them from the work about to happen. These cleansings can be especially important for those who need to communicate difficult things or who harbor hard feelings. The aches and pains of the ill can also be dropped into the bowl. When all are finished, the priestess stirs the water clockwise—the direction also known as sunwise or deosil—saying, "All that was released has been transformed. May we be blessed." Then participants can anoint themselves with the water as a sign of the healing or cleansing that has begun.

Next a priestess leads a grounding and centering. She says, "Imagine a root growing from the base of your spine. Send this root down into the earth, passing through all the layers of water, sand, and rock until it reaches the warm, pulsing heart of the Mother. If there is anything that still needs to be let go of, do so now. She can take it. Now draw easily up your root whatever strength, comfort, or energy you need. Let this fill your body and shoot through the top of your head like the branches of a great tree. Let the moon and sun shine down onto your branches, mingling with the earth-energy in your body. Let this energy fill the aura that surrounds your body. Use this energy to feed your Goddess self and to feed this working. Blessed be."

Next the priestess draws the circle or sphere of energy, using the athame or energy running from the fingers. "By the Earth that is Her body, by the air that is Her sweet breath, by the Fire of Her bright spirit, by the living Waters of Her womb, the circle is cast. We are between the worlds. What happens between the worlds affects all the worlds."

Then we call the quarters (the four directions) and the elements they represent—East = air; South = fire; West = water; North = earth; Center = the spirit—welcoming each in turn and asking them to guard the circle.

The Goddess and God appropriate to the ritual are then welcomed into the space. Deities are chosen according to the time of year, the phase of the moon, and the purpose of the ritual. Prayers, songs, and chants relating to deities associated with the seasons or the otherworld are presented throughout this book. This welcoming can be done by chanting, speaking, or dancing. In some circles only the Goddess is called in.

The ritual space is now set up. In the time following—the heart of the ritual—many things may happen. Spells to begin transformation may be worked, trance journeys may be taken, a just and healthy planet may be envisioned, thanks to the good earth for our sustenance may be given, or the season may be honored.

Songs raise energy; these can move into toning. We imagine the tones building a cone of energy that can be sent off into space, into the earth, into the spells or the people present, to lend power and strength to the intentions of the working. The singing can be gentle or lusty, the energy sparky or smooth. Besides all of that, singing is fun.

Extra energy can go to feed your God Soul, the Sacred Dove of your triple soul (see the essay "The Triple Soul" in chapter 5). Breath the energy up above your head. Any energy that you do not need yourself can be offered back to the Mother Earth. Touch the ground.

The priestess holds aloft food and drink, saying, "Blessed be the gifts of earth and sun, sky and water. We offer our gifts to those who have gone before us and for the sustenance of those yet to come. May all who are hungry be fed. May all who thirst have enough to drink. Blessed be." All in the room then feed each other. The words, "May you never hunger; may you never thirst," pass around the circle. Feeding each other is not only a sacred act, it replaces energy depleted by psychic work.

The priestess thanks the Goddess and God and says, "Go if You must, stay if You will. Hail and farewell."

The directions, starting with Center and moving backward, are thanked by whoever called them. All say, "Hail and farewell."

The circle is then undone, traveling widdershins (counterclockwise), being reabsorbed into the athame of the priestess, who then says, "The circle is open, but unbroken. May the peace of the Goddess go in our hearts. Merry meet, merry part, and merry meet again!"

All say, "Blessed be."

Every Pagan or Witch has her own particular way of doing ritual— a way that best suits her needs and that resonates within her. She may continue to do her daily practice exactly as she learned from her teacher(s), but just as often she adapts basic ritual techniques to suit her own personal preferences and needs. Reclaiming priestess Thorn offers an overview and some considerations and specifics to consider in developing your own daily practice.

Personal Practices of Pagans

T. THORN COYLE

Pagans honor the life-force that flows through and around all things. Our personal practices reflect our sense of the sacredness of life and the natural world.

A personal spiritual practice may involve ritual or meditation, or it may consist of practical acts of service. Witches tend gardens, feed the hungry, and care for the sick to honor the life-force. Political action is a way some Witches—particularly those in the Reclaiming tradition—express this reverence for the earth. We also dance under the moon and keep time with the solar cycles. Whether gathered in living rooms, in sunny parks, or on cold beaches, whether alone or with companions, Pagans have an active spiritual life. When all is sacred, every act becomes religion.

My own personal practices can include a daily grounding and centering, running energy, cleaning my chakras, and aligning the Trinity that is my self. Many of these practices are illustrated in other chapters of this book.

Poetry and music are important to many in the Craft. I write poetry as a sacred practice, the bardic thread being strong in my tradition. Reading poems to the earth or to favorite deities is often done as part of ritual. Some deities, such as Brigid or Gods of the Faery realms, are pleased by any beautiful poetry. For some Pagans, playing an instrument or listening to Pagan music can be a connection to the spirit.

Witches use tools to represent the five sacred elements. These tools are a pentacle (five-pointed star) or dish representing the body, material things, earth, and North; the athame (knife) for intellect, discernment, air, and East; a Wand for will, passion, fire, and South; a cup for emotion, intuition, water, and West; a cauldron or spiral representing the place of all things for Spirit and Center. The tools are used in most rituals to set up a space "between the worlds" and to awaken the ritual state of consciousness. These tools are charged with the Witch's essence and become, in their own ways, living things, foci for channeling energy and transforming it with ease.

Other tools are used for divination. Some of these are Tarot cards, runes, Irish oghamic representations, pendulums, and dowsing rods. I doubt you will find Witches reading entrails anymore! Divination is not used so much to foretell the future as to clarify situations and gain insight into life matters. One way of looking at divination is that these tools reveal to us that which is already known.

All tools are expendable. We use them to evoke emotion

and intuition and to get down to the heart of the matter with ease. We also use them because Witches tend to like objects and representations. Our homes are often cluttered with sacred things. That being said, all a Witch really needs is her body. Everything else is an aid and a comfort.

Pagans believe in the psychic realms as easily as they believe in the physical. Most of us believe everyone is psychic or intuitive. We use these skills on an everyday, matter-of-fact basis. This is another way of being in tune with the world. People are psychic in different ways; some "see" things, others "hear" or "feel." These skills are generally so much a part of our daily practice that they are rarely thought about.

Another common practice is leaving offerings. Pagans might leave offerings for various deities, for kitchen or garden Gods, for spirit helpers, or for ancestors. I leave offerings for the Fey ones, more commonly called the Faeries, who inspire me to write and dance. These offerings can include food, drink, flowers, or shiny objects. They can also be prayers of thanks.

Sacred baths are a way to cleanse, both physically and spiritually. Something as simple as Epsom salts or as elaborate as herbal infusions, rose petals, and candles can make any bath a sacred tool. Emotions or anxieties that need to be released can flow out into the water, and desired qualities (such as strength, healing, or a restful night) can be drawn in.

Prayer and meditation are strong components in the Wiccan life, though some of us have yet to reclaim the word "prayer" for our own use. When we sit at an altar with a lighted candle, we can center enough to hear things beyond the chattering of the brain. "Spells" are often just prayers of petition for those who pray more easily with physical objects, as many Witches do. Spells are our way of shifting things in this world and between the worlds. Dance, movement, and making love also constitute forms of prayer and honoring the Sacred. Anything that opens us up to the natural world and to divinity is acceptable.

A cornerstone of my daily practices is saying my prayer necklace. The prayer necklace is a practice I recommend for everybody, especially caretakers of the sick. The tradition was passed to me from Donald Engstrom, who explains prayer necklaces in chapter 3. A prayer necklace consists of a different bead for each prayer said in the ritual. My sequence includes prayers for the healing of earth, air, fire, water, and spirit, prayers for my ancestors and deities, my friends and various spirit realms I work in. I pray for personal areas that I need help with, and for the human world of nations and religions. I also name those who are ill, dying, or in emotional distress. My necklace has eighty-six beads in all, some beads being the same, for repeating prayers. The necklace can be short or long; mine, though many-beaded, takes very little time to say. The beads are a pleasing, sensual focus—colored and textured keys to memory. I also use a prayer necklace made by Cora Anderson, an elder of the Feri tradition of Witchcraft, which has white, red, and black beads in groups of ten. I use these to repeat the points of the Iron and Pearl Pentacles—"Sex, Pride, Self, Power, Passion, Love, Law, Wisdom, Liberty, Knowledge"—and on the marker bead, "I am Goddess."

Every Pagan probably has a unique set of personal practices. Though we are independent-minded, we share an understanding of the value of daily practice to our spiritual growth. We share a belief in magic and the art of transformation, and a love of the life of the spirit, life on earth.

3

Practices and Meditations

*J*ust as we must daily brush our teeth, exercise, and wash ourselves in order to remain physically healthy, our spiritual health is grounded in daily—or at least periodic—practices of meditation and cleansing. We include examples here that will introduce you to some of the basic concepts of the Goddess tradition: grounding, cleansing, the sacred elements, and the moon cycle. Some of these are oriented to preparation for dying or working with the dying, but all can be valuable in daily life. To end this discussion, an article on prayer beads offers a way to bring all of these elements together.

Before doing any ritual or magical work, we must "ground"—that is, establish an energetic connection with the earth. The energy we work with in ritual is stored in the earth and feeds the earth. When we are grounded, we can tap into that vast source of power instead of exhausting our own resources. And when powerful energies and emotions move through us, they can pass into the earth instead of burning us out.

The following meditation is an example of a grounding exercise. Something similar is done before every Wiccan ritual. Grounding is also a very basic and useful daily practice.

Grounding

Sit or stand comfortably, with your feet on the ground. Do not cross your legs or ankles.

Take a deep breath, down into your belly. Feel your chest expand as you inhale and contract as you exhale.

Imagine yourself as a tree, standing with your roots in the earth. Let your breath flow down through your legs and feet into your roots, and feel them push down through anything that lies between you and the living earth.

Imagine that your roots reach the soil and continue down, through layers of mud and rock and gravel, through pools of water, through bedrock, into the living fire at the heart of the earth.

Feel that fire as the earth's life-blood, her womb-blood that flows in great currents below the continents, her creative fire that pushes up to build new land. Take a deep breath and draw up some of that fire through your roots, through all the layers of rock and water and soil, up into your feet and legs. Feel your body come alive as the fire moves up, through your thighs and hips, up into the base of your spine and your sexual places. Draw it into any part of you that needs healing.

Imagine that your spine is a flexible tree trunk, growing and expanding as the fire moves up. Draw it into your heart; let it open and heal your heart. Breathe it down through your hands, and let your hands radiate healing. Breathe it up through your neck and throat, to ease your voice. Breathe it up into your face, into your eyes, into the third eye in the center of your forehead, to awaken intuition. Breathe it up and out the crown of your head, forming branches that reach up into the sky and sweep back down to touch the earth again, making a circle.

Decide how thick you want those branches to be. If you are swamped with emotions and energies that are not yours, make them thicker, a screen to filter out what does not belong to you. If you feel too distant, if you find it hard to be present, thin them out a bit.

Let those branches connect with the energy of the sky, with the sun if it is shining, or with the moon or the stars of the dark night sky. Feel their energy and breathe it in; let it feed your leaves and branches, just as light feeds the trees.

Draw the sky-energy down and in, down through your leaves and branches, down through the top of your head, into your heart and your hands and your belly, down your spine and down through your legs and feet into your roots, down through the soil and water and rock until it reaches the fire at the heart of the earth. Feel how the sky's fire meets the earth's fire in you, how they flow together, up and down, in and out with each breath. Soak up as much energy as you need, and when you are ready, return the rest to the earth by reaching down and touching the ground with your hands.

Now you should be grounded: in touch with the greater energies around you, part of a circuit, calm yet alert, relaxed yet energized. Find a place in your body you can touch, and a word or phrase you can say, to bring back this grounded feeling as you visualize your roots in the earth.

Anchor the feeling, so you can call it back whenever you need it.

Blessed be.

Besides anchoring yourself in the sustaining Earth, you can do a grounding meditation combined with a cleansing exercise using the image of a tree, as Reclaiming priestess Rose May Dance writes below.

Cleansing Meditation

ROSE MAY DANCE

Breathe deeply. Be the tree whose roots go deep into the ground, whose branches sweep the sky. Breathe and imagine that you are this tree. At the base of your spine is an energy center from which your taproot forms a channel into the earth. You can use this channel to release feelings, tension, thoughts, and busy-ness into the earth. There the energy is cleansed, transformed into fuel you can use. You draw up clean, renewed energy from the ground; up your taproot (which becomes your spine) and up through your body the clean, clear energy—power—comes, refreshing your body, mind, and spirit.

As you exhale, you discharge energy into the ground. As you inhale, you bring energy into your body and distribute it. As you breathe in, energy from the heavens also enters your aura at the top of your head and washes down through your body, going down into the ground as you exhale. Breathing in energy from above and below, letting it fuel and cleanse your body, and discharging as you exhale cleanses and renews your whole being. This is called "running energy."

Now, as you "run" your energy, again put your attention at the energy center at the base of your spine, your first chakra.[1] Here concentrate on imagining your body as healthy, vital, alive as you can be. You may be ministering to the dying or to the dead, but let it be clear to you that you are alive. Allow images to come to you, either as pictures in your mind's eyes, as words spoken inside you, or as smells, tastes, or other physical sensations. Call to mind the safety of your home and family, the nourishment that awaits you at your table, the comfort of your bed, the invigorating sensation of exercise or dance. Give life and love to your body. Fill the energy center at the base of your spine with life-force and let it flow down your legs and into your feet. Imagine these areas a glowing red color, or any other color that pleases you.

Now breathe the energy up your spine to the center of power located near your genitals, your womb—your second chakra. Again fill your mind with joyful images of the life-force in the form of sexual energy or creative energy. Know that creation and death are different sides of the same door, and honor that in your sexual/creative center. Recall the powerful feeling of orgasm and imagine that force cleansing

---

[1]The word *chakra* means "wheel." In our tradition, chakra refers to a center of energy in or near the body. It is a place where many paths of energy come together, near major organs. Chakras can be visualized as wheels, as flowers that open and close, as flames, or as globes of light and heat. I work with the seven major chakras mentioned in this meditation, and also with smaller chakras in the palms of the hands and soles of the feet.

your aura, traveling up and down your spine. Honor your own beauty, and the beauty of the person who is dying (or is dead). Honor the beauty of those gathered around. Breathe deeply and bring a warm coral color into your second chakra.

Now breathe the energy up your spine to your solar plexus, the center of your will, the power center of your body. Feel the life-force swirling and alive in your belly. Be aware of the power of your own will, your own choices. Honor the choices of the person who is dying (or has died). Honor the choices of the family, friends, lover.

Do you have enough energy to do the work that is before you? Breathe in energy from earth and sky to give you what you need, to relax and cleanse you, filling your third chakra with golden energy.

Now breathe the energy up into your heart—your fourth chakra—and also up to your shoulders, down your arms, and out your hands. Feel the life-force in its manifestation of love; feel it in your heart and hands. Allow yourself to spill over with love for yourself, for the dying, for the dead, for those gathered, for those concerned. Feel your happiness and feel your sadness. Let the feelings flow freely, rather than choking back with suppressed sobbing. Make sound and let your exhaling turn to audible sighing. Bring in energy from above and below, beautiful green energy to heal you and others, to heal sadness, to allow you to let go.

Now allow your breath to rise to your throat, jaws, ears, face. Feel how the life-force passes powerfully through your neck, moving out of your mouth as sound. Allow the power to come to you so that you will be able to say all that needs to be said in the time to come. Ask for the ability to hear what others are saying, be they living or dead. Breathe the energy and life-force into this fifth chakra, imagining a beautiful blue and the cleansing flow of water.

Now bring your attention up to your eyes, and to the energy center between your eyes in the middle of your brow, your sixth chakra. Feel the life-force pooling there, then releasing in the flow going down into the ground. Feel alive and alert in your own mind and eyes.

As you bring in beautiful indigo colors—the colors of the deep sea or night sky—ask for a cleansing and clearing of your mind. Ask that you will be aware of your boundaries, and not confuse your thoughts with the thoughts of others. Think about five physical differences between yourself and the dead or dying person. Do the same exercise for other people you are close to at this time. Breathe energy from the ground and make sure it comes all the way up to your head; draw in energy from the sky as well. Ask that you be fluid in your vision and thoughts.

Finally, bring the energy flow up to the top of your head, your seventh chakra. Ask that you be well connected to Goddess, God, Spirit—the divine source that is within. Ask to be inspired. Breathe violet energy in from above and connect with the earth-energy below. Breathe deeply, feel the life-force within you, ask to be at peace.

Let the rainbow of colors run through you as you continue to quietly run your energy. Feel that you are a fountain of light, colors swirling in from below, in from above, mixing, and releasing down into the ground. Breathe for a few minutes in this way, letting go of each thought as it occurs and returning to your breath.

When you are ready, let the color green—for growth— bathe you and renew you. Follow with an infusion of the color rose, for your own love for yourself. And end by filling yourself with the shining golden light of the sun. When you are ready, slowly bend down to touch the earth and then slowly come back up again, gently pat your body, and open your eyes. You are ready to begin ritual work.

The Elements of Life

The four elements—air, fire, water, and earth, sacred because they sustain all life—are cornerstones of the Goddess tradition as they are of many earth-based spiritual traditions worldwide. They correspond, in Reclaiming's formulation, with the four cardinal directions—air with the East, fire with the South, water with the West, and earth with the North. Together with spirit or mystery in the Center, they make up the magic circle we honor in every ritual. The elements also correspond with aspects of the self and of life. Air represents the mind, thought, vision, and inspiration. Fire represents energy, passion, and courage. Water is linked to the flow of our emotions, our sensuality, and intuition. Earth stands for the body and all the forces of manifestation into the physical world. Spirit, that central place of the mysteries that cannot be described or defined, is the place of change and transformation. The circle itself is an icon of wholeness. When the elements, and all they represent, are in balance, so are we.

The elements are often used in meditation and personal practice. Many books and resources provide practices and visualizations based on the elements that can be used in many contexts. The meditations that follow are specifically designed to let the elements teach us about the cycle of birth and death. The more often we acknowledge that cycle in life and practice moving through it, the more able we will be to accept and honor death when it comes to us or to those we love.

To practice any or all of these meditations, find a comfortable place where you can sit or lie in a relaxed position. Ideally, you would be outdoors in a safe place, in the presence of the elements. If you are indoors, you can open a window, light a candle, and place a bowl of water and a live plant in front of you, or on the altar. But you can also practice these meditations on a short work break in a high-rise office building where the windows do not open, on the subway, in an airport, or wherever you need them. Wherever you are, take a moment to ground yourself, then begin.

Meditation on the Elements

Air

> Breathe deeply. As you breathe, follow your breath as it moves into your lungs and out again. Each breath we take is itself a cycle of birth, death, and rebirth. We inhale, and life is born in us anew one more time. We pause for a moment, filling ourselves with life, holding it in. Then we exhale and let go. For just one moment, we are empty, suspended between life and death. Then we inhale again and are reborn.
>
> Take some time just to breathe, naming the cycle: birth, as we begin to inhale; life, as our lungs fill. At the moment of full-

ness and transition, let go for just an instant of names and thought, and just notice what comes. Then exhale, and feel your breath wane, naming the moment of emptiness as death. Be aware of the moment when your body automatically opens to fill with breath, the instant of rebirth as the cycle begins again. In that instant, let yourself be aware of the larger presence, the body we are all a part of, that breathes us back into rebirth and life as surely as our empty lungs gasp for air.

While we can control our breath, most of the time the body breathes for us, without our conscious awareness or volition. The body knows how to breathe, without being taught. Imagine that when the time comes to die, your body will know how to let go of life just as easily as it lets go of air when you exhale. Every breath is a practice for death.

Air is the matrix of life. We cannot exist without it for more than a few moments. We are not self-sufficient units: we must constantly interact with the world around us, taking air into our bodies, changing it, giving it out again. Air carries scent, actual molecules of other beings, other lives. When we smell a rose, we literally inhale tiny bits of the flower, transform them, and send them out. Everything that lives leaves traces of itself in the air, and that same air moves in and out of lungs, is taken in by pores in green leaves, and is carried around the globe. Just by breathing, we interact with all of life.

So as you continue to breathe, let your awareness expand to all of life. When you say "birth," think of all that is being born. When you say "life," feel your connection to all that is living. When you say "death," know that all living things die. When you say "rebirth," imagine that you consciously send your energy out to strengthen the forces of regeneration.

FIRE

All of life depends on fire. The sun's radiation supports all the living beings on this planet. Death is one way that energy is passed from creature to creature. Plants feed on sunlight. Animals feed on plants, or on other animals that feed on plants. Fire transforms itself into a billion diverse bodies.

Fire, in turn, can transform the seemingly solid body into vapor and ash. Fire unlocks the illusion of form, pries atom from atom, changes the most dense matter into energy, heat, and light.

Build a fire or light a candle. Watch the flame.

Imagine that you can take that fire into yourself. Feel your life as a living flame. Sometimes we flicker and nearly go out; other times we blaze up in a wild conflagration or burn steadily and cheerfully like a warm hearth fire. We are bodies momentarily suspended in a net of fire. Letting go, as much as you can, of words, names, and concepts, just watch the flame and allow yourself to be its mirror, another form of fire.

WATER

Life is born from water. Ocean water was the womb of life on this planet, and every womb that shelters a developing embryo is a small, enclosed ocean.

Water is part of its own cycle. Rain is wafted up from the surface of the ocean to sail with the clouds, congealing into raindrops that fall to earth. The rain soaks into the soil, feeds the roots of plants, or runs into streams that flow into rivers that flow on until they return to the sea. All the waters on earth are connected. Every drop is part of the larger flow, the continual transformation from wave to vapor to drop to stream, the alternation between salt and sweet.

Sit somewhere where you can watch water—whether it is the ocean waves curling and crashing, or a river's flow, or a simple bowl of water on your altar. Let yourself think about life as a process of return. From the moment we are born, we are flowing downhill toward death. Like a clear spring high in the mountains, emerging from the dark, we come into life at birth. In childhood and youth, we are like a dancing stream, full of energy, playful, strong enough to carve mountains. Sometimes our flow is blocked, but behind each dam we simply continue to build up power and momentum—power that will help us find a way over, under, or around. In maturity, we are like a broad river, a bit slower perhaps, but able to carry many things on our backs and irrigate broad fields. Finally, in the end, we return our waters to the ocean, merging with the greater tides and currents.

As you breathe, reflect on the cycles of water. Imagine that death is as natural as a river spilling its waters into the ocean. Let yourself dissolve, for a moment, into awareness of the great currents of life that surround us. Feel your own depths, or perhaps let yourself become light enough to evaporate. As the water vapor in clouds is the matrix from which raindrops form, know that within you is that which is the matrix of rebirth.

EARTH

It has been said that all of life is merely rock rearranging itself. We are made of the body of the earth, our bones and flesh composed of its minerals suspended in water, infused by air, animated by fire. The earth is made of the bodies of stars—stardust congealed into a ball. The ancient Egyptians were instructed to greet the Lords of Death by saying, "I am a child of earth and starry heaven." They were telling the literal truth.

Lie down on the earth in a safe place, if possible. If not, lie down on the floor or on your bed. Feel the force of gravity pulling you down as if it were the arms of the earth holding you close, reminding you of the physical being of your body.

Think for a moment of your physical, mineral being: the iron in your blood, the calcium in your bones. Part of you may have been red rock buried beneath the northern ranges that border the Great Lakes, dissolved by rain to be taken up through grasses and passed through body after body to reach yours. Part of you may once have been a diatom swimming in a pre-Cambrian sea, falling in death to the bottom to lie for millions of years beneath layers of bone and mud, compressed into rock, only to be uplifted by the rising of the great mountain ranges as the plates of the earth surged and crashed. Within you is the earth's geologic history. Her future lies within you as well, for someday you too will give your flesh and bones back to soil and dust. You are a momentary constellation of the same great forces that raised the Sierras and are grinding them flat. As you breathe, be aware of the incredible, seemingly accidental convergence of forces that make your temporary existence possible.

Now, as you continue to breathe, feeling the rising and falling of your lungs against the force of gravity, let your awareness deepen. Feel the presence of the creative power that weaves the elements together, that created *you* out of minerals, dust, and clay. Let yourself rest in that creative power, knowing that though the particular form you are will dissolve, the great forming powers of the universe will remain.

SPIRIT AND MYSTERY

The center of the circle is the place of change and transformation, the animating power of the universe.

When in your life have you actually encountered the sacred—the Goddess, God, or whatever name you choose? What has your real experience been of the great powers of life and death? What moments of transformation have you known in your life?

Ask yourself these questions in meditation. You might also wish to write about them in your journal, or draw or paint or dance them. Create your own spiritual biography.

Do your beliefs, rituals, practices, and values reflect your own real experience of the sacred? If not, what would? What does your own experience teach you about the nature of life and death?

The Goddess and God

In the Reclaiming tradition, we use the word "Goddess" in two ways. We speak of "the Goddess" as our symbolic term for the underlying consciousness and presence of the living being that is the cosmos. Other traditions might use God, the Great Spirit, the Creator, or the Nature of Mind in much the same way.

The more we awaken to this consciousness, the more we know that it is shared by all living beings. The more we communicate with it, the more the universe responds. That response is not in human speech, but it is nevertheless a powerful communication. When we talk to a tree, it does not generally respond with a rubber Disney mouth and a balloon of print in the sky. Nevertheless, something shifts. We become aware of the presence of a being aware of us.

From this awareness arises the second meaning of Goddess—the particular aspects of the sacred that we give names to, which in fact may be Gods as well as Goddesses. They originate as moments of communication with the great forces of life and death embodied in particular places, plants, elements, or experiences. Demeter, for example, the Greek Goddess of grain and agriculture, is the embodiment of Eleusis, in ancient times the most fertile area in Greece (today the most polluted area!). Eriu is the land of Ireland. Frau Holle is the elder tree, and she is also winter's snow and ice.

Goddesses and Gods also embody the cycle of birth, growth, death, and rebirth as it plays out in different aspects of nature and human life. The Baba Yaga is the dread keeper of the house of bones, while Morgan le Fay is guardian and guide to Avalon, the isle of rebirth. The Green Man embodies the vegetation cycle: from a tiny seed he grows into a strong, green shoot, to flower, set seed, and be cut down to die. Buried in the darkness of the earth, he is reborn and the cycle begins again.

Working with the named Goddesses and Gods, invoking them and meditating on them, allows us to experience the cycle of rebirth in many different aspects. The more familiar we are with the cycle, the more powerfully it is ingrained in our awareness, the more we will be able to trust it when we face death.

Moon Meditation for Facing Death

(This meditation can be used by the dying, but it is also helpful for caretakers to imagine themselves in the dying process.)

Lie down in a safe, protected place. You might wish to ground and cast a circle before beginning this meditation. Place your hands on your belly, and breathe deeply. Imagine that you are breathing into your womb. If you do not have a physical womb, you still have a center of creative, generative energy in your belly, roughly two inches below your navel.

As you breathe, imagine the dark sphere of the new moon filling your belly. A thin sliver of light curves to the right. Call her name: Artemis, wild Lady of the Woods, she who carries the moon bow, the Huntress. Think of all the times in your life when you have begun something new: school, work, relationships, friendships, projects. What were the qualities that sustained you? What were the energies that surrounded you?

Now you are beginning a new process, the process of dying. You are about to embark on a wild adventure into an unknown country. Call on Artemis, call on the fearlessness of the Hunter. You have the power to find your way in the wilderness, without maps or guides. New instincts awaken in you, the hidden wisdom of your body that has awaited this moment. Breathe in the power of beginning.

Time passes, and under your hands the moon grows, from crescent to quarter, from quarter to full. Feel the glowing sphere that fills you now. The full moon is the time of culmination. Think about the times of fulfillment in your life, the dreams you have realized, the plans you have carried through. What were the strengths that sustained you? What energies and feelings surrounded you?

Call on the qualities that bring culmination, and reflect on how fulfillment always brings an end. The ripe fruit falls from the tree. What is ripe, or overripe, in your life? What will you leave behind that is still green or that never had a chance to blossom?

Breathe in the light of the full moon and imagine that you are filling yourself with the freely given love of the Mother, she who pours her love out on the universe and asks for nothing in return. Call her name, Diana. Trust that her love will sustain you and her body receive you. Breathe in the power of the full moon.

Time passes, and under your hands the moon wanes, from full to quarter, from quarter to crescent, curving to the left, from crescent to a dark sphere. Now the end has come. The dark moon is Hecate, the Crone, Goddess of the crossroads who guards the way to the land of the dead. As you approach her realm, think about all the times in your life you have let go, have brought something to an end. What qualities sustained you? What energies surrounded you?

Call them up, call on the power of the Crone, call her name, Hecate, for now is the time to begin to say goodbye—goodbye to the people you have loved and cared for, goodbye to mothers and fathers, to children, to lovers, to friends. Where you are going, they cannot follow. Breathe deeply, and let them go.

Say goodbye to work—the work that fulfilled you and the work that sustained you, creative work and drudgery, goodbye,

goodbye. Let go of your successes and leave behind your failures. What have you left unfinished, undone? Say goodbye, for
you will never do it now. Breathe deeply, and let it go.

Say goodbye to your dreams—the ones you lived out and
the ones you postponed. Now it is too late for them; let them
go. Say goodbye to your fears. Soon nothing will be able to
harm you. Say goodbye to going new places, doing new things,
traveling and taking pleasure, eating and drinking, goodbye,
goodbye. Breathe deeply, and let go of the pleasures of love
and sex and touch. No caresses can warm cold flesh. Say goodbye to your eyes, to the bright colors of day, to the silver light
of the moon, to reading and seeing, goodbye, goodbye.
Goodbye to taste and smell, to hot coffee in the morning and
sweet fruit and newly-baked bread. Goodbye to shitting, piss-
ing, farting; goodbye to haircuts and brushing teeth and going
to the doctor; goodbye to healing, digesting, growing, and all
the things the body does. Goodbye to the scent of roses and
goodbye to sun and rain and the texture of a hand under your
touch. Goodbye to music, goodbye to sound and conversation
and murmured endearments, goodbye, goodbye. Breathe
deeply, and say goodbye to breath.

Give your body back to the earth, and rest in the silence.

But even in the silence of the earth, time does not cease to
exist. Change comes, and the dark moon grows a thin sliver of
light, curving to the right. Take a deep breath, and call back
breath and form. Feel your power to begin anew, to grow new
ears and new eyes, to spin a new form and weave new life. What
from your old life would you like to call back? What would you
like to leave moldering in earth?

Call on the power of Artemis, and let the new moon rise.

When you feel yourself filled again with the energy of beginning, thank the moon in all her aspects—Artemis, Diana, and
Hecate—and let the moon return to the sky. Slowly move and
stretch and bring yourself back. Pat your body; feel its edges.
Say your name, and clap your hands three times. When you are
ready, sit up.

Before the memories fade, you might wish to write in your
journal about your experience. Then open the circle and ground
yourself back in bodily life by eating something.

For those who are interested in learning about prayer beads, and perhaps in making their own prayer necklaces, Donald L. Engstrom explains his own prayer-bead pattern.

Pagan Prayer Beads

DONALD L. ENGSTROM

I suspect that prayer beads came to our distant ancestors not long after those people first started to practice what we now call prayer. The beads are the invention of many different people from around the world. Prayer beads are an ancient tool waiting to be incorporated by contemporary Pagans into our lives.

Prayer beads speak directly to one of Paganism's central mysteries: "We are our bodies until we are not." Prayers grounded in living flesh are much more than the sum of their parts. The beads can remind us with texture, color, and often sound to focus our magic and/or prayers through our complete being—flesh, bone, and living mystery. They can also be a powerful tool in our work with the Recent Ancestors and the Ancient Ones (both the Blessed Dead and the Powerful Dead).[2]

Here is an example of one of the simple prayer-bead patterns

---

[2]The Recent Dead are the folks who have just died and are still learning what it means to be dead; these people have not yet declared their ancestral jobs. The Ancient Ones are the folks who have decided not to reincarnate just yet; rather, they have chosen to continue their work from where they are. The Blessed Dead are people dwelling in Paradise who are healing, learning, and resting from their stay(s) on earth. (Paradise is a name, among many, used in discussions of the journey to, the arrival at, and the dwelling in the Place of the Dead, the Home of the Ancestors, the Healing Lands, the Beauty Lands, etc.; the journey, the arrival, and the dwelling are one.) The Blessed Dead are not focused on the living, but they do keep a close eye on their descendants. The Powerful Dead are folks who are committed to continue, support, and nourish large workings on the living earth—folks whose ancestral jobs are often focused on the living. These people consider all life their descendants.

that I use to honor some of my own ancestors (all those whose lives have made mine possible). I usually sit in my most comfortable chair, breath deep, and ground. I speak my prayers out loud as I slowly move the beads through my fingers one at a time.

A special bead of any color and design: "I honor the multiverse in which I dwell and which dwells within me."

A clear bead: "I dare to live in beauty, balance, and delight. I dare to see with clear eyes and an open heart."

A black bead: "I honor the black. I honor the Wild Realm of All Possibilities."

A clear bead: "I dare to dwell in beauty, balance, and delight. I dare to see with clear eyes and an open heart."

An indigo bead: "I honor the indigo. I honor the Borderlands. I honor the Edge Walkers."[3]

A clear bead: "I dare to dwell in beauty, balance, and delight. I dare to see with clear eyes and an open heart."

A yellow bead: "I honor the yellow. I honor the Eastern Clans."[4]

A clear bead: "I dare to dwell in beauty, balance, and delight. I dare to see with clear eyes and an open heart."

A red bead: "I honor the red. I honor the Southern Clans."

A clear bead: "I dare to dwell in beauty, balance, and delight. I dare to see with clear eyes and an open heart."

A blue bead: "I honor the blue. I honor the Western Clans."

A clear bead: "I dare to dwell in beauty, balance, and delight. I dare to see with clear eyes and an open heart."

---

[3]The Borderlands are the areas between life and death, night and day, enough and too much, and so on—the line between transformations. The Edge Walkers are beings—Mysterious Ones and others—who walk the borders paying attention to the tension between the fluid edges of change.

[4]The Directional Clans: Each of the five directions has powers, beings, and magics that hail from that direction. The Northern Clans include all who dwell in that direction, and so on.

A brown bead: "I honor the brown. I honor the Northern Clans."

A clear bead: "I dare to dwell in beauty, balance, and delight. I dare to see with clear eyes and an open heart."

A purple bead: "I honor the purple. I honor the Central Clans. I honor the Heart of the Spiral."

A clear bead: "I dare to dwell in beauty, balance, and delight. I dare to see with clear eyes and an open heart."

A gray bead: "I honor the gray. I honor the Mineral Queendoms."

A clear bead: "I dare to dwell in beauty, balance, and delight. I dare to see with clear eyes and an open heart."

A green bead: "I honor the green. I honor the Botanical Queendoms."

A clear bead: "I dare to dwell in beauty, balance, and delight. I dare to see with clear eyes and an open heart."

An orange bead: "I honor the orange. I honor the Zoological Queendoms."

A clear bead: "I dare to dwell in beauty, balance, and delight. I dare to see with clear eyes and an open heart."

A white bead: "I honor the white. I honor manifestation: the making and the unmaking."

A clear bead: "I dare to dwell in beauty, balance, and delight. I dare to see with clear eyes and an open heart."

A bead to represent deity: "I honor the Mysterious Ones,[5] the known and the unknown."

A special bead: "I honor the Goddess Terra, Mother of all who dwell on earth."

A special bead: "I honor Grandmother Bear, She Who feasts on sweet dead flesh."

A special bead: "I honor the Queer God, He Who loves me beyond all reason."

---

[5]The Mysterious Ones are all sacred beings—Goddesses, Gods, land and water spirits, clan animals, plant devas, and so on.

A clear bead: "I dare to dwell in beauty, balance, and delight. I dare to see with clear eyes and an open heart."

A bead to represent the ancestors: "I honor the ancestors. I honor all whose life has allowed me to live my own."

A special bead: "I honor my beloved husband, Aric Arthur Graf, carpenter, gardener, cook, community champion. May our love continue to feed us the powers we need to continue with our work. May our reunion be sweeter than honey. May our homecoming kisses be sweeter than wine."

A special bead: "I honor my dear boyfriend and true sister, David Grundy, gardener, cook, author, devotee of beauty. May our love continue to feed us the powers we need to continue with our work. May our reunion be sweeter than honey. May our homecoming kisses be sweeter than wine."

A special bead: "I honor my dear boyfriend, Donald Bossard, artist, cook, architect, master of sexual pleasure. May our love continue to feed us the powers we need to continue our work. May our reunion be sweeter than honey. May our homecoming kisses be sweeter than wine."

A clear bead: "I dare to dwell in beauty, balance, and delight. I dare to see with clear eyes and an open heart."

A white bead: "Farewell to the white. Farewell to Manifestation."

An orange bead: "Farewell to the orange. Farewell to the Zoological Queendoms."

A green bead: "Farewell to the green. Farewell to the Botanical Queendoms."

A gray bead: "Farewell to the gray. Farewell to the Mineral Queendoms."

A purple bead: "Farewell to the purple. Farewell to the Central Clans."

A brown bead: "Farewell to the brown. Farewell to the Northern Clans."

A blue bead: "Farewell to the blue. Farewell to the Western Clans."

A red bead: "Farewell to the red. Farewell to the Southern Clans."

A yellow bead: "Farewell to the yellow. Farewell to the Eastern Clans."

A indigo bead: "Farewell to the indigo. Farewell to the Edge Walkers."

A black bead: "Farewell to the black. Farewell to the Realms of All Possibility."

A clear bead: "I dare to dwell in beauty, balance, and delight. I dare to see with clear eyes and an open heart."

Then back to the first bead: "I honor the multiverse in which I dwell and which dwells within me."

"Blessed be."

I string my prayer beads as I would a necklace. Some folks do not connect the ends, allowing the beads to create spirals, zigzags, and other patterns. I have seen many different colors and textures used to represent many different directions, beings, and prayers. I find that using repetitive patterns, words, colors, and so on is very effective. I try to remember, when I design a set of prayer beads, that poetry and prayer go hand in hand.

I encourage you to string your beads in sacred space and time. The act of stringing the beads is often a time of deep feeling—one that generally leads me deeper and deeper into Mystery. It still delights me that such a simple and beautiful tool can lead me to places I have never been before.

Remember, though, that there is no one right way to string or use prayer beads. The most important thing to remember is that only you can design and make your own set of prayer beads. No one else knows your heart and mind quite as well as you do yourself. After all, we are our own direct contact to the Mysterious Ones.

Dare to dwell in beauty, balance, and delight. Dare to see with clear eyes and an open heart!

4

Myths of Descent and Return

*T*he cycle of birth, death, and rebirth is at the core of Pagan mythology. Many myths about Goddesses and Gods deal with journeys into the land of the dead. Often these are stories of descent and return. Working with these myths, retelling the tales, and exploring them in guided journeys and meditations can help us deeply integrate our understanding of the circle of rebirth.

In this chapter we explore the myths of Inanna's Descent, the story of Demeter and Persephone, and Lugh's Crossing. There are many other stories that follow a similar pattern: the myths of Ishtar and Tammuz, Venus and Adonis, Isis and Osiris. In part, they show us how the cycle of birth, growth, death, and rebirth plays itself out in the seasons. In some lands, summer's heat sears the growing things; winter rains bring renewal. In others, winter freezes all growth while the warmth of spring restores life. In the Inanna story, Geshtinanna, the vine, sends her grapes into the storehouse just as autumn rains renew the grasses upon which feed the flocks of Dumuzi, the Shepherd God.

The myths were not told to "explain" the seasons, but to personify the circle of death and rebirth. They can serve as fertile material for working through our own feelings about loss and death.

In the ancient Sumerian tale, probably the earliest known myth of its kind, Inanna goes down into the Underworld to visit her sister, Ereshkigal, Queen of the Dead. She passes seven gates, and at each must remove an article of her clothing or the jewels that mark Her royal station. Finally, naked, she stands before her sister, only to learn that she cannot return to the land of the living. She is hung as a rotting corpse on the gates.

On earth, vegetation dies and animals cease to mate. Finally Inanna's faithful helper, Ninshubur, pressures the Gods into giving her aid. They send down two sexless creatures, sometimes called flies, who win Ereshkigal's favor by sympathizing with her pains. They give Inanna the food of life and the water of life and bring her back to the living earth. But she must send a substitute to take her place down below. She cannot bear to send her faithful helper—but she finds her husband, Dumuzi, glorying on her throne, dressed in his finest clothes. Enraged, she sends the demons of the Underworld after him. Eventually, his sister Geshtinanna offers to share his fate, and now they alternate seasons among the living and the dead.

Descend and Return with Inanna

MEVLANNEN BESHDEREN

Inanna's Descent to Knowledge

Make yourself warm and comfortable in a dark or dimly lit room. Close your eyes, let your face and body relax, and come with me on a journey. Imagine the place you grew up in, and your favorite room in that place. Picture in the corner of that room a door. Come with me now, Inanna, to that place, to that room. There is a sign on this door; it says, "Sickness, Death, and Tears." To pass through this door, you must be ready to face those things. When you are ready, pass through the door. And I shall come with you, to be your guide on this journey.

There are stairs here. Descend, turning down and around, until you come to another door. The name of this door is

"Control." To pass through this door, you must surrender your ability to plan your life in detail. Now you must share that work with healers and caregivers, with friends and lovers. How does it feel to not know what will happen tomorrow? When you are ready, pass through the door.

Beyond the door, there are more stairs. Continue walking down, turning downward into the future. Keep going down until you find another door. The name of this door is "Objects." To pass through this door, you must let go of your possessions, the things you searched so diligently to find, you worked so hard to acquire. In the Underworld there is no place for them, and holding on to them will prevent you from passing this door. When you are ready to let go of your material wealth, you may continue onward.

And there are more stairs ahead of you. Continue down, down and around, down into the darkness. And you will find another door. The name of this door is "Comfort." To pass through this door, you must yield up all of the things that you do each morning to make ready for the day. In the Underworld, there is no place to wash your clothes; there are no warm showers; there is no coffee pot or radio. In the Underworld, there is pain, fear, and nausea, the crunch of bones, the shedding of hair, the spasm of bowels. Things taste and smell different here. And when you are ready to make that exchange, you may pass through this door.

The stairs continue down, down and around, down into the pain and crying and endless night. And here you will find another door, and its name is "Community." To pass through this door, you must surrender your relationships, your friendships, your great loves, your family. They are all at risk of severance here. Some of your relationships, some of your loves, will be lost to you, and some will grow stronger. Some of these people will be there for you, and some will not. And when you are ready to take this chance, you may pass through the door. Who did you lose? Who did you gain? How do you feel?

Continue down the stairs, down and around, down deeper now, down into knowledge. And before you, there is another door. The name of this door is "Identity." To pass through this door, you must surrender your work, your name, your face, the shape of your body. Here you take a new name, given to you by those who tend your mind and body. Say it to yourself now. Say your new name, in your own inner voice, and know that it is yours.

Continue down the stairs, down and around, deeper now, into a place you have never been. And here there is another door, and its name is "Madness." Here lies the unknown, the unpredictable, the loss of language, the forgetting of where and why you are. When you are ready to face that, you may pass through this door.

Beyond the door is a well, ringed by a thousand staring eyes. The well is filled with blue, liquid, shifting, burning fire. I cannot tell you what you may find there, but I will help you enter and leave the well. When you are ready, step into the well, past the watching eyes, into the fire.

Perhaps the fire is cool against your skin; perhaps it is hot. Perhaps it hums or vibrates or glows. Perhaps it tastes or smells of your lover, a summer's day, bones, or green growing things. Reach out, and find your answer in the fire.

And when you have that answer, I will help you climb out of the well of fire, with your own knowledge.

Inanna's Return to the Outer Worlds

And when you are ready to return to the world of words, come with me back to the door of Madness. And as you pass through this door, remember why you have come here, remember what you have learned. Perhaps you have a poem or a song, or perhaps you simply Know.

The stairs go up, up and around, up toward the world of names. And here there is another door, the door of identity. Here you must surrender the identity of illness, the cloak of disease, the name of suffering, and take on again the identity of your own work, your own name, your own face and body. And when you pass through this door, these things will again be yours to cherish and enjoy, to grow and change as you yourself desire.

Up, up and around, the stairs continue, as we climb together toward the world of manifestation. Here, at the door of community, you must look again at the relationships that were broken or lost or cast aside on the way down. This work will be difficult and challenging, but only you can do it for yourself. Which of your relationships and loves do you want to pick up again? Which ones can you mend? Which ones will you leave behind of your own free will? And when you are ready, pass through this door.

The stairs continue up, up and around, toward the world of taste and touch and smell, until we come to another door. This is the door of comfort. Here you may let go the burden of nausea, of dizziness and spasm and broken bones. To pass through this door, you must accept the responsibility of naming your feelings as they are. And when you are ready to again look after some of your own daily needs, you may pass through this door.

Continuing now, up and around, toward the world of form, we come to the door of objects. Some of the things you left here are gone forever, gone to pay the material price of your journey. Some have been put to use by your family and friends, and some await your desire to take them back again. Of the things that are here, which will you take, and which will you leave behind for another traveler? When you have made your choice, pass through the door.

Again up and around, up the stairs toward the world of plans and passions. Here is the door of control. To pass through this door, you must accept the responsibility of making your own decisions in life, for in the outer worlds no one else can make them for you. And when you are ready to take up that task, you may pass through this door.

And faster now, up toward the world of light, coming to the final door of sickness, death, and tears. Now that you have made this journey, know that you can come here again, to guide your own loved ones in times of need, and one day you may come to stay when the time is right for you. Open the door now, and step into the world of clocks and coffee pots, of dreams and hope and life. Take as long as you need in trance time, and just a few moments in clock time, to come back. And when you have returned, open your eyes and speak your name.

The knowledge that you have brought back from the Underworld is yours to do with as you will. Perhaps you may choose to share it with your friends and loved ones. Perhaps you will choose to keep silence. But the knowledge remains.

The myth of Demeter and Persephone is a much later story based on the same pattern. Persephone, first called Kore, is the innocent daughter of Demeter, Greek Goddess of agriculture and barley. While she is playing in the fields, gathering the wildflowers of spring, a chasm opens in the earth and she is carried off by Hades, Lord of the Underworld, to be his bride.

Demeter seeks for her all over the face of the earth, but finds her nowhere. She mourns and rages and withholds her life-energies from the earth. Crops die; animals no longer give birth to young. Eventually even the Gods go hungry. Questioning Helios, the Sun God, Demeter learns of Kore's fate. Zeus decrees that as long as Kore has not tasted the food of the Underworld, she can return to earth. But she has eaten three or four or six seeds of the pomegranate, and so each year she must spend the same number of months among the dead.

Still, she returns each year with the bright flowers of Spring, bringing hope and renewed life. The joy and comfort of that reunion are expressed in the poem below, from Mara Keller's work in progress, *The Greater Mysteries of Demeter and Persephone:*

> And every year, when winter is ending,
> You will be able to return to Me again,
> to enjoy the sweet light of Heaven, and
> the generous broad lap of Mother Earth.
>
> All the green shoots will burst forth,
> and the buds will begin to blossom,
> the colorful crocus and hyacinth,
> the glorious fragrant narcissus:
>
> flowers will open their lovely mouths
> to drink in the strong bright sunshine,
> to smile in the freshening rains,
> and grow sweet with the sap of spring.

Know My love shall never forsake You!
I love You as before, as I always will!
For no matter how far away you wander,
You are my Daughter! I am Your Mother!

Return to the Mother

Words and music by the Wind Hags,
after a poem by Judy Grahn

And so re - turn, re - turn re- turn———— Re- turn to the Moth - er

Just as the cycle of the day and the cycle of the year have dark and light times, so we can explore the cycle of our lives by going toward the light rather than toward the dark.

Lugh, the master of all arts, the one with the long reach, has somehow taken a shine to the Reclaiming tradition of Witchcraft and has revealed himself as the Sun god, he who gives his life with the grain, restores us with bread, steps into the dark, and lights and guides the way to the other side. Doug Orton and Beverly Frederick lead us to meet him.

Lugh's Crossing

DOUGLAS ORTON AND BEVERLY FREDERICK

Close your eyes and feel the warmth of the sun on your face. As children of the earth, we are sustained, nourished, and wholly dependent on the sun. The web of life is such that we are children of the sun as much as our Mother Earth. Let us then call the sun by one of its names. Let us call it Lugh.

Breathe in the air that still feeds your life. Acknowledge the three souls that together weave your being:

Vital spirit, our animal soul or Younger Self, belongs to the earth; when we cross, it returns whence it came.

Rational spirit, our ego or Talking Self, belongs to the sun; when we cross, it too returns whence it came.

We are witnessed and reclaimed by our parents earth and sun, while our guardian or Deep Self journeys to the gradation of its growth. But for now let us travel with our Talking Self back to Lugh. He waits even now—night or day.

Remember an occasion when you moved from one town to another, from one house to another. Once you were there, you were there.

Transition is frightening—in this world, in any world. Death frightens us; it scares us to think of death. That fear keeps us from greeting our death with open arms. Leaving everything we know is terrifying. So let us begin by giving ourselves to terror's dance—the resistance, the denial, the blaming. Let us stomp, rage, struggle, and scream until the dance is complete and we move from within into a place of grief.

While we are here, let us give ourselves fully to the sobs that come to us. Let the dammed-up disappointment burst forth in guttural wails that crash like waves upon the shore, until the wailing song is complete and we move from within to a place of acceptance.

When Lugh calls, there is no past, there is no future; the goodbyes are done. Remorse and expectation are over. They have simply ceased to exist. We are in a journey of the present. We surrender our future and let go of the past.

As our energy swells into the present, it becomes radiant. Our brilliance, like Lugh's, is complete and without effort. This is a place of healing.

Is this our work—our attention, our awareness in the experience of transition? What does the sun tell you?

(Pause here for reflection.)

Here in the present, the presence of Lugh, we leave all we have cherished. Yet all our lives on earth we have been connected intimately with the sun. Our mysteries are deeper than

Darwin's speculations. Even on earth, a part of ourselves lives in space. We have spent our lives at night dreaming, and we are larger than we know.

Lugh's gift to crossing has nothing to do with seasons and cycles of earthly harvest and weather. Feel Him beckon you to a new world with stardust memory. His gift is part of something larger than random selection and a consciousness aware of its death. Lugh shines down and says, "A part of you is always with Me. Transition is hard work. The very nature of matter is to hold on. I told you not to go there, but you never listen to Me. That is probably why we are such good friends."

Talking sun, Talking Self. Lugh holds no questions about earthly tidings. Lugh holds the promise of new forms beyond the horizon. His is the meaning in the moment of the present. For to be present is a glimpse into eternity.

And in that glimpse anything can happen. What irrational notions are coming to you? Let them come. What absurd feelings call to you? Go with them. Leave judgment behind. This is your time, your healing time—before you cross, as you cross, and after.

Lugh's Song

Words and music by T. Thorn Coyle

Lugh, strike Your spear in a shaft of sun - light, Dy - ing One, let
Lugh, strike Your spear in a shaft of sun - light, Sum - mer pas - ses a -

go, let go,_____ Lugh, strike Your spear in a shaft of sun - light,
way, a - way,_____ Lugh strike Your spear in a shaft of sun - light,

1.
Lead us in - to slum - ber.

2.
Show us the pas - sage, car - ry us home.

Spi - ral down - ward, burn in - to

1.   D.S.
dark - ness, Death to sleep in the tomb of birth

2.   D.C.
sleep in the tomb of birth.

Part Two

The Pagan View of Death

5

Lessons from Death

Birth, Growth, and Death as a Cycle

What is death? Why do we have to die, and what really happens when we do? We know that death is ultimately a mystery, yet what can we say about it, what can we hold on to and believe in when we are faced with loss and grief?

Pagans tend to be uncomfortable with the concept of "belief." Most of us have come to the Pagan tradition from some other religious upbringing, and many of us have spent a lot of time and effort divesting ourselves of our early conditioning. "Belief" and "faith" are too easily used as a rationale for oppressing those whose beliefs are different or unpopular. We value intellectual freedom, are wary of any sort of dogma, and find ourselves uneasy speaking of "faith."

But when we encounter death, faith can be our comfort and source of strength. Indeed, it is hard to face death without any belief in anything.

If we were writing this book as an academic exercise in thealogy, we would steer clear of any mention of faith or belief. We would carefully speak only of our "worldview," or perhaps our "construction of reality." But we are writing a work of help and comfort for the dying and those who love them. So we will take the risk of outlining what we believe about death and what comes after, cautioning the reader to weigh what we say against what your own experience and intuition tells you. For one of our core beliefs is that each of us has our own direct connection to the sacred. We need never simply accept someone else's truth, for our own powers of observation, discernment, and connection allow us direct revelation.

The heart of the Pagan understanding of death is the insight that birth, growth, death, and rebirth are a cycle that forms the underlying order of the universe. We can see that cycle manifest around us in every aspect of the natural world, from the decay of falling leaves that feed the roots of growing plants, to the moon's waning and waxing. Hard as it is for us to die, or to accept the death of someone we love, we know that death is a part of the natural process of life.

Therefore we can trust that death, like every other phase of life, offers us opportunities for growth in wisdom and love.

What Death Can Teach Us

Savoring Life

Death can teach us to truly appreciate and savor life. Because we know that our lives are short, we must fully enter into each moment. When we encounter beauty, love, ecstasy, or passion in our lives, we know that they are temporal. Flowers fade; lovers, no matter how faithful, grow old and die. That knowledge infuses our every response to the world and its offerings. The fear of loss and the pain of mourning can make us turn away from the world. But the Pagan way is to honor the fleeting nature of life's gifts, to know that their very ephemerality gives life a poignant beauty that enriches us.

Last year, I (Starhawk) and my partner David traveled throughout much of the late winter and spring. Because of the timing and route of our trip, we seemed to hit every region just when the fruit trees were blossoming and spring was beginning. Here in California, when the trees begin to bloom in late January and early February, I find their beauty overwhelming. I want to stare and stare, taking in their form and scent and the color of the petals against the sky. But last year, by the time May rolled around and we'd had four months of flowering trees, we were saying, "Enough already!"

Plastic flowers do not fade, but they do not have the charm of living blossoms. The awareness of death can help us to keep our relationships alive with the freshness of our first response to love or friendship. Knowledge of their fleeting nature deepens our joys and gives perspective to our conflicts.

Here is a meditation to affirm the preciousness of life.

A Meditation for Friends, Lovers, or Partners

Sit with your friend so that you can be comfortable while looking into each other's eyes. Take hands for a moment, and breathe together until your breath is synchronized. You may drop hands if you wish, or continue the contact.

Look into your friend's eyes and allow yourself to experience all you know and value about this person. Hurt, conflict, or frustration might also emerge. Let those feelings come. Do not push them away, but honor them as part of the rich whole that constitutes your relationship.

Imagine that you can see the small child your friend once was. Imagine that you can watch her or his first steps, hear those precious first words. Grow your friend up from babyhood through adolescence to maturity, acknowledging how each stage is fleeting and precious. Let yourself envision the old person your friend will someday become.

Now return to the present moment, allowing yourself to accept and appreciate the precise phase of life you and your friend share now. Consider how fragile life is. Imagine that you know your friend will die tomorrow. Reflect on how that knowledge affects how you treasure this moment in your relationship, how you memorize your friend's features, scent, tone of voice — all the ordinary, precious aspects of our embodiment in flesh and personality. Cherish the uniqueness of your friend at this moment, and let that emotion flow between you.

Become aware also how it feels to be loved and cherished in this way.

Know that something of this awareness can infuse every moment of your relationship. Make a commitment to remember this feeling and to evoke it again, especially in moments of conflict and impatience.

Thank your friend, hug, and end.

Owning Our Choices

The awareness of death also gives us perspective on our own lives. We cannot drift along waiting for our real lives to begin at some time in the future; we must acknowledge at every moment that this is it—not the rehearsal but the big concert, not the practice but the game itself.

A common plot in romantic fiction centers around a character who is diagnosed with a fatal illness and given only a short time to live. Facing death becomes, for that fictional character, a catalyst for truly living life. Such characters usually fall in love, a love all the more romantic because it is destined to be brief. In the movies, dying lovers remain stunningly beautiful until the end. They never smell bad or need their bedpans changed. And their terminal illness does not seem to prevent them from going on world cruises or climbing mountains.

Corny as this overworked plot may be, it does reflect a real truth about our experience. When we face death, we reevaluate our lives. We realize that we no longer have the luxury of putting off our plans and deferring our dreams.

In the last decades, countless men and women diagnosed as HIV-positive have lived the real version of this story, without the Hollywood gloss of romanticism. Most have not had the money to embark on long cruises; instead, they have faced the realities of painful and time-consuming medical procedures, discrimination, and fear. They have struggled to hold on to jobs, health insurance, and relationships, and watched family, friends, and lovers die with no soft-focus gel to cushion the pain. Some have succumbed to bitterness or despair. Others have found that the presence of death calls for a deeper level of care, support, and community, that it makes precious the most ordinary moments of life.

When my friend Stanford was losing his battle with Kaposi's sarcoma, I went to visit him in the new house he shared with his lover and life-partner, Paul. Because Stanford was a new friend, I had never been to his house before. We sat in his kitchen beneath a sunny window, drinking tea, laughing and chatting together, saying nothing particularly memorable or profound. Yet for me that ordinary occasion was luminous because I knew it might never come again. Each smile, each nugget of gossip became a moment of sweet and holy communion. Wherever I now am, whenever I visit and laugh with friends, I am conscious that these common acts of friendship are among the most precious gifts life offers.

At Stanford's wake, his lover reported to us something he said toward the very end of his life. "I never thought I would want to live like this, impotent, and incontinent. But life is still so sweet." When we are surrounded by love, life can be precious even in the midst of great suffering.

Death teaches us what is really important in life. Is it the amount of work we accomplish, or the number of sunny windows we have sat under with friends? What does not show on our resume or accumulate in our bank account may ultimately give most meaning to our lives.

Death may also challenge us to own our life choices. Lucia, a woman who was active in a revolutionary movement in Latin America, tells of what went through her mind when she and her friend Carlos were arrested at a border crossing. "I thought, This is it. This is the end. At first I felt angry with myself—why were we so stupid? Why did we try to cross here? Why couldn't we have come another day. But then I thought, No, we all have to die someday. I'm here because of my whole life, what my life has been. And I affirm my life. If I have to die for it—well, I'm willing to die. But I won't die in fear, cringing and begging like some people do. Then I became calm, and I could think what to do." In fact, Lucia's calm demeanor and lack of fear became an important factor in her eventual success in convincing the authorities to let her and her friend go. Had she not accepted her death, she could not have thought clearly enough to preserve her life. Had she not been able to affirm her life, she could not have accepted her death.

By the time we have a terminal disease, we may no longer have the strength and energy to realize our unfulfilled dreams. Death may come suddenly, without the grace of warning and time for preparation. Yet when we accept death as part of the natural cycle, we can allow that awareness to guide our priorities in every moment, and we can live fully and fearlessly.

Affirming Our Lives: A Meditation

Imagine that you knew, beyond doubt, that you had only one more year to live. What would you do today? Tomorrow? Next month? What would be most important for you to complete? What have you left undone that you would most like to do?

What unlived dreams would you choose to realize? What conflicts would you work to resolve?

What are the basic life-choices you have made that you can affirm? What would you change? What do you regret?

Suppose you had only one month instead of a year. Would your answers change?

If you knew you were going to die tomorrow, what would you do today?

Practicing Unconditional Love and Forgiveness

Death also teaches us about love, compassion, and forgiveness. "My love is poured out upon the earth," the Goddess says (see "Charge of the Goddess" in the epigraph to this book). Just as we offer a new-born unconditional love, "a dying person most needs to be shown as unconditional a love as possible, released from all expectations," says Sogyal Rinpoche in *The Tibetan Book of Living and Dying.*

Unconditional love means that regardless of conflicts we might have had with our friend, regardless of whatever still lies unfinished between us, we can honor our deep connection of spirit. Unconditional love means that we recognize the Goddess in our friend's eyes, that we allow ourselves to accept her failures, her annoying behaviors, her mistakes and weaknesses as part of the rich brew of her personality. When my mother was dying, I remember feeling an enormous pang of grief at the thought that she would never yell at me again.

When a child comes into the world, we are instinctively moved to love and cherish him. So too when someone leaves this world, great reservoirs of love may be called forth. The magnitude of death dwarfs our minor annoyances and petty grievances. The suffering of death evokes our compassion.

"My law is love unto all beings," the Goddess tells us in "Charge of the Goddess." Yet there are many times in life when we may doubt that the primary ground of the universe is love. Certainly when someone we love is dying, or when we are experiencing pain and suffering, the world does not seem like a loving place. But when the gates of life and death stand open, at death as in birth we may catch a glimpse of another country in which love *is* truly the law. When personality disintegrates and intelligence is gone, sometimes only love is left.

When my Uncle Hi was hospitalized in the late stages of Alzheimer's disease, I took my Aunt Ruthie to visit him. Hi was not a religious man; he came from the Communist side of the family, those who had rebelled against the Orthodox Judaism of their parents. But we found him on the hospital ward with a prayer book open, chanting and swaying in the fashion of our forefathers. In the place of the traditional skullcap, he was wearing a pair of Mickey Mouse ears. He could have appeared to be a tragic figure of humiliation, but when he caught sight of my aunt, he was transformed. Such love shone out of his eyes! He stood tall with an inner dignity that made his odd attire completely insignificant.

Suddenly I could see what he must have been like as a young man, a lover, a hero. He came over and kissed my aunt with such tenderness and passion that I thought I would cry. "Take me home, Ruthie," he said. "Let's go home." Heartbreaking as the moment was, I felt privileged to be granted a glimpse of his secret soul. With his mind, his defenses, his judgment gone, all that was left was the essence of his being—and that core was love.

Sometimes the dying revert to the same innocence that makes a newborn easy to love. However, we cannot always feel kindly and loving toward the dying. Our suffering friend or relative may be angry as well as innocent—or crotchety, complaining, demanding, self-centered, whining, or given over to self-pity or despair. In addition, our personal history may get in the way. We may be unable to forget the wounds we have inflicted upon each other, the unforgiven hurts, or we may feel angry at our friend for dying or for choices she or he made while living. Try as we will, we may not be able to set aside our own hurt or anger. The "Forgiveness Meditation" offered later in this chapter can be helpful in allowing us to acknowledge our less-than-loving feelings. Naming and accepting our feelings may allow them to move aside and let us contact a deeper layer of love, just as clouds may part to let a ray of sun shine through. The sky is still cloudy, but the colors around us may be more intense, the distant hills standing out more sharply than they would under a clear sky.

Death calls forth our ability to forgive. Forgiveness means clearing the slate, letting go of the past, starting anew. One aspect of this process is letting go of our own attachment to our hurt. Another aspect is forgoing an accounting of the wrongs done, relinquishing a need for punishment. I am often wary of calls for forgiveness. Too often victims are pressed to forgive their victimizers, when justice may be more in order. When someone has the power to harm us, forgiveness must wait upon repentance. Otherwise, we may simply perpetuate the damage.

But someone who is dying generally no longer has the power to hurt us, at least physically. Most of the hurts people inflict upon us in relationships fall far short of crimes meriting the death penalty. Often the dying are suffering enough to redeem any pain they might have caused us.

When we are dying, we may need to forgive for our own well-being, our own peace of mind. We may face death with hurts unresolved. Our loved ones may care for us imperfectly, or wound us by neglect, we may have good reason for anger, but hate and resentment carried across the veil can be enormously draining of our energies and soul-reserves. Forgiveness can help us to let go, ease suffering and release us to continue our soul's journey unfettered. Forgiveness can become a free gift of love that shifts the balance of the universe.

Death can sometimes teach us great spiritual lessons even when we are less than eager to receive them. Those lessons may come through unlikely sources. Those who live well, keep our trust, and die with courage may teach us much about living and loving, but those whose lives are filled with mistakes, failures, and betrayals may also be true teachers of compassion.

Last Spring, Macha and I sat at the bedside of a dying friend. Raven was a longtime member of our community, much loved as a teacher (for he had introduced many people to the Craft) and for his charm, his unique imagination, and his handsome face and lithe body, now ravaged by AIDS. However, Raven also had a long-standing drug problem, and when the need was upon him, he would lie and steal. Many of us, over the years, had felt hurt and betrayed by him. We could not trust him in our homes, and our efforts to help him seemed to only further his destruction.

When he became seriously ill, however, his old friends gathered around him once again. We were able to move him out of his grimy apartment into a hospice and help him arrange his affairs. At his deathbed, many of us kept vigil through the long hours while he lay unconscious, listening to his labored breathing, singing and chanting and holding the energy to help him cross. There were many people in that room whom I loved dearly—but as I looked around I realized there were also people there with whom I'd had major conflicts over the years, toward whom I still held grudges and resentments. Yet because we were all engaged in the greater work of helping Raven die, I could put my unhealed wounds aside and acknowledge the love I felt toward everyone in that room.

At the end of the long vigil, my coven-sister's daughter Bethany came in. When Bethany was a young girl, Raven had stolen magical objects her parents were saving as gifts for her First Blood ritual. At the time of Raven's death, she was a beautiful young woman in her mid-twenties, a paramedic and ambulance driver who could sit at a deathbed with the calm confidence of one who daily holds the lives of others in her hands. She took Raven's hand, whispered in his ear, and he let out a long breath, almost a sigh of relief, and died.

Raven was an unlikely teacher of great spiritual lessons about forgiveness. But his death taught us all something about the power of community. We can trust our community only if we know that we will care for our own in times of great need without judgment or blame. And the effort we make to let go, to forgive, to focus on what is truly important may also bring healing that can flow out beyond the dying person's bedside to the circles within circles of lives that he touched.

The following meditation can help us acknowledge hurt and move us toward forgiveness. It can be used before working with the dying, or by a dying person to help clear away lingering wounds or resentments.

Forgiveness Meditation

Begin with a discernment process. Ask yourself the following questions:

Why am I angry or hurt by _____? Is _____ aware of my feelings? Have I expressed them? What have I asked for in return? What response did I get?

Is there anything I need to do to hold _____ accountable for his actions, for my protection or the protection of others?

What are my feelings doing to me? Are they serving me in some way? Binding me? Bolstering my sense of self-worth? Eroding it?

How do my feelings keep me connected to _____?
Am I willing to break that tie? If not, why not?

What am I hoping for?

Can I imagine what life would be like without this tie? What
feelings arise?

If I let go of this hurt, what new connections might arise
between me and _____?

Is _____ in any way a mirror of forces and emotions
within me?

Other questions may also occur to you. You may wish to
write out some of your answers in your journal.

When you are ready, sit in a quiet place with a bowl of salt
water. Ground, and if you wish, cast a circle in a simple way.

Gazing into the water, allow all your emotions to surface as a
muddy stream. Let them flow into the water.

Let yourself acknowledge any feelings of revenge that arise,
any sense of satisfaction in _____'s suffering, or any
belief that _____ deserves to suffer pain, to die.
Those thoughts are human; you can simply let them arise and
flow through you.

Imagine for a moment that you could step outside yourself
and see your body energy like a glow around you. Are there any
cords, any threads of light binding you to _____?
Where do they hook into you?

Here is a very rough guide to the energy centers of the body
and their traditional meanings. (Note: Some of these correspond
to the chakras, for those familiar with that system; others are
simply areas where attachments may occur.) (See also the meditation on page 28.)

Crown of the head: spiritual connection

Third eye: psychic connection, intuition

Throat and neck: expression

Heart: emotion

Hands and arms: action

Solar plexus: power

Belly (two inches below the navel): life-force, nurturing, creativity, body-centered intuition

Sexual organs: sexuality

Base of the spine: survival

Feet and legs: grounding

If any cords exist, imagine that you pluck them out and return the energy to _____ with compassion. Cords are fixed patterns of relationships. Releasing them does not necessarily mean cutting all connections. When the cords are gone, energy may actually be able to flow more freely between you.

When you feel empty, sit for a moment in stillness. Allow yourself to experience the space that has opened within you. Imagine it as a dark womb, where something new can begin to grow.

Now call on the love and compassion of the Goddess. Think of the moments in your life when you have been touched by love, the instances of grace, of beauty and joy that do not have to be earned. Imagine that love as an inner warmth, filling the empty space as the sun warms seeds in the dark, cool soil of spring.

Does this feeling have a color? Bathe yourself in it. Does it have a rhythm or a tone? Let yourself make sounds.

Imagine pouring this feeling into the salt water, charging it with color and sound and the radiance of love. When you feel the water has been transformed, take a sip to take back, in a new form, the energy you have released. Put some of the water any place on your body where you have let go of a cord.

Thank the Goddess, open the circle, and pour out the water on the ground, into a running stream, or (if need be) down the drain.

Use this meditation whenever you need to call forth reserves of love and compassion.

Seeing Death as Sustaining Life

Death serves life. Death is an integral part of life, a gift not a curse, for it allows for change, making room for what is new. The existence of death allows for infinitely more variety and diversity among living things.

Medicine Story, a Mettanonquit storyteller and teacher, once told a group of us the following tale:

HOW DEATH CAME INTO THE WORLD[1]

After that Maushop was sitting by the fire late at night as the moon started to rise through the woods. Suddenly the frogs stopped singing, and he looked up to see what was the matter. There was Matahdou coming back in the moonlight, but he didn't seem all there. It was like he was made of smoke, and part of him was missing.

Maushop called out, "Brother, I don't think you are supposed to be here. You have left some of yourself somewhere else!"

Matahdou was sad as he spoke. "Brother, it is very lonely where I am now. The healing powers have made me the keeper of the door of the land of souls, but there is no one there, and I am all alone."

Maushop said, "I guess it is time for us to consider the question of death in the world. We will have a council here, but you should go back to that other place now."

So Maushop called everyone together. Of course, in those days all the animals and the human beings lived together as one family, and all spoke the same language.

Maushop spoke to them all and said, "You all must have noticed how the family of Mother Earth is growing very quickly. That is because you have all been having babies, and your babies have grown up to have more babies, and they have grown to have more babies, so that as the generations go on, the world is starting to fill up. Just now there is plenty of room and enough food for

---

[1]From *The Children of Morning Light: Wampanoag Tales,* as told by Manitonquat (Medicine Story), New York: MacMillan Publishing Company, 1994.

everyone, but as we go on bringing more and more into the world and not sending anyone away, after a while there won't be enough room for everyone, and there won't be enough food. Plants will all be destroyed, animals will starve, and Mother Earth will suffer.

Now, I can see two possible ways to solve this problem. In one of them you could just stop having babies and keep the same number as you have and just go on living in this way forever. In the other, if you want to keep bringing babies in through the door which you call Birth, then we should make another door, which we will call Death, and when you have been here for a while and experienced this world, then you would go through that other door and experience a different place.

Of course they all wanted to know about that other place, but Maushop said he hadn't been there and he didn't know much about it. He said that Matahdou was there waiting and had made a star path in the sky for them to follow down to the southwest. He said they would have to leave their bodies behind for Mother Earth to make into new life, because only their spirits could enter the land of souls. He said that it was an important decision that they would have to make for themselves, because whatever they decided, that's how it would be for all the generations to come.

So the animals and people all went into their clans, and the clans went into the male and female groups, and each group began to council about what Maushop had said.

After a little while the men's groups were all finished, and when they came together they found they were all in agreement. They had all decided that they should stop having babies so that the world wouldn't get too full and they could all just go on living as they were forever. Then they looked around and saw that the women were coming out of their councils.

The female creatures had made one big circle, and so the men all went over and peeked into the circle to see what was going on. There in the center were all these little cubs—little lion cubs, wolf cubs, bear cubs, human-being cubs, all playing with one another, wrestling and biting one another's ears, and the women were all laughing and saying things like: "Oh, look at those two over there, aren't they cute!"

So the men all looked to the oldest clan chief and said, "Grandfather, speak for us."

So the oldest clan chief stepped out and said, "Well, the men creatures have had their meetings and we all agree. We all think it should be like this, that we will stop having babies so that the world won't fill up too much and we can just go on living as we are forever. Thank you."

There was silence for a moment, and everyone turned toward the oldest clan mother. So this grandmother stood up slowly and looked around at everyone and said, "Well, the women have had their meetings, too, and they have also come to an agreement. And that's not the way it's gonna be. We have decided that we want to go on having babies and bringing new little ones in through that door called Birth, and so we must have that other door called Death that we can go on through after a while. This is the reason we decided that: We have noticed that we do not know enough yet about life and Creation here. Especially the human beings do not know enough. We keep making the same mistakes, and then we find new mistakes to make. But these little ones that come to us from the Creator, they are messengers. They bring us new teachings all the time from the Creator. They keep us on our toes so that we will do right for them, and not just for them, but for their children as well, and for all the unborn generations that are waiting to come here. When we understand that, then we must keep making a better world for them."

So, since it was the women who were in charge of birth and of raising those little ones, they were the ones who had the last word, and that's the way it has been ever since.

Another tale comes to us from traditional Japanese lore.

IZANAMI AND IZANAGI[2]

Out of the primeval oily ocean mass arose three deities: a reed-like substance and a male and a female. These three produced

---

[2]It was Beth Carlson who points out to us that this story is also relevant, indicating an Inanna-type story for the Shinto Creatrix Izanami, "She Who Invites." Part of this story is in *Japanese Mythology* by Julia Piggott, copyright 1969, The Hamlyn Publishing Group Limited, pp. 13, 14. Ms. Piggott has cited the *Kojiki* (C.E. 712) and the *Nihongi* (C.E. 720), the earliest extant Japanese books.

generations of Gods and Goddesses until Izanami and Izanagi, She Who Invites and He Who Invites, were created. Izanagi dropped his spear into the primeval ocean, and the drops from the tip, congealed and falling in, created a land called Ono-Koro (self-coagulating). Izanami and Izanagi married on Ono-Koro, learned the art of lovemaking by watching the birds (wagtails), and gave birth to the Japanese landmarks, trees, herbs, winds. The last child born to Izanami was the God of fire, and His birth killed Her. She went to the Underworld, Yomi, the Land of Gloom, but Izanagi followed Her in spite of Her protests, and shamed Her by bursting in upon Her in Her decomposing state. She chased Him, aided by hideous female spirits, back out into the world. At the entrance of Yomi, She screamed that in revenge She would denude the world of its inhabitants by destroying a thousand daily, thus creating mortal death. He responded that in return He would create fifteen hundred new lives each day. Thus Their marriage created the pattern of nature for all time, and Their divorce created mortal life and death.

Death is part of nature's strategy of change. Because we die, leaving room for new beings to be born, species can adapt to new conditions. Nature herself can create new forms and try new experiments. If this possibility did not exist, any change in the environment could result in mass extinction, in a final termination of life. Death preserves life.

What dies decays, and decay is the matrix of fertility. Today when I finish writing, I will prepare a new garden bed, piling on half-rotted compost, spoiled hay, manure, vegetable scraps—anything I can find that was once living. Over the next months, all this material will rot down into fertile soil, feeding the worms and the soil bacteria, making a good home for eggplants, tomatoes, squashes that will feed me and my family. Our bodies are sustained by the processes of decay.

Reconciling Death and Consciousness

When we face death, we must mourn the loss of that consciousness which makes us who we are. All our hard-won skills, knowledge, and experience will soon be gone. Our memories will be no more. We know that our bodies can return to earth and feed something else, but we fear the loss of the intangibles, the very things that make us most ourselves.

Because of the way the Goddess tradition teaches us to view the world, we can feel confident that consciousness is never lost from the universe. Death is not an extinction, a final end. It is a transformation, a dissolution of one form so that new forms can be created.

Pagans see the earth, and in fact the universe, as alive, an organism rather than a mechanism. As a living being, the cosmos has a consciousness in which we all participate. The living tapestry of being is woven of this underlying awareness.

Our individual awareness and personality is like a standing wave in a flowing river. That wave has a unique form, but the form is created by motion. And the substance of consciousness is not unique; it is common to all the filaments and currents of the river.

The scientist Rupert Sheldrake comes close to describing the Pagan conception of consciousness in his theory of morphogenetic fields. He postulates that every species and every grouping within a species shares a form-generating field of being. Knowledge acquired by individuals can, in time, become part of what he calls "the group mind." The popular version of this idea is the story of the "hundredth monkey." As the tale goes, on an island off the coast of Japan, a very smart monkey one day discovered that if she washed her food before eating it, she did not have to chew on dirt and grit. She showed her technique to her fellow monkeys, and they also began washing their fruit. When a certain number, perhaps a hundred, of them had learned to wash food, the monkeys on the next island also began washing their fruit, even though they had no direct contact with each other. It was as if the idea of washing fruit had spread through enough of the underlying monkey "group mind" that it had become a feature of monkeyness.

Sheldrake's theory is akin to the esoteric teachings of many spiritual traditions. Indigenous people around the globe have prayed to the

Deer Spirit or the Buffalo Spirit to send food in the form of individuals of their kind. The gardeners of Findhorn learned to work with "devas"—the spirits of individual species of plants and the overarching deva of the garden itself. Jung spoke of the collective unconscious. We all know the feeling when a group "jells" and becomes something more than a collection of individuals.

Because as individuals we affect the group mind, everything we learn is important. As we evolve and develop, the collective mind also grows. Every insight we have, every moment of growth in love and compassion, makes those experiences easier for others to achieve. Everything we learn has a value that extends beyond death.

The Three Souls

Reclaiming draws from the Feri tradition of Wicca in our understanding that each person is made up of three selves. Our rational, adult, verbal self, the personality we most often identify with, is only one aspect of a human being. We call that self the Talking Self. Younger Self is our emotional, preverbal, instinctive, and creative self, who responds more to images, sounds, rhythms, and smells than to words. Finally, we each have a Deep Self—that part of us that does not disintegrate at death, but extends through many lifetimes. Our Deep Self mediates between our personality and the great powers of life and death. In some traditions, Deep Self is seen as the personal God or Goddess; in others Deep Self appears as our Guardian Angel.

If our consciousness is like a standing wave, then Deep Self is the underlying rock that creates the form our awareness takes. Deep Self shapes our fate, lines up the lessons we need to learn, and guides our evolution.

When we are in contact with Deep Self, we feel a sense of rightness in our choices and actions—not self-righteousness or complacency but a visceral sense of knowing we are on the right road. Whatever happens, whatever the consequences of our actions, we know we are doing what we are meant to do.

When we face death, our contact with Deep Self must be strong. For death dissolves Talking Self and Younger Self, who are bound into the physical body. The core of our being retreats into Deep Self, to begin the journey that eventually will bring us to the place where Deep Self can weave a new form and personality.

The more we strengthen our contact with Deep Self in life, the easier it will be to stay connected in death. Deep Self is contacted not through Talking Self but through Younger Self, by way of images, emotions, colors, and sensual cues rather than words.

Meditation for Contacting Deep Self

Sit in a quiet, comfortable place. Ask yourself, "What is truly sacred to me? What do I most deeply value? What would I take a stand for, risk myself for?" When an answer arises, ask, "When are my life-energies directed toward serving what is truly sacred for me? How do I feel in that moment?"

Concentrate on that feeling. Link it to memories, colors, kinesthetic sensations, sounds, and smells. Maybe you imagine it as a deep forest of ancient trees, dark green, smelling of earth and rain, filled with the sound of the wind in the branches. Or maybe it is a playground in the park, filled with the sounds of happy children playing, enlivened by bright colors and the scent of flowers.

When you are steeped in the feeling, and the scene is real to you, imagine a presence hovering about three feet above your head, as a sphere of blue fire. Call the presence down and let her or him enter your scene. Imagine that you can see a person, looking very much like yourself. Greet your Deep Self and take some time to speak together, to ask for guidance and strength. Your Deep Self may suggest a daily practice for staying in close contact, or give you a name to call or an image to use.

Take the time you need, and then thank your Deep Self. Imagine the presence floating back into the sphere and then dissolving. Say goodbye to your image of the Sacred, open your eyes, and come back.

☾

Victor Anderson, the Feri tradition mentor of many Reclaiming members, has guided T. Thorn Coyle in creating the following explanation and meditation. Thorn uses different names for the three parts of the self. What Starhawk calls Younger Self she calls the Sticky

One. What Starhawk calls Talking Self she calls the Shining One, and Deep Self becomes the Sacred Dove. These variations reflect personal preferences. Starhawk prefers the imagery created by using the adjective "deep" for the God/dess self, to challenge our assumption that getting close to divinity means going up, up and away out of the world. Victor himself generally uses the Hawaiian terms Unihipili, Uhane Malamalama, and Aumakua. In Hebrew the three selves are Nefesh, Ruach, and Neshama; in Arabic, Nafs, Ruch, and al Sir. We encourage you to adopt the terms that feel most comfortable to you.

The Triple Soul

T. Thorn Coyle

"The body makes the spirit and the spirit makes the body." So says one of my teachers, Victor Anderson, on the nature of the soul. Our tripartite soul is the part of us that continues on after our death, unlike our physical flesh, which remains only in the form of composting matter. Nonetheless, this does not make the soul a being separate from the body; it is simply another, albeit etheric, part—a part just like our hands. This nondualistic thinking is not unique to the Feri or Reclaiming traditions of Wicca or to Wicca itself. Nor is the thought of soul as trinity unique: this concept appears in Hawaiian, Jewish, and Celtic cultures as well.

The three parts of the soul have distinct functions and work together like three atoms that together make a molecule. The Sticky One is that which draws flesh to bone, whose energy extends two or three inches out from our physical self. It is the vital body that creates the life-force and stores our memories. The Shining Body is our auric self, the egg of light that surrounds us and communicates with the rest of the world. The Sacred Dove is our personal God-self, which lives just above our heads. It is our true parent, or ancestor. The Sacred Dove is also our muse and teacher.

Through upbringing, cultural imprinting, or day-to-day stresses and psychic strain, the atoms of our soul can become out of synch with one another. The following meditation to align the three souls comes from what I have been taught by Victor and Cora Anderson.

Meditation to Align the Triple Soul

Begin with your breath. Inhaling deeply, center yourself and ask the Sticky One to store Mana (or life-force) in your physical body. Breathing in and out through your nose, from the well of your belly, take in the life-force that swirls around you. Your vital body stores it, easily and naturally. After a while, you may feel the edges of your body begin to tingle. When you feel a rightness in your body, a fullness of life, tilt your head back and send out a breath, releasing the Mana to flow up to your God-self. The Druids called this "feeding the dove." This causes the three parts of your soul to align within you. You may feel this as a gentle snapping into place, a straightening. The life-force then descends back into your auric and physical bodies from the Sacred Dove. This often leaves you full of a good, warm, sexual awareness. Close with the Hawaiian prayer taught by Victor, "Who is this flower above me, and what is the work of this God? I would know myself in all my parts."

Another way to attain this alignment is to simply breathe deeply and say, "All three souls are one." You may also use set patterns of breathing (e.g., take four breaths, pause, four more, and so on) if a longer meditation is helpful to you. This practice is good for all but can especially be an aid to those who are sick or dying. We want to die with our triple soul in alignment, so all parts go into their next phase as one being. If the souls are fractured, the Sticky One can remain behind as a poltergeist. Since the Sticky One holds both Mana and memory, it retains a force in the physical world. This can happen when a person has not made peace with her actions on the earth or has done things that are considered evil and not right with the universe.

If you feel that one who has passed on has done so in an unaligned state, perhaps because she left behind the restless ghost of the Sticky One, you can ask your God-self to help that person. It is not recommended to try to realign someone in any other way. Your God-self knows more than your brain could cook up or your Shining Body sense. (Sometimes, too, it is not our place to help.)

Alignment of the Triple Soul makes us stronger, healthier beings. It helps us in our daily work and spiritual quest, which are one. It lends energy and ability to cope, transform, and grow. As Feri Elder Cora Anderson says, "When you have all three souls, you can ask anything you want of the Gods and get it. You just have to learn how to ask."

6

The Land of the Dead

The Otherworld: What It Is and How It Affects This World

If something of the soul—the Deep Self—continues to exist after the death of the body, where does that something go? As we have seen, there are many different conceptions of the land of the dead. They rest on the Pagan understanding that the visible world is not all of reality. The physical world emerges and is formed by a realm of energies and spirits.

Imagine that you are looking at a waterfall. The water takes on form and dimension in its motion because of the underlying form of the rocks below. The shapes it takes may seem to have an independent existence, but they are really reflections of the forms below.

So too, material reality is formed by what lies behind it. The difference is that material reality seems rock solid, while the forming powers seem ephemeral, changeable, fluid. We might think more of water flowing through a limestone cave, leaving stalagmites and stalactites as remnants of its passing.

To say that there is a spirit reality behind the physical implies no disrespect for the material world. In the Pagan view, spirit and matter are an unbroken continuum. Matter—which comes from the same root word as *mother*—is sacred, infused by spirit. The spirit world in turn is shaped and informed by matter. They interpenetrate each other to sustain life and change and growth.

Once when I (Starhawk) was leading a trance based on the story of Demeter and Persephone, this message came to me: "The land of the living needs a representative from the land of the dead, and the land of the dead needs a representative from the land of the living." Persephone becomes such a bridge, a healer, Witch, shaman, artist, one who in life is a walking reminder of the inevitability of death and in death comforts us with the surety of rebirth. To encounter death is to become such a bridge between the worlds, for great moments of transformation and creativity occur when those worlds meet. As physical birth is an opening of the gates, so too the birth of ideas, of poems, of music or stories or new inventions occurs on that creative edge where imagination becomes form, where form takes on substance and ideas are made real.

Our physical senses and our embodied brains allow us to perceive only a small fraction of reality. We cannot see microbes or ultraviolet light, for example. We can hear only a small range of sounds. When we try to describe the otherworld of energies and spirits, we are limited not only by our bodily constraints but by the expectations, assumptions, and language patterns ingrained in us by the culture we were raised in.

What is the otherworld, really? We can never know, never truly describe nonbodily reality with our tongues of flesh, in words that must be interpreted by the cells and synapses of our brains. So we resort to myths and metaphors, always taking the risk that we will confuse the map with the territory. Having issued that warning, I will nonetheless try to outline the geography of the otherworld.

Cultural Conceptions of the Otherworld

Different cultures create their own visions of that other realm and their own expectations of where we go at death. The Tibetans have elaborate descriptions of the planes of what they call "the Bardo realm." Inanna descends through seven levels. The Greeks saw the land of death as being below this world, a shadowy realm reached after crossing the river Styx and drinking the waters of forgetfulness. The Christian Heaven is a realm of light, its Hell a place of eternal and relentless fire; while the realm of the Scandinavian Goddess Hel is a cold place of ice and eternal snow. The British Celtic paradise, called Summerland or Avalon, the Isle of Apples, is found in the West after a journey across a dark or misty sea. The Irish otherworld is Tir Na N'og, the Land of Youth, the realm also of the Sidhe or Fairy folk who exist on the boundaries of matter and spirit.

Images as Creations of Mind

While the energies and powers of the otherworld have an independent existence, the shapes in which we perceive them and the names we give them are creations of mind. Some may be individual creations, others cultural creations of the group mind of a people. Because the substance of the otherworld is malleable and fluid, it can be shaped and influenced by mind. So what we create, what we expect, becomes real—or at least becomes a constellation of energies and patterns we experience as if our metaphors were real.

The more focused the concentration we direct toward a particular set of images, the more fixed become the energies and patterns those images represents. If we believe in angels, we feel protective presences around us. If millions of people around the world believe in a fiery Hell, focusing powerful emotions of fear on that vision, a fiery Hell will exist in the otherworld, and those who die expecting to go there will experience those fires. Those of us who have experienced depression or panic attacks or moments of obsessive anxiety in life know how the mind can indeed create its own Hell. The images of the otherworld reverberate in the physical—believers in Hellfire, through the centuries, have burned many a heretic and suspected Witch with the justification that they were saving them from a greater fire.

Because the otherworld is fluid, even the most sinful believer will not remain in Hell eternally. Eventually the mind's constructs dissolve, and we move on. We can help release the dead from realms of pain and suffering with the time-honored techniques of prayer and offerings. Many of the prayers and chants in this book can be used with the conscious intention of helping our beloved dead break free of their own fears and expectations and move into contact with the great love and compassion of the Goddess. Offerings of food, lighted candles, or libations poured out on the earth are tangible gifts of energy to help bring the dead to a place of renewal.

Changing Our Beliefs

We can also prepare for death by looking honestly and clearly at our beliefs and expectations for what happens afterward. Even if we have intellectually rejected a childhood faith, the images we were raised with may still be deeply embedded in our minds. To change them may require serious and focused work.

Changing Our Images of the Otherworld: A Meditative Practice

Over a period of a few days or weeks, develop your own personal spiritual biography as it relates to death. (You may want to do this exercise with a friend and share your histories.) What were your earliest beliefs? Experiences? Did these change as you grew? Keep a journal or make a series of drawings.

How do you feel now about these early beliefs? Do they reflect your current understanding? Are there images you would like to change?

If you suspect that images of fear and punishment lurk in the depths of your mind, begin to collect pictures and artifacts that reflect those fears. You might find a print of a Hieronymus Bosch painting of Hell or a statue of the Devil, for example. Put the various artifacts on your altar at the full moon, or place them around your room, and let them remain during the two weeks of the month when the moon is waning. Sit with them for some time each day and consciously imagine them dissolving into patterns of light. Say to them, "You are only a creation of mind."

At the dark of the moon, burn the pictures, smash the artifacts, or bury them or give them away. (*Note:* You may need to repeat this practice over several months. Use your intuition. If you do not feel done with the images, take the pictures down but save them to work with again.)

Now place on your altar, and around your room, images that represent the beauty and mystery of the otherworld, that reflect your current beliefs and evoke the love and compassion of the Goddess. Spend some time each night calling in that love, imagining yourself wrapped in the Goddess's cloak and under her protection. Ask for a name you can call her by as death approaches, or for any specific practices you should do or ask others to do for you.

The Isle of Apples: Our Vision of the Otherworld

We cannot just banish old images; we must replace them with something. The Reclaiming tradition favors the Celtic vision of the otherworld: that the soul takes a journey across the sunless sea to the Isle of the West, the Isle of Apples. We are greeted by our ancestors and by those we have loved in this life and other lives. There we wander among the sweet groves where the trees are in blossom and in fruit at the same time, where it is always summer. The Goddess and God are with us, revealing the great beauty and love inherent in the universe. All hurts are healed; all pain is forgotten. We review our life—the challenges we have faced, the lessons we have learned—acknowledge amends that need to be made, and form the outlines of challenges to come in our next lives. We might also make what Yoruba priestess Luisah Teish calls a "contract with Creation"—we may take on a task that needs to be done; we may volunteer to bring forth a new idea or to care for something or someone who needs protection. In this place beyond time, we grow young again. Eventually we grow so young that we are ready to be reborn.

Every Samhain, every Halloween, our community takes a trance journey together to the Shining Isle, to meet our own beloved dead at the time when the veil between the worlds is thin and to become familiar with the way between the worlds. Here is a personal guided meditation adapted from one version of that trance journey, based on our Spiral Dance Ritual on Samhain 1992:

A Visit to the Shining Isle: A Guided Meditation

LEE HENRIKSON

WITH LIBERAL BORROWING FROM STARHAWK

Note: You can read this to someone who is grieving or to someone who may be crossing over soon. Speak slowly, letting the rhythm of ocean swells set the rhythm of the story. You can repeat the lines of the journey across the sea to help deepen the meditative state if it feels right. You may find the mood enhanced if you light a candle and dim all other lights or play soft, dreamy music.

Take a few deep breaths and relax. Let yourself just be in your body. Let your body sink into the earth. And breathe, breathe into your whole being. Let your breath go to tense or tight places in your body and allow them to let go. Breathe and relax and let yourself be present in the moment.

Continue to breathe and to be aware of your breath. Let your breath go into your heart. Imagine that your breathing opens up a place in your heart—the place where you keep your sadness, your fears, your grief. And as you continue to breathe, go into that place. Step into that place that is tender in your heart. You do not need to do anything with any feelings that come up here. Let your feelings, your sadness, your grief open up a door, and let yourself step through that door to the other side. And as you step through, you find yourself on the shore of the Sunless Sea. You are on the shore of the sea whose face never sees the light of the sun, whose face never sees the light of the moon. Do not worry if you do not remember this place. It remembers you. Listen to the sound of the surf. Feel the wind that blows off the waves. Feel the beach beneath your feet. Smell the salt air. *(Short pause.)*

Across those dark waters, beyond the rim, is the Shining Isle, the Isle of the Dead. It is the place where the Dead go and the place where the yet-to-be-born reside. It is the source of all creativity and inspiration. It is the place where all souls find peace.

From that sacred island a boat comes for you. And as you look out across the waves, you see the boat gliding toward you. What color is the boat? What shape? It skims the waves and you hear its keel scrape the beach before you. Step into the boat. Make yourself comfortable for the journey.

When you are safely in the boat, it glides back into the sea and carries you toward the Shining Isle. You have set sail for the Isle of the Dead, the island of all possibility.

Feel the wind blow as the boat glides across the dark waters. Feel the gentle swell and sway of the waves rocking you gently, cradling your boat as you journey. The wind gently blows, and the boat gently rocks in the waves, as you travel onward toward that sacred isle.

(Repeat if you wish.)

When you feel the boat scrape the shore of the Shining Isle, step out onto the island. Feel the energy of this place, the Shining Isle; here is all that ever was, ancestors, Gods, Goddesses, spirits. Feel how the land welcomes your feet; feel how the land shines. Smell the air of this sacred place. And as you look around, notice the landscape: Are there forests or meadows? Do you hear bird song? *(Short pause.)*

As if from the land itself, someone steps forward to greet you. An ancestor of the bone or spirit. What does this being look like? What is your ancestor wearing? Greet her or him. Ask her name if you do not know it. And walk with your ancestor, walk through the meadows and the forests to the apple orchards of the Goddess. Sit with your ancestor beneath one of those blessed apple trees whose branches hold flower and fruit and seed. Sit and talk. Is there something you need to say to your ancestor? Something your ancestor wants to tell you? Say it now.

(Long pause.)

Begin to finish your talk with your ancestor. Is there a pledge you wish to make? Is there a challenge you wish to accept?

(Another pause.)

It is now time to leave this lovely island. Take your ancestor by the hand and let her or him lead you back to the shore where the boat waits. Thank your ancestor and any other spirits you have met here. Exchange farewells and climb back aboard the boat. Feel again the boat leaving the shore and journeying back across the Sunless Sea. This journey across the sea takes but a heartbeat, and then you feel the boat scraping the shore of the Land of Night and Day.

And you stand once again on the living side of the Sunless Sea. Bid farewell to the boat and walk up the shore and back into your heart. Feel all that you bring back from the Shining Isle. Let your pledge or your challenge rest there in that space in your heart.

And breathe again into your body. Touch your body. Say your name to yourself. Snap your fingers. Clap your hands. Feel yourself once again on the living earth.

Now that you know the way to the ancestors, they are never far from you. And you can return to them whenever you have need. But for now, the journey is over. Blessed be.

The following meditation is a partial example of a group trance journey led by Deborah Oak Cooper for nearly fifteen hundred people at Reclaiming's Spiral Dance Ritual at Fort Mason, San Francisco, in 1996:

Samhain Journey Meditation

DEBORAH OAK COOPER

Bring your attention inward, to your own body and breath. Feel yourself in this room which is itself a pier, with dark, dark salty water beneath us. Let your animal self feel that water. It is so near; feel it lap around the pilings beneath us. And as you breathe and feel the closeness of that dark water, imagine in your mind's eye that we all are on the shore of a Sunless Sea, a dark and salty Sunless Sea, a sea made up of our tears, our loss, our grief.

So many have died this year. So much has been lost. And this is the time of Samhain, the time when we remember those who have died, and—if we have the courage, if we have the need—we look beyond the veil, beyond the Sunless Sea. And we call our beloved dead. We call them and we travel to meet them, between the worlds at the Shining Isle.

For when we travel between the worlds, we can change all the worlds. And in both of our worlds healing can occur. So we stand here on the shore of the Sunless Sea of our tears and grief, and with our courage, our need, and our love, we travel to meet our beloved dead.

Feel the waves lap on the shore. Feel how your heart sails out to meet the waves upon waves of beloved dead. And as you breathe, imagine that this room itself transforms to a mighty barge. As you breathe, feel yourself on that barge with the dark sea beneath us—the dark sea of our grief and tears. This is the sea that will take us to the meeting place between the worlds.

As each name of our beloved dead is called, our loss, our grief takes us closer to the meeting place, the Shining Isle between the worlds. Let us begin our journey.

Let us sail out to the meeting place, the island between both of our worlds, where we can dance together and make magic and heal each other. Let us sail, listening to the sea and hearing the names of the beloved dead in the waves, those who come to meet us. They are setting sail too. As we set out over this sea, we both set sail to meet on that sweet island between the worlds. As we travel, feel them travel too. With each name you hear, we both come closer to each other. Over this sea of tears, of loss, of grief, we come closer to each other. As each of their names is called, we ride another wave toward the meeting place.

As the veil parts, let us journey toward them over this Sunless Sea. With each name, each memory, coming closer to that sweet, sweet place.

Wave upon wave of our beloved dead rise to meet us. We come closer. With each name called, each memory invoked, we come closer to that sweet place between our worlds, that island in the distance. See it through the veil—the veil that is thinning as each name is called.

As the dead travel to meet us, we have so much to say to each other, there is so much we need from each other; as each name is called, we get closer.

See it up ahead. We are almost there—the sweet island between the worlds. We call it the Isle of Apples. Apples holding the pentacle of life; apples that are mystery and wisdom. Let us come closer to the island between the worlds. Let us see the beauty of this place between the worlds.

And if you did not hear the name or names of your beloved dead called, say them in your heart or whisper them. Let this propel the boat over the last remaining waves.

The boat lands. We are here. Step ashore; step ashore.

After such a journey you may need to stretch. Allow yourself to rise. You can still stay in trance time, dream time.

Let yourself walk. Let yourself move on the island, eyes soft-focused, attention inward. Feel your feet on this island, this place between the worlds. Open all your living senses to this place. See the trees, their leaves moving with the spirits of the dead. Smell the air, salty with the sea and containing the sweet smell of apples. Walk up the path you find. Everywhere there are whispers. Feel and hear the dead walk among us on this sweet isle.

The dead are arriving too. With such joy and such grief, we both arrive tonight.

How happy they are to know we have not forgotten them. How much we miss each other!

Hear them arrive among us. Listen. This room is the island between the worlds. This place is full of the living and the dead. Hear them walk among us. Listen to your heartbeat; listen to the whispers of the dead. Listen. There is so much we have to say to each other. Listen. . . . Who is here? What do they have to say? Who is here? Who have you called to this sweet place? Who has called you?

Perhaps you have called someone specific, someone you dearly miss, someone whom you need to talk to, someone you need to listen to. Perhaps you have called someone who needs something from you to be at peace. Perhaps you need something from that person to be at peace yourself. Say her or his name in your heart; say the name. The beloved dead you seek to find tonight—some person or persons—have they traveled over the waves to see you? Call them in your heart; look for them on the island. The path is there; follow it until you find them among all these other faces, the living and the dead who have traveled here.

As you call them, you may find that they are calling you too. Your voices reach each other. Take your time. You will find each other. Say their names in your heart. Follow the path. Listen for them calling your name. Find your beloved dead. Spend the time here talking and listening to each other. Know that you will dance together and make magic that can change things for both of you on either side of the veil. Decide between yourselves what that change could be. And know that magic will begin tonight—with each step you take together when we dance, you will change things together

Some of you may not have any beloved dead whom you need to work with or find here. If that is so, then think of what needs to be done. What do you want to see happen in the coming year?

There is so much work to be done. Some of us need changes in our personal lives. In this place between the worlds, think what that change would be, *could* be.

We will dance tonight with the dead, and with each step make magic together that can change our lives for the better.

All of us need to do magic that can change the world, that can restore the balance. The dead are here to help us with that.

In this place between the worlds, this place of possibilities, imagine what you can do to help restore and renew the earth. Feel how the dead want and need us to do that. How they are willing to help. Look around: perhaps one of the dead comes forward, whispers to you. Perhaps you knew that person when she or he was alive, and perhaps you did not.

Someone may need to talk to you, to listen to you. Someone who needs what you have to give, someone who has something to give you. So many have traveled here. The dead are all around us. They know we have to work together. They come here to tell us so many things. They come to listen.

Now listen. Go deep inside and listen to who calls you. What change needs to be made? What magic can be set in motion as we dance together tonight? Listen.

(Silence.)

They have so much to tell us, so much to give.

The dead from many ages swirl around us. They come to delight in our living bodies, to hear the music of our heart-beats, to remind us how precious that sound is; how they miss it; how fleeting life is. Rejoice, they say. Every moment is a treasure and a responsibility. Everything we do in our life, every step we take, we can impact what comes after us. Tonight, as we dance, decide if you want to do the work that could ensure that someday your name will be called and that you will come to dance with the living. What steps can you take to help ensure that this dance of life and death will continue? That sometime in the next century the children of our children will call our names and dance with us the double spiral of life and death on this wondrous green planet earth?

The dead swirl among us, reminding us how wondrous this world is, how sacred the earth is. Life is sacred. The dead know that in their bones.

Feel the blood, the precious blood, coursing through your bodies. Rejoice in it. It is sacred.

Know that you dance tonight with the dead, to remember how sacred the life-force is and to renew your pledge (or make it for the first time). To protect it, to protect the living body of our Mother Earth. And to take delight in her, to not only fight for clean water, clean air, and preservation of the wild places, but to relish and to delight in them, to breathe them in, and to delight in our life, to delight in our senses.

The dead exist to remind us that life is sweet — oh so sweet. Savor it. It is also oh so short.

This is what the dead come to remind us.

Feel them around us everywhere tonight. So many dead; so many ancestors from so many different lands and cultures. They come to dance with us and to dance together, to make magic, to make change. Magic that will help us renew this sweet green earth and the beauty of the wild. Magic that will open hearts and senses with each dancing step.

So come now. It is time to dance with the dead and with the living, to work our magic so that this dance will continue, so that life will thrive on this green planet. And as you dance, feel the power build both above you and below you, increasing power and magic in both worlds. Feel that power as we dance the double spiral which is our own genetic code, the symbol of this glorious cycle of life and death.

Move back now. Move back, staying with your intention, holding the changes you want to make for yourself and for this world. And move yourself into a circle.

This is the true mystery: how we can do this. Somehow every year it does happen. Move into a circle and hold hands, remembering that the dead too are among us. They smile at our impatience and our human fumbling. And remember as you dance that we are human, of human flesh and blood. And unless we are careful and intentional, those of us who come after can be injured. By this I mean that moving in and out wildly will result in arms being pulled or yanked down the line. This is not the time to crack the whip.

This is the time to dance with intention, knowing that each step we take tonight is a spell and an intention, a building of power. So keep holding the hand of the person who is next to you and you will eventually look into the eyes of all who dance in this room.

Do not stop holding hands and dancing the spiral until we all are facing the same way. Then we will continue building the power both above us and below. This is the dance. This is the magic. Let it begin now. (Note: After the spiral dance, participants were guided back from the Isle to ordinary space and time).

C

We may believe in the literal existence of the Shining Isle, or we may see it as a useful metaphor for directing our consciousness into realms of learning, compassion, and beauty. However we view it, the more familiar we are with the imagery, the more practiced we are at taking the journey, the easier the journey will be at death.

(Of course, there are those of us who prefer ten-year-old Bowen's theory about the stretch limo driven by the Faery Taxi Service—a limo that picks us up when we die and conveys us to the otherworld while we sit back and have our choice of drinks and videos.)

The Cauldron of Rebirth

A related myth tells us that the souls of the dead return to the cauldron of Cerridwen, the place where all possibilities are generated, where the dead and the unborn swirl and dance like the spiraling of the galaxies in the cauldron of space. Here we dissolve back into our original elements and are brewed into new life. The cauldron appears in many myths as the cauldron of plenty, or the font of inspiration and wisdom. In Ireland, the cauldron falls under the care of the Dagda, the Good God, who uses its regenerative powers to feed the people. In the Second Branch of the Mabinogi, the Medieval compilation of Welsh mythology, the cauldron becomes the ultimate weapon of war: dead soldiers are tossed in to be revived so they can fight again. Eventually the cauldron is destroyed when a living man jumps in and sacrifices himself. The resulting explosion prefigures a nuclear blast, destroying the land. The myth warns us of the dangers of misusing the regenerative powers of life.

The cauldron is a powerful image of renewal. It teaches us that the realm of the dead is also the home of the unborn, the fertile, creative seedbed of new growth and birth. What we create in that realm with our focused imagination reverberates in the world of form and substance. What we learn in life, the qualities we nurture in ourselves, the love we give and receive—all this goes into the brew.

Cauldron Visualization

JENNY SILL-HOLEMAN

Washing in Cerridwen's Cauldron can help cleanse you of your fears and concerns around death and dying, transforming those feelings into peace and clarity.

Ground and center, bringing your awareness inward to find the center of calm within, letting go of the everyday distractions around you. Cast a simple circle around yourself if you wish, perhaps using candles and incense to aid your concentration. Close your eyes and imagine yourself standing before an immense Cauldron, one large enough to contain you completely. Invite Cerridwen to be with you, for it is Her

Cauldron before which you stand. Ask Cerridwen for Her help in discovering those fears and concerns you would like to transform. Be aware, as well, of what you would like to transform them into. Do you want peace instead of fear? Understanding instead of anger? Be as clear as you can.

Now imagine Cerridwen lifting you up and placing you in the Cauldron. In Her wondrous Waters of regeneration, you find yourself dissolving. Feel all those things you wish to change being dissolved as you dissolve. Feel yourself floating there for a while, at one with Cerridwen's transformative Waters.

When you are ready, feel yourself reforming in the cauldron, renewed by Cerridwen's Waters, with your old angers and fears replaced with a clean feeling of understanding and peace. As you step out of the cauldron, know that those new feelings will remain with you. Gradually bring yourself back into awareness of the outer world, refreshed and renewed by your rebirth in Cerridwen's Cauldron.

If you wish, you can use an actual bath for this working. Fill your tub with fresh water of whatever temperature you like. When it is filled, stand before it and look deep into it, seeing it as Cerridwen's Cauldron of cleansing and regeneration. Call upon Cerridwen Herself to aid you as you work with Her Cauldron. Hold your hands over the water, palms down. As you do, feel Her standing behind you, enfolding you, Her hands over yours. Feel Her regenerating energy flowing through you and out of your hands into the water, charging the bath and transforming it into Her Cauldron of regeneration.

When you feel that the water is sufficiently charged, bring your hands back to your sides and reflect for a moment on all the thoughts and feelings around death that you would like to have transformed. When you are ready, step into the bath and begin washing in the waters of the Cauldron, imagining the magic of the water soaking into your skin and loosening the feelings you wish to transform. Be aware of your fears and anger dissolving in the waters of Cerridwen's Cauldron as you are charged with new feelings of peace and understanding.

When you are done with your bath, drain the tub and take a moment to watch the waters swirling away, taking down into the earth those feelings you have let go.

Cerridwen's Cauldron
The Pitch Black Witch of the Poison Glen

In the cauldron, Cerridwen's brewing.
From the cauldron, Cerridwen's treasure.
Through the cauldron, Cerridwen's doing —
A draught, a spirit, will make your measure.

Another powerful image of death and rebirth is the spiral. When a spiral twists, turns, and backtracks, it becomes a labyrinth, a winding road into the heart of mystery, and a powerful meditation tool:

Walking the Spiral:
Labyrinth Meditations

VIBRA WILLOW

Labyrinths appear in many different forms all over the world.[1] The form sometimes called a "Cretan labyrinth," has a single path and seven "layers" (counting, as if they were rings in a tree trunk, from the center to the edge). Many scholars believe that originally the labyrinth was a dance form, and it is associated with very early images of women's

---

[1] Sometimes the words "labyrinth" and "maze" are used interchangeably. As I use them, however, they are different: a labyrinth has one path, however complex, that leads to the center with no false turns, and a maze has false paths that dead-end. In a labyrinth you may *feel* lost, but in a maze you can actually *get* lost.

spirituality. The labyrinth forms that were designed much later for the cathedrals of Europe are divided into quadrants, and a cross usually appears in the middle. In modern times, artists and Pagans are creating many variations of labyrinth designs, with innovations such as a processional path leading directly out of the center or a labyrinth forming the shape of a Goddess.

In many places, the labyrinth is used in rituals as a physical metaphor for death and rebirth, or simply for birth. The following meditations can be used in any shape or size labyrinth, so long as it has only one path leading to the center and the only way out is the same path. And the meditations can be done either while actually walking a labyrinth path or while tracing a path that has been drawn in sand, sculpted in clay, or drawn on paper, with your finger, a wand, or simply your gaze. If you are using a two-dimensional labyrinth, remember that the path lies *between* the lines that form the shape of the labyrinth.

I. Through the Labyrinth

As you approach the labyrinth, look at it and find the center. *Know that the center is your goal.* Notice the overall shape of the labyrinth, and the many twists and turns of the path. *Know that to reach the center, you will often head away from it.* As you follow the labyrinth path, you will probably become confused or disoriented. *Know that the only way out is through the center.* When you are ready to begin, focus your gaze at the beginning of the labyrinth path, not beyond. Find the entrance and take a moment to be sure you feel solidly in your body and connected to the earth. Breathe easily into your relaxed belly. If you are walking a labyrinth path, before you begin touch the ground, then stand and enter.

Going In (Release)

As you begin, reach back to your youngest memory. Then, as you travel inward, with each turn of the path feel yourself becoming older.

Let your memories arise, and let them fade. Remember the sweetness and the bitterness, the joy and the pain. Remember your past and imagine your future. Feel your body changing as you remember and envision each age. As you travel the path, reflect on your own infancy, your childhood, then your youth, adulthood, maturity, decline, and approaching death. As you move through each age, when a painful memory or vision emerges ask, *What does this teach me?* And let it go. And when a memory or vision of special joy emerges, ask, *What does this teach me?* And let it go.

On the path, you may feel lost or disoriented. You may think you have not followed the path correctly, or that the path itself has gone wrong. When that happens, *know that you can stop for a while.* And when you do stop, notice how it feels to be lost, to be confused. *When have you felt this way in your life?* Look down at your feet. *Know that there is no decision to make; trust the path.*

Center (Death)

When you reach the center, give in. Forget your memories. See the visions of sweetness and pain spinning off into the sky, beyond the stars. Let the last of your resistance be gone. Take your time. Allow yourself to be here, *without thought, without anger, without regret.* Be still, be at peace, and wait.

And then, remember:

Remember your face before you were conceived. Remember emerging from beyond. What else do you remember? Remember the water. Remember the heartbeat. What else do you remember? Remember the comfort. Remember the peace. What else do you remember?

Remember the constriction. Remember the urgency. What else do you remember? Remember the waves. Remember the struggle. What else do you remember? Remember emergence. Remember release. What else do you remember?

Coming Out (Rebirth)

Feel the spirit in the center of the labyrinth, and *know that here you are whole.* When you are ready to begin the outward path, take a deep breath and feel the earth beneath you. As you travel outward, the path may seem both familiar and unfamiliar. *Know that you have been this way before. Trust the path.*

Before you begin, be aware of the four directions. Then travel the path slowly, allowing yourself to open to each new layer. There are many answers to the questions in this meditation, so you will ask and answer them many times. *Know that the elements sustain you on the path.* At each turn of the path, take a deep breath, call in the power of air: *What is your name? Who are you?* As you begin to travel each new layer of the labyrinth, call in the power of fire: *Where does your passion lie? What will you do?* As you walk along each layer, call in the power of water: *When do you feel best? Where do your dreams lead?* And as you approach each turn, call in the power of earth: *What will you eat and drink? Where is your home?*

As you emerge from the labyrinth, take a moment to look again at the path and the center. Remember your name and who you are; remember where your passion lies and what you will do; remember where your dreams lead and when you feel best; remember what you will eat and drink, and where your home is. Step out of the labyrinth. Touch the ground.

II. Chant of the Butterfly Goddess

It is believed by some that the shape of the earliest labyrinth derives from the "labrys," the double ax of ancient Crete, a symbol that in turn is associated both with the Amazons and, even more anciently, with the Butterfly Goddess. This meditation is inspired by that possibility, and explores the mystery of metamorphosis, a transformation achieved through death and rebirth within life. Try to slow yourself way down and enter a state of caterpillar consciousness before you begin.

Each of these verses should simply be chanted, rhythmically, over and over, as you move along the labyrinth path, and the end of each part will blend into the beginning of the next. In the center, chant until everything is liquid; then be still for as long as you need, until you feel a change. On the way out, begin slowly; when you are close to emergence, you will need only the second part.

Spiraling in: spinning

From all that I am
I spin my cocoon.
I spin my cocoon
For safety

The center: dissolution

Inside my cocoon
I dissolve what remains.
I live through my fear
In the dark.

Spiraling out: transformation

From spirit and earth
I take new form;
I spread my wings,
I am free.

    May the wisdom of the labyrinth stay in your heart.
Blessed be.

7

Karma and Reincarnation

Embracing the Wheel of Birth and Death

Loss and Rebirth

The Goddess tradition teaches us that death is not a final end, but a point on the cycle that includes rebirth. The dead become the unborn, who return again to life after an interval of rest, healing, and renewal. Death is transformation, not termination.

We share this concept of reincarnation with many other cultures and traditions, but the Pagan view has its own unique characteristics. For us, the Sacred is embodied in the living world, present in all of nature and human life. The wheel of birth and death is the living being of the Goddess. We are not striving to get off the wheel, to get beyond the need for rebirth, to transcend the sufferings of life. Rebirth is the Goddess's great gift to us, and we embrace the wheel. The reward of a life well lived is to live again, to meet once more with those we have

Let the Spiral Turn and Turn

Words and music by Starhawk

Let the spi-ral turn and turn,   Wind will blow and fire will burn.

Wa-ter flows u-pon the earth,   As we dance from death to birth.

known and loved, and to love again. This worldview is reflected in the two songs included in this chapter: "Let the Spiral Turn and Turn" (above) and "All Things Must Pass Away" (page 150).

Despite the Pagan emphasis on rebirth, death is still a great loss. Our essence, our Deep Self, is reborn, but our particular personality is wedded to a body, a gender, an ancestry, a life history. That personality will dissolve at death. Lessons we have learned will become part of our essential being. Traits, preferences, and knowledge may in some way be carried on. But much of what makes us unique in this life will be gone.

The Limits of Memory

Many people remember their past lives. Many more people *think* they remember their past lives. As a novelist, I (Starhawk) know of the mind's ability to create stories and characters that seem as real as (or more real than) anything experienced in the body. As an often overstimulated human being, I am aware of how much of this life I forget. A few years ago, I had the sobering experience of looking over my college transcripts. Not only could I not remember what I had learned in many of the classes, I had no memory whatsoever of taking quite a few of them. I certainly could not have named the professor or found my way back to the classroom. Why, then, would I expect to remember the details of a previous life?

We forget most of our life experiences almost as soon as we live them. Yet we know who we are, and memory creates a being with a coherent existence. The knowledge and skills we acquire become part of us even if we do not remember the details of their acquisition. So while I cannot remember the name of my first-grade teacher or the faces of most of my classmates, I remember how to read. Likewise, what we carry over from life to life is knowledge, deep traits of character, a sense of familiarity with certain people and places, patterns of behavior and understanding, and (if we are lucky) inner wisdom; detailed scenarios are left behind.

The Pagan View of Karma

Belief in rebirth can teach us compassion when we acknowledge that, over many lifetimes, we have probably been just about everything. We cannot cling to prejudice against people of a different race or gender or religion when we believe that we ourselves may have been among that group or may yet be reborn among them in another life. We cannot judge others too harshly, claiming that we would never behave as they have done, if we suspect that in some life or another we probably *have* done that very thing or something worse. The great range of human capacity for good and for harm is shared by all of us and played out in our life-dramas over the ages. We may choose to do good, but we must be humble enough to acknowledge that we are capable of doing ill.

Reincarnation also inspires us to take the long view. Native Americans teach us to look seven generations ahead when making decisions. When we believe that we will be here again seven generations on, we have a deep identification with the consequences of our actions. We cannot complacently destroy our ancient forests for immediate gain, pile up debts our grandchildren will have to pay, or risk the destruction of the environment for short-term profits. Whatever we love, we must work to preserve.

Many traditions that believe in reincarnation also have a doctrine of karma, or cause and effect—a doctrine stating that what we do in one life determines the level of fortune to which we will be born in the future. Karma is a comforting philosophy when life is going well for us, for at such times we like to think we deserve our fate. However, when we meet misfortune, when we become ill or suffer losses, must we then also feel guilt for hypothetical misdeeds of a previous existence? If we say yes, then karma can easily become a rationale for blaming the victim, for accusing the oppressed of creating their own oppression.

Yet karma can also motivate us to work for social justice. In our world today, the opportunities for lives of abundance and freedom are much more limited than life circumstances of poverty and hunger. Perhaps we should think of the poor as being like those selfless souls who forego their share of cake when there is not enough to go around. By taking up lives in painful circumstances, they have allowed others room to live in privilege and comfort. And unless we who enjoy abundance work hard in this lifetime to improve opportunities for everyone, our turn at poverty may come next. This understanding of reincarnation inspires us to work for economic and social justice for all, to forego complacency and respect the poor.

Challenges from the Goddess

The Pagan view allows for a certain degree of randomness in the universe. Certainly our actions and choices bring consequences with them, but sometimes bad things just *happen*. Fate is not always fair. Perhaps the randomness of life is the price we pay for freedom, for a world that is not completely predetermined.

But the universe may not be as random as we like to think. Pagans see the Goddess as offering us challenges that spur us to grow and evolve. The Goddess does not punish us; She provides no Hell for wrongdoers. If we refuse Her challenges, or fail to meet them, She simply continues to offer us the same challenges over and over again in different forms. What we might perceive as rotten luck or undeserved suffering may actually be an opportunity for gathering power. We may spend lifetimes working on one aspect of growth.

Those challenges may be painful. We might continually find ourselves in abusive relationships, for example, changing one partner for another of the same kind until we learn new ways to love and value ourselves. We might suffer continual losses until we acknowledge and heal an old wound. At moments we might be tempted to beg the universe to simply punish us and get it over with.

But the challenges we face can also be exhilarating. We will feel stronger in facing the vicissitudes of life if we ask ourselves not "What did I do to deserve this?" but "What opportunity for learning and growth does this challenge present?" We may never know the cause of our fate, but we can choose how to meet it.

If we meet the challenges the Goddess offers, She presents us with new and often more difficult ones. But we will have grown in power and creativity, reaping the rewards of spiritual evolution.

Death is among the toughest challenges the Goddess presents us with. Facing death with courage and love can shift the patterns of lifetimes and move us into new realms of liberation and renewal.

We Have Taken

Music by Anne Hill, Words by Starhawk

We have ta-ken, we give back, Re-lease all and no-thing lack.

The Rule of Three

Our actions, our choices—these do influence our fate. Pagans speak of the Rule of Three—that what we send out, especially magically but also in how we live our lives—returns to us three times over. If we focus our being toward love, healing, and compassion, we attract those forces to us, because energy attracts energies like itself. That does not mean that nothing bad will ever happen to us or that we will become immune to grief or loss. It *does* mean that we will have the inner resources and the outer support to deal with the inevitable sorrows of life.

If, on the other hand, we obsess on revenge and focus our minds and energies on hate, we will undoubtedly attract hostility and conflict to us. When misfortune occurs, we will have alienated those who might have helped us.

The emotional and energetic patterns we develop in one life may carry over to the next—much as the emotional patterns formed in early childhood influence our responses as adults, even when we do not remember the incidents that created them.

When a spirit is moving toward rebirth, we are attracted to energies that match our own, to situations that will provide us with the challenges and opportunities we need to grow, or to fulfill our contract with creation.

We should beware, however—as I suggested earlier in this chapter—of adopting a simplistic, judgmental view that blames people for the circumstances of their birth and perpetuates oppression. When I returned from Nicaragua in the early eighties, I described to a student the extreme poverty I had seen there. "Wow, those people must have done something really awful in another life to be born into that conflict," was her reply. Such attitudes have been used for generations by the privileged to justify their state, allowing the rich to feel complacent, the enslavers morally pure. But my student's response reflected a complete misunderstanding of the complexity of factors surrounding rebirth.

To use a simple metaphor, we might think of choosing a womb for rebirth as being somewhat like renting an apartment. You might have the ideal apartment in mind, you might be able to list all the features necessary to your health and growth, but you are going to have to take what is available at the time you need to move. If the city you live in has lots of pleasant, airy, roomy flats at reasonable prices, your choices will be wide. But if housing stock is limited, overpriced, or rundown, if the landlords have not invested in improvements and there is no rent control, you might end up in a dank, cramped cockroach-ridden studio through no real fault of your own. And if we do no work in this life to improve choices for everyone, our options will be limited in the next.

When our own lives seem fraught with difficulties, when we wonder why we chose our neurotic parents or how we got into a defective body, we can take comfort from the insight of Reclaiming member Deborah Oak Cooper, who recently returned from a trip to Disneyland with her small son. "Now I understand how reincarnation works," she said. "The best rides have the longest lines. Sometimes you end up on a really lousy ride just because you didn't have time to wait."

The Ancestors

The dead remain part of the human community. We can call on them for guidance, inspiration, and support. They become ancestors who guide and protect their line. Because they exist in a realm beyond our linear conceptions of time, our ancestors may be available to us even when they have gone on into new lives. They may spin new personalities and inhabit new bodies, but their Deep Selves are timeless.

Traditionally, the job of the ancestors is to offer protection to us and to provide guidance in the form of inspiration, deep knowledge, and help in acquiring skills they may have had. We honor the ancestors by remembering them—if not by remembering their names, then by remembering what we know of their struggles and achievements. We may build altars to them or make offerings of food, drink, or light (as in candle flames), giving energy to the dead. When we die, we hope to be remembered with love, so that our Deep Selves become the ancestors of the future.

Part Three

The Dying Process

8

Preparing for Death

○

Preliminary Thoughts Toward Midwifing Your Own Passage

DIANA L. PAXSON

One of the most positive contemporary developments is the natural childbirth movement, including Lamaze training and family participation. What is needed is to develop a similar preparation for death. According to one theory, hauntings occur when the spirit does not realize it is dead and cannot proceed, or died in the midst of an emotional crisis that ties it to a specific place. Numerous psychics and occultists have described "exorcisms" that consisted of making contact with the ghost and guiding it home. Joan Grant in particular includes a number of such stories in her autobiography. Obviously the speed and ease of the transition will be increased if (as in childbirth) one knows how to work with the process. The difference is that here one is giving birth to oneself, and there is no coach to point the way.

Where can we find information or models for this process? Sources include ancient texts such as *The Egyptian Book of the Dead* and *The Tibetan Book of the Dead*, contemporary accounts of death/revival experiences in the work of Elisabeth Kübler-Ross and in Dr. Raymond Moody's *Life After Life*, and accounts of shamanic visions in the writings of Mircea Eliade and elsewhere. The *Books of the Dead* are instructions to the spirit on how to get past the dangers of the otherworld and pass the final judgment so that it can dwell with Osiris, or achieve Nirvana. "The Death of Vivien LeFay Morgan" in Fortune's *Aspects of Occultism* describes one view of how an adept might consciously discorporate. In theory, at least, an adept experienced in astral projection might be able to accompany a departing spirit at least part of the way.

Accounts of the experience of dying vary in details but are surprisingly similar in structure, suggesting that there is a common transcendent experience that can be described only in images preconditioned by culture and experience. The major elements of the experience as analyzed by Moody include the following:

- The ability to hear conversations taking place around one after all vital signs have ceased

- Feelings of warmth, peace, and quiet, often in a womblike darkness

- Buzzing or ringing sounds

- The feeling of being sucked through a long, dark tunnel (compare with shamanic descents, the birth process, etc.)

- An out-of-body experience—leaving the body and hovering nearby, able to see and hear but unable to communicate with the living

- The welcoming presence of friends and relatives who have died before

- Confrontation with a "Being of Light," who in a non-threatening way requires the spirit to evaluate its life and decide whether it is time to go on

- A review of that life's experiences, as part of the above evaluation

- Progression toward some kind of barrier—a gate, a far shore, etc.

Those who revive turn back before they cross this barrier. Presumably those who go through it have completed their transition and this incarnation.

The theologians of Egypt and Tibet developed an elaborate mythology of this journey, concentrating on helping the spirit to face the judgment and make its way through a series of doorways to the land of the blessed. It is clear from contemporary evidence that the way the "Being of Light" is perceived is conditioned by culture and background. Many Americans identify that being as Christ. An ancient Egyptian would have known it for any one of the preliminary examiners, and finally as Osiris. The hope of the Egyptian believer was that through virtuous living, proper preparation, and the protection of Isis, the soul would "become Osiris" itself.

There is obviously a universal spiritual reality behind all this, which suggests that one may be able to develop a positive and useful "myth" in advance through active imagination and meditation. Reading Moody and Kübler-Ross will help convince the mind that something happens. Developing a vivid image of a protecting deity ought to increase the chances that one will encounter the Judge in a familiar and comforting form. Initiations that involve passage from one stage of life to another provide models for the experience of dying. Trance work and out-of-body experience help to convince the consciousness that it can exist separate from its physical vehicle.

Being aware of the common sensations in the after-death experience detailed by Moody will make these things less frightening when death does happen. Our spirits will be less likely to wander about or become disoriented, and more likely to proceed properly to whatever lies ahead for us.

✺

Working with the Dying

Among the things that Pagan priestesses and priests can do for their dying loved ones, or for anyone who is gravely ill and requests their presence and involvement, are explorations of their conceptions of spirit and of their expectations of what may follow. The following exercises can be empowering to someone who is disempowered by the failure of the physical body, and enlightening to someone confronting personal mortality.

Pentacle of Pearl Meditation

If you are helping someone else prepare to die, you may find it helpful to go through some of the work yourself first, as if you were the one dying. What follows is a meditation based on the Pentagram of Pearl, a meditation tool that comes from the Feri tradition of Wicca. Its five points are Love, Wisdom, Knowledge, Law, and Power.

Sit in a comfortable position with a bowl of salt water. Read the questions but do not necessarily attempt to answer each one. Breathe slowly and deeply, gaze at the water, and let feelings, images, and thoughts surface. Take as much time as you need for each section of the meditation. You do not have to do it all at one sitting—just work with as much as feels comfortable.

Whenever you need to, and especially when you are done, imagine that any feelings or energies you do not want to carry away with you flow into the bowl as a muddy stream. When the flow slackens, imagine sunlight, moonlight, and the fire from the core of the earth flowing into the bowl and cleansing it.

LOVE

The Love point on the Pentacle of Pearl encompasses our relationships, our connections with others. Ask yourself:

Whom have I loved? Who has loved me? Who loves me now, among the living and the dead? (Recite their names slowly, as a mantra.)

What is unfinished in my relationships with others? What is unsaid that I need to say? Are there people I need to forgive in order to free myself to move on? Are there people I need to hold accountable for actions that have harmed me, so that I can leave this life with a sense that justice has been done? Are there amends I need to make, is there forgiveness I need to ask for?

WISDOM

Wisdom stems from love. Wisdom is the learning we get from making mistakes. Knowledge implies answers; wisdom is the willingness to sit with deep questions, to contemplate mysteries that have no answers. Ask yourself:

What are the challenges I have faced in my life, from the time of birth up to the time of death, which I am facing now?

How have I met each one? What have I learned?

Are there challenges I have failed to meet? What have my mistakes taught me?

KNOWLEDGE

In the world of the living, we are used to being judged by what we know, what skills we have acquired, what abilities we have developed. In dying, we lose all of these, but something deeper remains. Ask yourself:

What areas of knowledge have I cultivated? What is it in me that was drawn to those particular realms? What knowledge is complete for me in this lifetime? What have I only begun to explore? If I am not the knowledge but the knower, who am I?

LAW

The law we are concerned with here is natural law. The basis of that law is that all that is born must die, and all that dies is reborn in some new form, some new way. Ask yourself:

When in this lifetime have I died before, changed, or transformed? What have I lost, and what have I found in its place? Where can I see nature's laws in operation? What cycles, what turnings of the wheel, do I know?

POWER

In one sense, death is the ultimate loss of power. In another sense, death is a yielding up and joining with the great powers of the universe.

What energies do I want to carry with me into death? What do I want to leave behind?

This meditation may or may not be useful to someone who is preparing for her own death. Death has its own timing and pacing; we cannot impose on it our ideas of how it should be without doing a disservice to the dying. But if these questions are alive and working within you, about your own life, they will be present in your friend's dying. If you are sensitive, you will know how to work with the questions as you help your friend. For some people, it might be appropriate to lead them through the meditation. For others, it might be more helpful to let them read it alone, in solitude. For many others, it might not be appropriate to do any structured meditation or questioning. The questions may arise spontaneously in conversation, or they may simply inform the way you listen.

You or your dying loved one may have more familiarity with Tarot cards, or may find visual imagery to be an easier way to reach beyond your rational self. The following meditation by Mary K. Greer may offer you insights into the process you are undergoing.

Tarot Death Card Meditation

Mary K. Greer

In my Tarot classes I sometimes take people through a meditation on the Death card. You may want to tape-record this meditation and make your own journey:

Ground yourself in a sacred circle and invoke spirit protection and the presence of the Gods. Imagine you are at a very interesting and exciting party with lots of people, both friends and strangers, all around you, and lots of things happening. Although you have enjoyed the party, you realize it is time to go. You wave goodbye and turn around. Perhaps a little sad, but also anticipating the next step, you open and walk through a door that closes behind you. You find yourself in a silent anteroom or cloak closet with an exit door in the opposite wall. You realize, though, that you cannot go through that door in the clothes you are wearing. They will no longer be appropriate. So you take off your clothes, one by one, until you are completely naked.

However, you now realize you have not taken everything off after all. There is still another cloak, another layer to be removed. And so you reach up and find that you can unzip your skin and flesh from the top of your head to your crotch, shrugging it off like a one-piece coverall. You strip it off until you are down to your skeleton, down to the bare bones. You have taken off everything that is inessential, that is not truly yours. Only your most basic, elemental structure—your raw scaffolding—remains.

To your left is a full-length mirror. Look at yourself in the glass. See the skeleton of who you are, now that no cloak, mask, or personality covers you. Without rank, race, or social class, face the bare truth of yourself. See what is left after everything you thought was you is gone.

It is time to go through the other door. It might feel frightening to enter the unknown stripped bare, for you have no idea what awaits you on the other side. You open the door and step through and into a realm of light. As your eyes adjust, a form in the distance becomes more and more tangible. It is an angel similar to that on the Temperance card of the Tarot. The angel steps forward to welcome you, and then begins to dress you, clothing you in the garb of your highest self—perhaps in a rainbow waterfall of shimmering colors or in a flood of ethereal essences. With soothing, healing motions, the angel adjusts and arranges your raiment until it fits just right. Look down and see yourself robed in your spiritual essence. Breathe in the light and aroma of this place. Fill yourself with its life-energy.

Thank your guardian angel for being present to help make

your transition easier. Perhaps you will want to stay a while in this wonderful, healing place.

When you are ready to return to the material world, you find that you can step easily and effortlessly back into your physical body, your normal consciousness, and your regular clothing, but an awareness of your spirit raiment stays clearly with you, although out of sight. You may want to recite your chosen song or chant or poem at this time.

Thank and release the spirits you invoked, and open the circle.

Some people are tactile, hands-on types; they can learn and experience more by digging their hands in and getting them dirty, by creating something new from disparate materials, by exploring and manifesting their experiences through tangible objects. If your dying loved one is one of these folks, and has the time, energy, and inclination to explore maskwork, such activity can offer rewards and insights. The following exercises, by Canadian Kate Slater, offer another sacred technology of empowerment.

Maskwork: Creation, Protection, and Transformation

KATE SLATER

We are born without separation between body and mind. Growing, learning to think in words, we become divided, attempting to reconcile our bodies' urgings for care and comfort with the rules that our minds impose. Eventually we may deliberately try to regain wholeness, to "be one" with our bodies, to savor our other senses by shutting off the stream of words.

Aging, we see and feel our bodies giving up their powers and turning inward. Our senses diminish, our bodies become troublesome or invisible. Normally and inevitably, we must let them go. Terminal illness does this too, without the resignation and reward of having lived enough years. Illness and pain leave complex emotions and fear of the unknown journey. Words may fail us, so we need to learn new communication techniques: between our consciousness and our hurting bodies; between inner and outer, this world and another; ourselves and others. People may be afraid to listen to us talk about dying. Understanding what we ourselves feel is hard. We swing between emotion and acceptance, acceptance and denial. Finding words is hard. Images can hold more.

Death is a profound mystery. The tools we use to explore other mysteries may help us here: images, symbols, masks — ancient keys to understanding the things too complex to be told in words.

The keys of maskwork are creating our mask, wearing it, unmasking, and the option of looking directly at it and talking to another part of our self. Creating and wearing masks lets us explore and communicate emotion, transformation, and personal reality. Our masks can be personal and explicit while we hide our spontaneously naked thoughts; we can choose the face we put on or take off. With a mirror we may witness our own transformation. With a companion we can use the mask to focus and express our feeling, with or without spoken words.

Masking — choosing the way we present ourselves to the world — is natural to us. When we are healthy, we are often urged to give up the most extreme of our natural masks and advised that they may block us from clear communication, but we rarely strip completely. Severe illness and exhaustion leave us exposed and vulnerable. Losing our natural masks, we may find self-expression and renewed control in building a mask of paint and paper, once again choosing a face. If we have used masks in ritual, we know that they can let us express hidden feelings, feel more deeply, explore other identities, and dance other music.

In ritual we *are* the mask, in play we *imagine* we are the mask, in theater we are ourselves *enlivening* a mask, and in therapeutic art we *express* our inner selves by creating it. We can do all of these things.

Life Masks: Reality and Transformation

Make a mask to express your known but hidden self. How do you now feel? What color, shape, texture is that feeling? When you put your mask on, do you feel this more intensely? When you take it off, can you leave that feeling stored in the mask? Are you willing to let others see it? Who? Is there emotion that you are culturally constrained not to show?

As you look at your mask, can you reflect on the experience it records and understand it more clearly? Your mask is what you attribute to it—body, thought, magic, emotion, concealing or revealing your self. You might want a series of images, each different in time or intent. Try having your companion hold or wear your mask so you can see it without mirror reversal. You can talk to this face of your self.

Make a healing mask with wellness and wholeness as its intent. Incorporate bits of your hair and your usual healthy makeup or appearance. Bless it or charge it with intent. Put it on and look into a mirror. How does being well feel? How does looking at the world through this face change what you see? Absorb all of the feelings of wellness that you can from the mask. Let someone care for it and keep it blessed.

Express an identity: a new one or one that is already yours but does not ordinarily show. Warrior, Lover, Magician. Shaman, Pilot, Raven. Your hidden male or female animus or anima. Light and shadow. What do these masks tell you?

Explore the unknown with a mask that represents your body. Try taking off this mask and watching it from a distance; look at it from above, as so many reported near-death experiences describe. What does it feel like to leave your body? How does your body look? Is taking off your body hard or easy?

Try a shamanic journey to the place where you will go when you die. For each person this journey will differ, but most of us reach a barrier of mist or light (or a door) beyond which we cannot see. When it resists us, we know that it is not yet time for us to proceed further. We may visit this place often, each time turning back when the barrier appears, learning that we can go back and forth and gradually losing our fear of this increasingly familiar territory. And perhaps at last, when we are ready, we may go into this journey and choose to pass the barrier, never to return.

Make a journey mask. Think of the Egyptians, dressing in their golden masks to resemble Osiris, their God of resurrection, to help them travel. What Goddess or God will you seek out? Would you appear as priestess to Gaia or to Artemis? As priest to Odin or to Dionysus? How will your deity recognize you? Will you travel as hawk or human? What things will you bring on your journey? Will you include coins for travel, magical formulae, or a map ("Turn left at the cypress by the spring; don't drink the water")?

Make a mask as you were or as you will not be. How did you look in your youth? How would you look as the sage old person you will not have the chance to be? What are the powers of these people? Remember them, or dream them.

What are your powers now? Can you express this in your mask? What are your vulnerabilities? Do you want to express these?

What does your spirit look like? Your soul? Are they different or one and the same? Can you convey those intangibles tangibly? (Masks may go to varying depths in what they show of our souls.)

As you wear your mask, what are your powers? Can you speak as an oracle? See deeply into the hearts of people around you? Be invisible? Shape-shift to another form? Unite with your power animal? Tell the truth? Feel one with your deity?

What do you want to do with your mask? Wear it? Keep it? Display it? Dance it? Destroy it? Use it in ritual? Add things to it? Give it to a friend? Tie it to a tree in the forest? Leave it with or on your body? Your mask should remain yours to do with as you will.

Remember that your illness and your threshold state make you awesome to some people. Wearing your mana-filled mask, you may inspire more dread, be harder for some people to approach. Use your mask wisely. You will encounter masked nurses and doctors: Would they understand your mask?

Symbols We Might Dream

Our dreams might reveal important symbols we may wish to explore in making our masks. For instance, we may dream of huge visionary eyes that perceive the cause of events, see the Gods. Minimal or nonexistent eyeholes show trance, sleep, or death. The Green Man, living, growing, ripening. Flower crowns, sun disks, and rays. Storms and fire for transition. Sunrises, sunsets, stars. Snakes shedding their skins. Animals. Wings to move between the worlds. Butterflies for Greek souls. Mandalas for serenity. Apples, pomegranates, poppies. Mergings: half one thing, half another, you and your totem. Light and dark. A candleholder built into a crown. Images we hear in music. Colors from our dreams.

Burial Masks: Ancient Instruments of Hope and Continuity

Ancient cultures from Siberia to South America used burial masks to honor and protect their dead and to preserve their identity during the transformation into the otherworld.

In Egypt great effort went into preparing the dead for the long journey to meet their Gods. Each mummy had its mask made of plaster or layers of linen and plaster. Both men and women were dressed as Osiris, a God who had died and lived again in full physical form. Vision was important, so the masks had strongly painted eyes. The ability to answer challenges on the journey was important, so the mask mouths held small inscribed tablets. (Similarly, the Greek Pythagoreans carried folded sheets of hammered gold with obscure travel directions.) Inscribed on Tutankhamen's golden mask were these words: "May you [the mask] make him [Tutankhamen] to be a spirit, may you subdue foes for him, may you guide him to the fair places of the realms of the dead, . . . that he be one who is enduring, enduring, enduring like Re, forever."[1]

---

[1]Quoted in Sue D'Auria, Peter Lacovera, and Catharine H. Roehrig, *Mummies and Magic* (Boston: Museum of Fine Arts/Northeastern University Press, 1988); exhibition catalog.

An inscription on the coffin of another ancient Egyptian beseeches, "O Mother Nut, spread yourself over me, placing me among the imperishable stars which are in Num."[2]

In Greco-Roman Egypt, portraits were made of persons in their full strength or youth and hung in the home until placed as masks over their model's mummy. This could give hope to someone who believed that the afterlife would restore them to this optimal state. Some European cultures reversed this idea: items placed in graves were deliberately broken, because what was broken here would be whole in the otherworld.

Continuity After Death

In Rome, masks were made of wax or metal and kept in the home, to be brought out and worn to represent ancestors in the funeral processions of their relatives. Along the Ivory Coast, the Yaure kept funeral masks in a sacred grove outside the village, to be used during funerals to assist the spirits of the deceased in joining their ancestors in the afterlife.

In Western Europe today, casts are made of the faces of the dead, especially of famous men. These life-size, solidly three-dimensional, eye-closed heads have an intense quality of still-ness. Admirers buy copies for their homes. Is this magic? Could these images be like the Celtic severed heads, able to talk, be an oracle, take part in feasts? The dramatic casts make us wonder, Who was this person? What was his mysterious power?

How to Create Your Own Masks

The kinds of masks you and a friend (or friends) can make vary from quick and simple to slow and elaborate. Capturing dreams needs speed; exploring the deep mystery of a haunting image requires a slower process.

Starting with the easiest, your options include (but are not limited to):

- A child's peek-a-boo behind fingers or a sheet

---

[2] Quoted in D'Auria, Lacovera, and Roehrig, *Mummies and Magic.*

- A veil

- A purchased domino (eye) mask, plain or trimmed in moss, feathers, glitter

- Face-painting. (This can be done by you while looking in a mirror or done by a friend, with your input. After you look at your painted image in the mirror—and perhaps take a photo—remove the paint and look again. Good paints help produce satisfying results. This sort of mask is easy to repeat but messy.)

- A cut-and-paste mask mounted on a stick

- One or more plastic forms from a craft shop, painted with acrylics and trimmed. (A basic set of acrylics and three brushes will do. Clean the brushes well with water. This is the easiest way to do a series of masks.)

- Plaster-cast gauze molded on the face. (This is a very satisfying, messy, and easy technique, though it requires a helper. The resulting mask feels and looks more like your own face than the other options listed, but you can build in sun rays, a beak, or antlers. Study the mask before you paint it: you may find that your face is finer than you thought or recognize the bones of your ancestors. Instructions for making this kind of mask are included in Appendix A.)

- Masks constructed of papier-mâché, foam, hammered metal, or found objects. (These can be simple, if you choose, or they can be complex, labor-intensive projects that give you the freedom to deeply explore images.)

- Face casts. (These can be made by several techniques, including making a plaster-cast gauze mold of the face, oiling it or lining it with clay slip, supporting it, and then filling it with plaster of paris. This cast may in turn be used to build more masks or used as a rough display. Better molds can be made with plaster or dental alginate. For directions, see *The Prop Builder's Mask-Making Handbook*, by Thurston James.[3])

How to Help a Friend with Mask-Making

You can assist with the creation of a friend's mask, finding materials and reference pictures, helping her build the mask, or finding purchased forms (if this is more within her capability); in some cases, you can help by faithfully building your friend's imagery for her, if she cannot. But however you are involved, let this remain her project, her thoughts, her magic. Prepare yourself to accept her expression, whether her choice is serene or angry, a Green Man or a skull.

Then devote the time to let your friend—the owner— explore the mask's potential, over several sessions, in talk or mime or other ways. Be there to listen and witness. Your presence and empathy will be enough. Accept and reassure; do not try to offer interpretations or probe for reasons. You might be asked to wear or hold the mask so its owner can engage in dialogue with it. And finally, you should be responsible for seeing that this powerful object ends up wherever its owner wants it to go.

Thinking about death is part of living.

I think that what we will find after our last breath will be some combination of what we most need and what we expect to find. The spark of thought and creation outlives our hands. For a full and honest book about creating art to understand crisis, I strongly recommend Pat Allen's *Art Is a Way of Knowing.* Allen says, "Images are messages from your soul and never come to harm you. . . . Intention empowers. . . . Attention transforms. . . . Anyone can do this."[4]

Blessings on your hands and hearts.

---

[3]Thurston James, *The Prop Builder's Mask-Making Handbook* (Crozer, VA: Betterway Publications, 1990).

[4]Pat B. Allen, *Art Is a Way of Knowing* (Berkeley, CA: Shambhala Publications, 1995).

9

Working with the Dying

A deathbed vigil feels oddly similar to the vigil as we wait for a birth. Death is its own form of labor.

Many years ago, when Macha's husband, Rod, lay dying, she asked me (Starhawk) to come and be with her, to sit by his bedside. As we sang, chanted, and did all we knew to try to ease his passage, I watched his labored breathing. In the last stages of cancer, his wasted body worked and sweated to stay alive. I could tell that the effort to take one breath, for him, was like lifting weights or straining to push a heavy cart up a hill would be for me. Recovery was hopeless; consciousness was gone. He was clearly ready to die. Each breath simply prolonged his suffering. Yet his body continued to struggle to breathe, to live. At that moment, I had a profound realization: although we had always invoked death as the Implacable One, life too can be a relentless, implacable force. Death may come as a release into a new dimension, as a liberation, just as an infant's birth is a release into a new world.

To be present when someone is dying is both a gift and a challenge. This chapter offers advice, meditations, chants, songs, and prayers for those who are helping someone cross over.

A Crash Course in Being Present with the Dying

SHARON JACKSON

I should have known better, I suppose, than to sing "Donald, Where's Your Troosers" to the elderly Scottish lady in the palliative care ward at the hospital. After all my training, I ought to have been a little more cautious about barging in, striking a pose, and launching into a rollicking song in an amateur Scottish accent. "We-e-e-e-l-l-l, I just got back fro' the Isle o' Skye," I sang cheerily as she sank lower under the covers and stared at me with beady, slate-colored eyes.

"All the lassies say, HELLO, Donald, where's your troosers!" I ended on a smashing crescendo and stood smiling at her, waiting for her to acknowledge my gift.

There was a long pause, and then, in a very thin voice, she said, "Aye, that was verra nice. Now get out."

That is a sterling example of how *not* to be with dying people—invasive, abrasive, full of assumptions.

Beyond examples such as that, what can I offer you that you cannot read in other books? As Witches, we learn to feel or to "read" energy, to be sensitive to the energy level in others, though we may not know *exactly* what someone else is feeling or needing at that moment. I learned to use that ability more and more as time went by.

I learned to be still, to wait until the dying person gave me a clue. I learned to leave my own agenda at the door and to follow where I was led.

As a volunteer, I learned not to take it personally when someone did not want company. My job was simply to be there as a compassionate listener, a tea-bringer, a foot-massager, a fingernail-painter, a pillow-puffer, a soup-spooner, and sometimes a hand-holder. On one remarkable occasion, on the request of a woman in my ward, I got rid of the evil spirits coming at her out of the ceiling in the upper-lefthand corner of the room. I neither saw nor felt them myself, but I did apparently banish them quite nicely, to the appalled audience of two nurses standing at the door. I learned to be a willing servant, but not a slave.

I made some wonderful friends, and then they died. It was hard, until I figured out that their friendship was one of the last gifts they were able to give, and then it became an honor and privilege. Death is pretty smelly sometimes, or ugly, or painful, or all of the above. But I was always reminded that this was not *my* death; if I was to be of any use at all, I had to stay focused on my purpose, stay centered and grounded. When a volunteer starts wailing or gagging, or brings her own emotional baggage into the room uninvited, that is the time to put her behind the hospital gift-shop counter down in the foyer.

It could have been that singing "Donald, Where's Your Troosers" the day before, or even the day after, would have been perfect. My mistake was not to simply wait for a moment, feel the energy, talk to the woman, and discover how she was. Good old common sense, a little sensitivity, and a little love — generally that is all you'll need.

Working with the Living

TIMOTHY WALLACE

For those directly involved in magical work around crossing over, the world may take on a melancholy shade, become a place of shadows and departures. Caregivers may find their activities focused on the dying one. Priests and priestesses may discover that, due to their nearness to the gate, the energy of death bleeds back into their lives. The friends, colleagues, and loved ones of the caregivers and ritualists also have a task — to restore their joy of life and sustain it.

For the most part, this involves serving the "beer and pretzels" of ordinary life. Caregivers and ritualists need food, drink, rest, casual conversation about simple matters, and a loving, invigorating touch. They need to get away from the realm of death and enjoy the living world.

One simple thing to do in support of caregivers and ritualists is to take them away from the site. Take them out for a movie, a meal, a coffee, a walk in the park—whatever seems appropriate and affirms the continuing presence of the ordinary world. I have learned that this helps caregivers to broaden their focus from the narrowness of death's gate. Going out into the everyday world refreshes life's hues for them.

Another thing to do is to take on some of the caregivers' mundane burdens: feed their companion animals, do their dishes, clean their homes, weed their gardens, provide childcare, hang out with their families, and the like. This relieves them of some of the feeling of being overwhelmed by the combination of the major task at hand and the tasks of ordinary life. Such assistance enables them to maintain their focus on the dying process.

Those who are working around crossing over may find that their desire for life is sharpened, that they have a greater need for caring gestures, comfort, and loving. Hugs, kisses, and massages may affirm their physical beings and restore the emotional and spiritual energy that goes to the dying process. The solidarity of a community of colleagues and friends balances the growing intangibility of the departing one.

Beyond this, caregivers may experience keen erotic appetites and need the renewal of life that sex provides. Here the need to use good judgment and consider what is appropriate is paramount. Nonetheless, a life-affirming sexual magic is associated with nearness to crossing over.

Beyond the "beer and pretzels," people can support caregivers and ritualists with a variety of magical acts and practices. Colleagues can make talismans or amulets or other charged items for them, so that they will enjoy energy and support that helps anchor them in the living world. Friends can create a ritual of a particular form or involving a certain element, place, or deity on behalf of the caregivers. This ritual may involve themes of purification and rejoining the ordinary world of the living. Those who have journeyed near to death's gate need to be reembraced by their still-living friends and colleagues.

In addition, working with the dying is very likely to transform the caregiver or ritualist, and this transformation needs to be commemorated. For the caregiver, new talents or skills may reveal themselves, new ways of relating with others or with the world may offer themselves, or other changes may become evident. The caregiver's friends, loved ones, and magical community can welcome such "gifts from death" with celebration and understanding. Such celebration is especially useful if these "gifts" are difficult for the caregiver to assimilate all at once.

Following a crossing over, the caregivers and ritualists themselves undergo something of an initiatory experience: there is a period of struggle to return to the ordinary world and to a magical practice that does not so fully involve the powers of death. Support of these caregivers is therefore not a short-term process, but one that may take several months to a year.

All in all, working with the living who are themselves directly involved with crossing over may become a significant personal challenge and a major magical undertaking. In my view, it is firmly rooted in the earth and sustained by earthly acts and passions. It is as plain as a California poppy—and as vibrantly alive.

Death, Health, and Hygiene

M. A. BOVIS

Each time I have experienced the death of someone close and dear, it is as if I have gained instant access to all the other little deaths I have experienced. I may not remember them, they may not be that important in the overall scheme of things (for example: encountering a rude stranger, breaking a treasured possession, enduring a disappointment from a friend), but I have access to a huge sea of sadness. The grieving period that follows such a death is a chance to transform myself and create something positive out of one of the most difficult times in my life. Presented below are some of the tools I have used to help take care of myself during and after a friend's crossing over.

1. *Shower daily.* Dancers and athletes towel off quickly after exercise because there is an acid in sweat that stiffens the muscles. For the same reason, you should rid yourself of the sweat that accompanies emotional stress. In addition, there are toxins in tears that damage the skin of your face, and you need to keep your aura clean. A shower is better than a bath because the water, having absorbed all your negative stuff, goes down the drain so you do not soak in it. If you feel you want a bath, be sure to put salt in the water (sea salt, Epsom salts, *any* salt) or some herbs (see herb section), but *always* shower off afterwards.

2. *Sleep and eat.* Get as much sleep as you can so your immune system and your unconscious mind can work on your healing process. If you cannot sleep, at least try resting quietly during the time you would normally sleep. Eat regular meals as much as possible; your body needs fuel during this time as much as any other time. Lots of fruits and veggies and less sugar—but you knew that already, I'm sure!

3. *Take vitamins and immune system boosters.* Remember that death is one of the big-three major stresses, which means that it depresses your immune system. Take care of yourself: if you cannot sleep or eat, at least give yourself some fortification for the processing you are doing. Some good boosters are echinacea, golden seal, or pau d'arco; go to your local health food store and ask for some advice.

4. *Move your body.* Create a movement-only ritual. (If you must use sounds, use only wordless sounds, and feel the sounds you make resonate in your body.) What is important is to acknowledge what you are going through (something *big*), and to be *in* your body and *out* of your mind. Movement is the best way I know to do that. Dancing seems to work better for this purpose than simple exercise or ballistic stuff like running; the creative part is pretty important. Remember that this is not a performance; it is for your health, so do what feels good.

5. *Get a massage, a haircut, a manicure, a pedicure, a shave, a waxing, a tattoo.* Adore your lovely, dear body that holds yourself.

I emphasize healing because in my experience grieving has
been similar to recuperating from an operation or a long illness. I must stress here that it is so important to be gentle to
yourself. Be loving to you. After all, how would you treat an
invalid who was convalescing from a long illness? Certainly
not with impatience and sharpness when that person was
unable to "bounce right back." Sometimes a need to "bounce
right back" is escapism, and it is certainly okay if you *want*
that. But if what you need is a longer convalescence, you must
honor your process, being gentle to yourself along the way.

Of course, in the end what will help in the personal grieving process varies for each person. The above is what worked
for me, but your tools may be different. In any case, be sure to
consider how death and dying affect your whole self—your
body as well as your mind and emotions—and honor that
whole self in the process.

Minerals, Herbs, Oils, and Teas

M. A. BOVIS

This section on minerals, herbs, oils, and teas is written in the
hope of sharing my experience with others. I have read books
on the subject, but the advice and suggestions of others have
played a greater part in my education. My friend John
McClimans' report that he carried black tourmaline in his
pocket for protection means more to me than what I might
read in a book, because he can give specific examples of when
it worked; furthermore, my friend is more immediate in my life
than a list in a book, however reputable. (Even so, you are
reading this in a book!)

When my brother died and I had to pack (lightly) right
away for a trip to the opposite coast, I did not think twice

when I grabbed lavender and vetiver oil and a quartz crystal necklace. These were my tools to work with; as a Witch I saw them as much a part of my wardrobe as clean underwear. I also brought some oils and some waters of the world to wash and bless my brother's body with. Of course, Pagans tend to have more of these things around the house than regular folks do, so it is easier to grab them when grieving deeply.

If you find some of my suggestions more or less effective than others, I would be grateful if you would let me know by writing to me in care of the publisher. Blessings and best of luck!

MINERALS

Put stones on your body in little bags, carry them in your pocket, hold them in your hand, or wear jewelry (a potentially expensive option). Cleanse them frequently in sunlight or salt water and leave them on your altar for a while periodically to recharge.

Quartz Crystals:

Any clear quartz crystals can be used to store and release grief. Use or wear one during the day and a different one at night.

Rose quartz is good for loving yourself in a difficult time.

Smoky quartz is good for spiritual grounding—the darker the better.

Amethyst quartz is good for spiritual healing.

Other Stones:

Black tourmaline offers very strong psychic protection in a very vulnerable time.

Jade gives intense healing, can help with a lack of physical energy.

Bloodstone contributes insight and healing of wounded heart/feelings/spirit.

Hematite offers good protection.

Violet sapphire is great for healing and protection.

HERBS AND OILS

Oils:

Any of these oils can be used on a handkerchief, spread on a thick ribbon,

or dropped into water; they can also be used in bathing (but it is
    good to add salt to the water as well).

Lavender is for cleansing, purifying, aiding clarity.

Citrus is for cheering (often easier, better, and cheaper used
    fresh rather than from a bottle; just peel a grapefruit, for
    example).

Vetiver is for grounding, helping one be practical, strengthening.

Peppermint is for cheering and energizing.

Rose is for love, calming, and healing.

Jasmine is for love, calming, and solace.

Rosemary is for clarity and cleansing.

Carnation is for purity, clarity, and cheering.

Sandalwood is for grounding and spiritual strength.

Rose geranium is for cleansing and clarity.

Useful oil combinations:

Rose and jasmine.

Sandalwood, carnation, and peppermint.

Sandalwood, rose, and lavender.

Herbs:

For bathing:

Always use either Epsom salts or sea salt with these herbs. Salt is a
    good neutralizer and purifier.

Lavender and rosemary (dried or fresh) are good for cleans-
    ing, energizing, and cheering (either in the bath or in pot-
    pourri).

Fresh flower petals from roses are calming, from carnations;
    purifying, or mums; energizing.

For use around the house:

Eucalyptus leaves, available from any florist, are refreshing.

Fresh lavender, basil, rosemary, peppermint, or oregano in
    food, teas, or little vases will help clear the air and cheer
    you up.

Citrus is a good brightener; for a quick and easy pick-me-up
    any time, simply peel an orange or grapefruit, cut up a
    lemon or lime.

TEAS

<u>For drinking:</u>

Chamomile is calming, soothing.

Peppermint is good for the central nervous system. I like to blend it with lemon verbena. Try to avoid too much caffeine, as it can interfere with healing

<u>For burning (above small charcoals):</u>

Sage and sweetgrass are great cleansers, either in combination or alone.

Lavender (again!) is good for cheering and clearing.

Frankincense and cedar resin (if you can get it) are spiritually soothing and calming scents.

Purification

When someone is dying, everything we have ever felt about that person surfaces with great intensity, both the positive feelings and the negative. Relationships are rarely clear and simple, and our love for the dying person may be laced with anger, envy, bitterness, or other unpleasant feelings. Such feelings are real, they are valid, but they are not appropriately expressed when a person is dying.

Because death is the ultimate loss of control, we can be helpful to a dying person only by letting her or him be as much in control of the process as possible. If unfinished business lies between you, let the dying person bring it up (or not). Be careful not to do or say things you will later regret.

In the Craft we are taught to acknowledge our feelings but not necessarily to act them out. We need to develop the inner power to hold a feeling without immediately expressing it, to contain strong emotions without repressing them. The salt water meditation can help us do so. Some part of us feels love and compassion for the one who is dying. We can be in that part and set the other parts aside for the moment. (*Note:* If *no* part of you feels love or compassion toward this person, you should not be priestessing her passage.)

Salt Water Purification

Before being with the dying, sit with a bowl of salt water for a moment. Breathe deeply, from your belly, and be sure you are grounded. Allow your thoughts and feelings to arise, and let them flow into the bowl as a stream of colors. Do not censor yourself. You may feel grief or fear, but you may also feel anger at the dying person (or at aspects of the situation), resentment, exhaustion, anxiety, even eagerness to get the ordeal over with. Allow all those feelings to flow into the bowl as energies.

Ask yourself some of the following questions:

Why am I here? What do I really feel about being here? What are my fears?

What needs of my own might interfere with the dying process? What am I getting out of this? How important is it to me to be needed? To feel that I personally control the spiritual atmosphere? Can I let go? How do I feel when I am not in control?

Just let the answers surface, and let the feelings and energies that arise with them continue to flow into the bowl. Remember that we ask these questions not to judge ourselves, but to bring to light the forces working within us that might otherwise rule unseen and to transform them into useful energies.

When you are ready, take another deep breath; imagine that you can draw up energy from the earth and call down energy from the sun, moon, and stars, and let that energy flow into the bowl to charge the water. When you sense that the energy has shifted, take some of the water back by sipping some of it or touching it to your body, wherever you need it. This act symbolizes that we are not trying to rid ourselves of any of our emotions. Our feelings are energies. When we put them into the salt water we acknowledge them and take back the energy they represent, to use as we need.

Pour the rest of the water, if possible (and if the solution is not too salty), onto the earth or into a running stream. If that is not practical, go ahead and pour it down the drain, with the water running.

When time is too short to do the full meditation, do a quick version of it with water in the bowl of your cupped hands. Traces of salt on your skin will be present in the water.

This is an excellent meditation to do regularly before you go to sleep at night, at this or at any other stressful time in your life.

.☺

Simple Ritual for the Ill

T. THORN COYLE

This section modifies the basic ritual described in Chapter 2 (see "Ritual Basics" on page 19) for use in hospitals or hospices. (I recommend that you read "Ritual Basics" before this section.)

Times of illness and transition call out for ritual to help all involved. Sick or dying individuals may need help carrying out ritual, or at least a reminder that it is still possible to partake of their most basic spiritual practices. Let them know that though they may be in a hospital or confined to a bed or wheelchair, their spiritual needs can be attended to.

If possible, set up the ritual space with an altar in each quarter, representing North, earth; East, air; South, fire; West, water; Center, spirit or ether. Use colored cloths instead of candles, or use the objects and tools that represent these elements (see "Personal Practices of Pagans," page 22 of Chapter 2). If there is no space for directional altars, one altar will do. Do not worry if it is not elaborate. In a space devoid of the things of home, a single picture can become an altar. Simple things bring comfort and reminders of the sacred. A plant, shell, or feather becomes a connection to the spirit that dwells in all things, connecting the sick to the world they may no longer walk upon.

Earth or salt water cleansings are preferred to incense for most hospital rituals, because health care institutions cannot allow burning things in a room that has highly flammable oxygen; furthermore, ill people are sometimes not hearty enough to breathe smoke. You can follow the salt water cleansing in "Ritual Basics" or make up your own.

You may then set up sacred space following the outline set out in "Ritual Basics": grounding, circle-casting, and invoking the elements. If time needs to be short because of energy constraints, simply say, "By the earth that is Her body, by the air that is Her breath, by the fire of Her bright spirit, by the water of Her living womb, and by the Spirit which is the center of all, the circle is cast." This will do for both casting and invoking the elements.

The Goddess and God that the dying person is closest to, or who will be most helpful to her in this time, should then be welcomed into the space.

Now is the time for the core of the ritual. Use your intuition and imagination to combine various helpful elements. The sick one could be given a healing massage, for example. Any of the meditations in this book could be used as a trance journey in this space. Spell work for a safe and easy passage or a mending of old wrongs could be done as well. (This work could take the form of a simple pouch full of seeds of good intention, feathers for swift flight, and so on.) Perhaps a space for grieving and letting go could happen here too. Whatever feels appropriate probably is.

Sing a favorite song—either one especially loved by the sick person or one that you think will have special resonance for her (perhaps from among those presented in this book). Give the energy raised to the healers, the friends present, and the ill person herself.

Offer food and drink if you have it, and if the ill one is still able to eat. Thank all that you have called into your sacred space. Open the circle. Your ritual is done.

Fates Chant

Words and Music by T. Thorn Coyle

Sitting Vigil with the Dying

M. Macha NightMare

It has been my great privilege to be present as a priestess to
two dying friends in the past year. Both were men. Both were

Witches. One wanted to live; he wanted more days to wake up and be a man in this magnificent world of earth/the material. The other chose to take control of his failing body and to approach Death with his eyes wide open.

Both of these men shared a Pagan worldview with me and with the other priestesses and priests at their deathbeds. This was helpful—to them and to us—for it meant that we shared a common vocabulary of the sacred, common symbology, common magical techniques, and common songs, chants, and prayers. I will tell you some of the ways in which these commonalities aided our work, but I want to make certain that you not be discouraged or inhibited from involving yourself as much as possible in the immediate experience of the dying person just because you do not share a common spiritual tradition and practice.

Some of the things we can be attuned to and use with the dying are as common as the feel of wind in one's hair, of sun on one's skin. They need not be esoteric. They are things that everyone whose spirit inhabits and animates a human body knows.

Everyone needs human contact, care, and concern in his last days and hours. Every human deserves that. Elsewhere in this book are some specific grounding and purification exercises for you to do before being with the dying person. For now, I will simply tell you some of my experiences with Raven and John.

Raven died just about one year ago as I write this, just after Spring Equinox. Raven had AIDS and was an addict. A loved member of our collective for many years and a very powerful priest, he had estranged himself in recent years because of his return to substance abuse. But it was important to him, even in his deteriorated mental and physical state, to celebrate the sabbats (that is, holidays) with his community. Most of the celebrations were in public places like parks; and Raven attended.

Just after Brigid, Raven was admitted to Maitri Hospice so he could be cared for as his strength and health declined. Shortly before Spring Equinox, Raven had his first seizure, followed by meningitis. He was hospitalized and could not be taken to our community ritual. So four of us went to his bedside at Maitri to celebrate with him there.

At that sabbat, Spring Equinox, when earth's regeneration is so visible all around, we five Witches called the God to our circle with an old English song called "Jack in the Green." The song is about grain god and his cycles—"Though He dies every autumn, so He's born every spring."

Raven remembered a guided visualization that Kat, one of those present, had created years before. He requested that she do it again. The visualization involved an old blind woman in a cave, scritch-scratching marks into its walls.

In the quiet of Raven's room, as we listened to Kat's voice suggest/describe where we were together, Raven weakly but intently whispered, "Scritch . . . scratch . . . scritch . . . scritch . . . scratch." He was inside the cave, watching the woman make the marks, or perhaps making them himself.

The marks are DNA codes; the cave is an egg, sacred to the Goddess of spring, Eostar.

This reassurance of Raven's spiritual beliefs and repetition of lifetime practices, like some of the chants we did, gave him comfort and solace. I believe it helped him to see his death less as something to be feared and thereby easier, smoother, less painful.

So when you find yourself with a dying person with whom you share a common faith, pray, sing, chant, talk, do things to help your dying loved one focus on the spiritual nature of her transition, on the sacredness of the work she is undertaking and the experience she is undergoing. You will both take comfort in the practices.

One of the things Raven told people in his dying weeks was, "I've been so bad. The Goddess is going to be mad at me." Fear and the notion of guilt reappeared. Raven had been raised in a tradition that stressed guilt and retribution and punishment, and he had reverted to that notion when faced with the specter of the seeming annihilation of death. I could see no benefit from this attitude, so I mentally noted it in case an opportunity to explore it presented itself—which it did, as it happens, on his final night.

On the night Raven died, many, many people came to his room in San Francisco General Hospital's Ward 5A—a place where beautiful, compassionate people work. When I arrived, there were already four Witches with him, two of whom had been seriously estranged from him for years because of his addiction-related betrayals. All five of us stayed until after Raven's passing. People came and visited with him (he was unconscious for the most part), exchanged hugs with others and hugged him, held his hand, and sang and chanted together. We did a chant that Raven himself had written about the wake of Lugh the Sun King.[1] We chanted to Kali Ma, to Hekate, to Cerridwen. We chanted of our love for him:

Listen, Raven, listen to my heart song.
Listen, Raven, listen to my heart song.
I will never forget you. I will never forsake you.
I will never forget you. I will never forsake you.
Listen, Raven, listen to my heart song.
Listen, Raven, listen to my heart song.
I will always love you. I will always be with you.
I will always love you. I will always be with you.

Raven's non-Pagan father chanted this with us, his Witch friends. Love, tears, open hearts surrounded Raven as he lay there leaving his body.

With the bed circled by chanting Witches, I sat by Raven, stroked his skin with raven feathers, and talked, and talked, and talked him over the threshold. Raven and I took on our bird forms; I could see our shiny black feathers. To the others who surrounded Raven's bed, chanting, I have been told that we appeared as a man on a bed with a woman whispering in his ear—but somehow different, not really there. To me—and to Raven, I know—we were not in human form, but rather we were corvids, soaring together far away into the vast, starry night.

I told Raven how his Dark Mother loved him. He could feel how She loved him as he approached Her. Whatever he

---

[1]See also "Lugh's Crossing," by Douglas Orton and Beverly Frederick, on page 51 of Chapter 4.

had done while he lived a life in San Francisco had no rele-
vance now. She was his Mother; She gave him this life. He
was returning to Her lap, to Her bosom. She had no concern
for what he had done in life. She loved him unconditionally.
She would give him rest and renewal. She would restore him
to life in a body at the proper time—another time. Raven and
I saw Her black, black skin and Her dazzling, bejeweled toes.

All this while, the chanting around us continued. The circle
around Raven held us safe. And for me, the sound of voices
was my lifeline back to my body, back to the hospital room,
back to this existence. Without that as something to call me
back, the risk I took could have had unfortunate consequences.

Raven's death effected a psychic toll on me, I believe
because I went so far into another world with him. That night
after he died, I craved heavy, heavy food. I was dazed,
ungrounded, slightly out of my body. In the days and weeks
following his death, I was gradually restored with massages—
both deep and strong, and gentle and nurturing—and by eating and making love and exercising. And three months later, at
Reclaiming's Midsummer ritual on the beach, by a plunge in
the cold, exhilarating, cleansing, salty Pacific Ocean with
Raven's and my community of Witches.

So I was able, with the use of my intuition and in the safe
circle maintained by our sisters and brothers, to use the information Raven had provided about his fears of punishment. I
was able to see those fears vanish as he and I approached the
Dark Mother in the glittering sky, and he felt the pull of Her
love for him and Her desire for him to return to Her for a
time.

My friend John McClimans, who died about eight months
after Raven did, was a priest of the Goddess in several Pagan
traditions. First and foremost, he was devoted to Hekate,
ancient Goddess of the liminal realms. Though John and I did
not share the same Craft tradition as Raven and I did
(Reclaiming), all of the priests and priestesses at his deathbed
were Pagans and all but one were Witches. We too had a common worldview to help us work together.

John was a victim of a lifetime of bad habits that had left
him, at age forty-eight, morbidly obese, diabetic, a double

amputee, wearing a pacemaker and having recently suffered a stroke that left him unable to move much of his body or to speak except with great difficulty. After many months in and out of surgery for the amputations, and in and out of hospitals, John needed much specialized care from his wife and loved ones.

Bad health aside, John was a man of honor and principle, humor and compassion, righteous indignation and curmudgeonliness, questing mind and spirit, and unbounded love for his friends. He decided, several weeks after suffering the stroke from which he found it so difficult to recover, to refuse medications and to go home to die in his house, with his loved ones around.

He took up residence in a hospital bed in the middle of his living room. Friends came to visit; his coven came to circle with him; people phoned from all parts of the country. He had previously discussed his feelings about his dying with his wife, his partner, and a few close friends. In accordance with his wishes, we took shifts staying with John. I was privileged to be one of the people he wanted with him.

When someone is dying, he is neither here among the living, engaged in the business of living, nor is he there, on the other side, gone. He is in a liminal realm—neither here nor there. This is not true for everyone, perhaps, but many Pagans understand and appreciate this concept. They may already have experience with the Goddess called Hekate in their magical workings and worship. This liminal realm is Hers.

Hekate rules the space *between* here and there. She dwells in the liminal. She presides over the time which is neither past nor future and the place which is neither in this world of the living nor on the other side of the veil that separates the world of flesh from that of spirit.

Though we who are not approaching death are not actually in Hekate's realm, we can observe that our dying loved one is *not* firmly planted in this world. He is drifting toward another world. He could be said to be sailing on a boat, approaching a threshold—any number of images that convey the fact that he is not engaged in living but is not devoid of life and animation either. *We* are not in Her realm, but we can see that *he* is.

John, as I mentioned, was a priest of Hekate. So we knew that he was choosing to meet Her in his own way, consciously, with his eyes open. During those last two weeks of John's life, I was acutely aware of Her presence. Sometimes I could see Her mantle sweep around to enfold John. The inside of Her cape seemed like the star-studded night sky. Sometimes I could see John through a misty curtain of stars. Sometimes the curtain was opaque, sometimes translucent, sometimes not there at all.

All the time I was in the room, day after day, I tried to keep within eyeshot of John, while not intruding on his conversations with visitors. I noticed that some people tended to be less sensitive to the dying person's needs than to their own. Yet when you are with a dying person, it is very important to let him set the tone. After all, there may be little else he *can* set: someone like John, who had little ability to physically control his body, is in a state of relative disempowerment. As an example of the importance of tone, John *hated* it when someone spoke of him in the third person in his presence. He felt discounted, objectified. He told us that. Speech was difficult for him, but if we listened with patience, and if he did not have the distraction of other activity or conversation in the same room, he could say what he wanted to say.

Still, sometimes the general energy in the room became fragmented by cross-conversations and other static—none of it ill-intended. At these moments, John would seek out my eyes and we would link thoughts. These were precious, loving interchanges for both of us. I would—very quietly, almost in a whisper—chant, "Weaver, Weaver, weave his thread, whole and strong into Your web. Healer, Healer, heal his pain. In love may he return again."[2] John looked so very deeply in my eyes in those moments that I felt we were truly connected.

As with Raven, this activity—the intense personal communion combined with chanting of words that reflected John's and my shared thealogy—brought comfort. It also

[2]The words and music of this chant by Starhawk appear on page 171 of Chapter 12.

included the introduction of a new practice in the form of the specific chant, which John had not known and which I had learned only in the last year.

Another reason this employment of deep, clear, direct eye contact and chant was useful was that John was sensitive to sounds and light. Dying people often are highly sensitive to changes in temperature, to light, to sound. They prefer their rooms to be dimly lit (though not dark) and relatively quiet.

As explained elsewhere in this book, we Witches honor four elements of Life: air, fire, water, and earth. Many of us have observed that people usually leave their bodies one element at a time, although this is not always noticeable to someone watching. First, the dying one seems to feel heavy and immobile, unable to move, to lift arms or head. This is the element of Earth pressing in on him. At another point, he becomes dehydrated and wants water, water, Water. He also becomes cool to the touch as fire leaves him. At the end, the last thing to leave is breath, the element of Air.

Another common experience I have noticed in sitting vigil with the dying is my own openness. I have felt a profound opening of all my chakras, those seven vortices of energy that reside along the spine from tailbone to just above the crown of the head. My heart overflows with love and feels very vulnerable and undefended. The vision in my third eye, in my brow, is much more acute than in ordinary circumstances. My crown feels open. My solar plexus feels open. And oddest of all to me, my genitals feel open.[3]

This is not a "bad" feeling, but it is one to be alert for. I recommend taking precautions not to have to interact with the mundane world any more than absolutely necessary when you might be in such a state of consciousness. Allow some time to reorient yourself before driving or trying to conduct business. Eat, take a brisk walk, breathe deeply, pull yourself back together. It may help to shower — not because you are dirty but because you need to be refreshed. It is kind of like having to drink your

---

[3]This is not sexual stimulation; it is something else. I am not exactly sure how to articulate it, other than to say that it is an openness.

coffee in the morning before you begin to interact with others.

My experiences with dying people have taught me much. They have taught me the value of holding hands, massaging, touching. They have taught me that the right chants, at the right volume (never too loud), give comfort. They have taught me to observe the state of the dying person so I can become aware of where he is in the liminal realm. They have taught me to be sensitive to sound, light, humidity, temperature, touch— so I can modify the sounds in the room if necessary, dim the light, draw the blinds, offer water, draw up a blanket or take it off, take a hand, stroke a brow. They have taught me to differentiate between the state of the dying person's body and the state of his mind or consciousness or spirit. Most of all, they have taught me to trust my intuition so I can work to help make my dying loved one's last days and weeks as pleasant, pain-free, and spiritually meaningful as possible.

I hope that my sharing of experiences with you, the reader, will help you to be more prepared for those times when you are privileged to attend to your dying loved ones. I hope that you can share those precious times in an absence of fear, and instead with an open heart, savoring your last times together, trusting your knowledge of the person and your own intuition, so that both you and your dying one can fully realize the strength of your connections, the depth and magnitude of your love, and the peace of a passing borne in caring and compassion.

Prayers for Caregivers to Say or Sing While Someone Is Dying

EMBRACE THE CHANGE

All that ever was exists now
in the living body of the being
we call universe, Goddess.
She breathes in —
we are born.
She breathes out —
we die.

But birth and death are on the same wheel
which is always turning,
like the tide
or the changes of the moon.
We become ancestors, the unborn,
newborn,
the guardians of those to come.
Cherish the turning,
the letting go and the bringing forth,
decay and growth,
life and death.
All points on the wheel are sacred.
Embrace the change.

CARRY ONLY LOVE

Beloved one, you are dying (dead),
but you are not alone.
We are here with you,
the beloved dead await you.
You go from love
into love.
Carry with you
only love.

May our love carry you
and open the way.

Prayers for the Dying Person to Say

LISTEN PEOPLE

Listen people,
the universe is alive,
and I will always be,
flowing in and out of form,
dying and being born,
forever.

FOR ALL THE GIFTS

For all the gifts of life
I have received
I give thanks.
To the mother who bore me,
to the father who seeded me,
to the ones who held me, rocked me, nursed me,
who fed and taught and nurtured me,
to those who played and danced and laughed with me,
to those who pleasured me and touched me,
to those who challenged me,
to those who love me,
to the ones who shared my life,
and to whom I have given life,
to each animal and plant
whose life I have eaten,
to the sun and moon and stars,
to the moving air, the flowing water,
to the earth who sustained me
and will receive me,
I give thanks.
Now I make room
for something new.
Now it is my turn
to feed,
to nourish,
to become soil
where roots of strong trees
may flourish.

BIRTH, GROWTH, DEATH, REBIRTH

Birth, growth, death, rebirth—
all points on the wheel are sacred
In some new form
I will live again.

10

The Moment
of Death

Our Energy Bodies and Their Dissolution

To understand what happens at death, we must first understand that our physical body is surrounded and interpenetrated by energy bodies linked to the three selves. The *etheric body* is our basic life-force and vitality, linked to Younger Self; extending out about a centimeter from the physical body, this is what is affected by acupuncture and other energetic healing techniques.

The *astral body* or *aura* is the body of our thoughts, images, and emotions, linked to Talking Self. It can grow or shrink with our state of mind but generally extends out about as far as our breath. Some people can see the aura and observe the colors and images within it. With the help of a friend, you can learn to feel the aura by sitting still and breathing deeply, grounding, and moving a hand back and forth into the field surrounding your partner. At about the edge of your partner's breath, you will feel a change: a tingling, a slight change in temperature, sometimes an urge to stop. With practice, much information about a person can be absorbed by feeling her energy field.

The Deep Self connects to the physical body through a cord of light attached to the energy center just below the navel. It hovers above our crown chakra as a body of light, often appearing in art as a halo. The aura and the etheric body are also linked to the physical body by an energy cord—a sort of spiritual umbilical cord.

As death approaches, the energy bodies begin to break up and dissolve. The energy cord linking them begins to fray, as does the veil or membrane that keeps the physical world and the otherworld apart. Symbolically, we say the gates between the worlds begin to open.

The Presence of the Mysterious Ones

A great vortex of powers and energies is created as these gates swing wide. The ancestors of the dying person or others close to her or him draw near. The dying person's helpers and guides on the otherworldly journey—all the Mysterious Ones ranged in his service—approach. If he has a strong connection with a particular Goddess or God, that deity's power and love can be felt.

The Goddess, the Gods, and the ancestors can also consciously be called to aid our own or our friend's dying. This book contains many prayers and chants that serve that purpose. But the simplest and most heartfelt way to invoke them is as follows:

Invoking the Mysterious Ones

Sit quietly, breathe deeply, and focus on the great powers of love and compassion in the universe. If you have particular deities or ancestors in mind, visualize them or simply concentrate on the feelings you identify with them. Speak to them from the heart, and ask for their presence, their help and support. Know that the great compassionate powers are always ready to come to our aid when asked.

Uniting with the Deep Self

At the moment of death, the energy cords break. If the dying person has a strong connection to her Deep Self, consciousness will unite with Deep Self. Watchers might perceive a movement of energy or light up through the belly cords, or flowing directly out of the crown of the head. Alternatively, they might sense that the dying person's spirit is gathered in by an aspect of the Goddess, the God, or one of the Mysterious Ones. Emotion fills the room: grief, of course, is present, but sometimes, before sorrow sets in, we may experience a feeling of joy, release, and liberation, akin to what we felt as kids on the first day of summer vacation, or a sense of relief and comfort, akin to what we feel when returning home after a long and arduous trip. The presence of such emotions strengthens our intuitive sense that the dead have indeed crossed over successfully to the realms of renewal.

After the relief comes the grief. While death is part of the natural cycle, so is our grief. The Reclaiming tradition has a saying that the Sunless Sea is made of tears. Our grief provides the energy the dead need to reach the dimensions of the otherworld where healing and regeneration are found. The unmourned dead have a difficult crossing.

But if, in our grief, we cling to the dying person, unwilling to let go, our sorrow can hold our friend's spirit back.

Prayers for Immediately After Death

The following prayers can be used just after a friend's death, to help the spirit cross over, perhaps in conjunction with a song such as "All Things Must Pass Away," found on page 150 of Chapter 10.

BLESSING OF THE ELEMENTS

May the air carry your (her/his) spirit gently.
May the fire release your soul.
May the water cleanse you (wash you clean of pain and sor-
    row and suffering).
May the earth receive you.
May the wheel turn again and bring you to rebirth.

BLESSING OF THE DEAD

Be free, be strong, be proud of who you have been, know that
    you will be mourned and missed, that no one can replace
    you, that you have loved and are beloved.

Move beyond form, flowing like water, feeding on sunlight
and moonlight, radiant as the stars in the night sky. Pass
the gates, enter the dark without fear, returning to the
womb of life to steep in the cauldron of rebirth. Rest, heal,
grow young again. Be blessed.

GODDESS OF DEATH, GOD OF GRAIN

Goddess of death,
you who are the end inherent in the beginning,
scythe to the ripe grain,
the fall of berries,
and the coming of night.
You are called the Implacable One.
but we know you
as the most gracious Goddess.
Healer,
end of sorrow,
relief of pain,
Receive our sister (brother) _____.
May she/he become a star
in your night sky cauldron
and be brewed back to life.

God of grain, God of seed,
You who every year's end
are cut down and buried,
You who know the dark places
underground,
the way down and the way up,
the fall and the rising,
guide our sister/brother _____,
show her/him the long road
through the maze
to the place of rebirth,
to the place of return.

All Things Must Pass Away

Words and Music by Starhawk

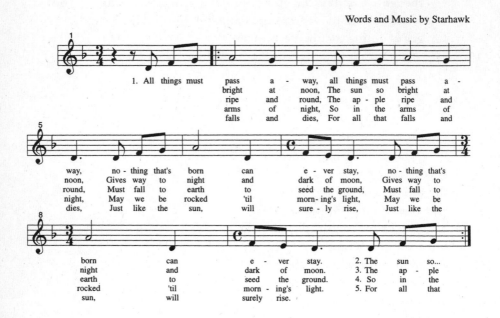

1. All things must pass a - way, all things must pass a -
   bright at noon, The sun so bright at
   ripe and round, The ap - ple ripe and
   arms of night, So in the arms of
   falls and dies, For all that falls and

way, no - thing that's born can e - ver stay, no - thing that's
noon, Gives way to night and dark of moon, Gives way to
round, Must fall to earth to seed the ground, Must fall to
night, May we be rocked 'til morn - ing's light, May we be
dies, Just like the sun, will sure - ly rise, Just like the

born can e - ver stay. 2. The sun so...
night and dark of moon. 3. The ap - ple
earth to seed the ground. 4. So in the
rocked 'til morn - ing's light. 5. For all that
sun, will surely rise.

Passage

Words and music by T. Thorn Coyle

Wa - ter en - gulf me, Fire scorch my skin,

Air suck my breath, Earth re - ceive me— in. In - to the arms of

mys - te - ry, My spi - rit soars, o - pen the gates

11

What We Must Do for the Dead

Washing the Dead

The dead should be washed with clear spring water, if possible. Add a few drops of waters of the world, water from a sacred well, ocean water, or water from a favorite place, if you have such water handy, or a drop or two of scented oil. Rosemary added to the water will bring purity and protection.

During the washing, the following blessing can be said. Feel free to add to the blessing or change it in any way. (Some lines—those that are gender-specific—obviously will not fit everyone.)

If you cannot actually wash the body, for whatever reason, you can still say the blessing and visualize the washing.

After the washing, smudge the body with sage or any appropriate incense. Then smudge or cense the shroud or clothing and wrap or dress the dead. (We suggest a simple sheet of white cotton, but it is up to you.)

Blessing for Washing the Dead

I bless your hair
that the wind has played with.
I bless your brow,
your thoughts.
I bless your eyes
that have looked on us with love.
I bless your ears
that listened for our voices.
I bless your nostrils,
gateway of breath.
I bless your lips
that have spoken truth.
I bless your neck and throat;
we will remember your voice.
I bless your shoulders
that have borne burdens with strength.
I bless your arms
that have embraced us.
I bless your hands
that have shaped wonders.
I bless your breasts
that nurtured us,
formed in strength and beauty.
I bless your heart
that loved us.
I bless your ribs and lungs
that sustained your life.
I bless your solar plexus,
seat of power.
I bless your belly,
sacred storehouse of the body.
I bless your womb
that gave life,
that bled with the moon.
I bless your hips,
the child's first cradle,
strong support.
I bless your vulva,

gateway of life,
jewel of pleasure.
I bless your cock,
its rising and its falling.
I bless your testicles,
carriers of the seed.
I bless your buttocks,
smooth and round.
I bless your thighs,
strong foundation.
I bless your knees
that knelt at the sacred altars.
I bless your legs
that carried you.
I bless your feet
that walked your own path through life.

Orienting the Dead

Many cultures share a belief that death can be confusing, that the spirit may not realize it is dead unless the living tell it so, that the dead may get lost unless they are guided. *The Tibetan Book of the Dead* is perhaps the most complete example of a guidebook to the after-death realms.

There are elaborate shamanic techniques for guiding the dead, but unless we are trained in such methods, we do better to stay with simpler practices. If you sense that your friend's spirit is confused, imagine that you are speaking to her or him. Tell her what has happened; let her know that she is dead, that you care for her and grieve for her but are willing to let her go. Use the prayers, chants, and songs in this book to send her energy and love. Speak to your friend's Deep Self and imagine your friend's life-energies flowing into that essential part of her being. Call on your friend's ancestors to help and guide her. Invoke the Goddess, the God, the Mysterious Ones, and the great powers of compassion to surround your friend.

All of these things can be done whether or not you are physically in your friend's presence. Regardless of the circumstances of death, we can trust the boundless power of compassion to guide souls into places of healing.

The First Three Days

Victor Anderson, a priest in the Feri tradition, teaches that the soul remains close to the body, or to the home, for three days after death. During this time, the spirit reviews his life. For this reason, a recently dead body should not be left alone. The company of caring friends singing, chanting, invoking, and meditating can help orient the soul and guide it toward healing and comfort. Try to wait at least this amount of time before cleaning out your friend's rooms or giving away his belongings. The familiarity of his home base may help orient him to his changed state.

This is also a time to say anything to your friend that you could not say or forgot to say in life, and to reassure the spirit of your love and forgiveness. After three days, or after the burial or cremation of the body, the soul moves on. After that time, if you sense that your friend's spirit is still closely bound to home, greet him gently and lovingly and remind him again that he is dead, that the time has come to let go.

Anything that people believe in exists in the otherworld, somewhere, as we have said, the spirit crossing over goes wherever in the otherworld it expects. If you believe, you will go to Avalon and walk with the Goddess beneath her flowering apple trees, you will. If you die expecting to go to the Christian Hell, that's exactly where you will end up. (The only difference is that you will not stay there for all of eternity, but only until you become aware that you can move on.)

Therefore, souls can conceivably stray into the wrong realm— especially if they died suddenly or violently. Prayer, ritual, and meditation can help lost souls find their way to the land of the ancestors appropriate to their people, and can truly release souls from the fires of Purgatory or Hell.

Whether we believe literally in the other world, or take its descriptions as metaphors, they assure us that something of us continues after our physical body is gone, that the lessons we learn in this life are not wasted, and that the human community extends into the past and the future. When we assist a dying person, when we provide comfort and support, we can ease fear and help her passage be a smooth one. When someone dies unexpectedly, ritual can help ease her transition. Most of all, ritual is a comfort to those of us who remain alive.

Imperfect Death

The ideal death is as rare as the ideal life. Death may not come to us peacefully as we lie on a bed surrounded by sorrowing loved ones chanting, praying, and sending us energy. Death may come unexpectedly, in rush-hour traffic, on an airplane surrounded by strangers, or alone on a mountain trail. Death may come violently, accompanied by humiliation and violation. It may interrupt us in the middle of a project or cut short a love affair.

We may envision a perfect death for our beloved friend and yet be unable to relieve her pain or his fear. Our own horror, weariness, or grief may overwhelm our best efforts at staying grounded and compassionate. We may be as irritated at our friend in death as we have been in life. Or we may be far away from our friend at the moment of death.

Death does not have to be perfect in order to be successful—that is, to be a death that enables the spirit of the dying person to move into realms of healing and renewal and enables the survivors to grieve, let go, and heal.

When someone you love dies and you cannot be there, you can still ground yourself, cleanse with salt water, chant, pray, and send energy to your friend's spirit. Light a candle to help guide your friend's spirit, saying the "Blessing of the Elements" and "Blessing of the Dead," found in the previous chapter on page 148. (Please follow candle safety rules and never leave an open flame unattended.) Set out an offering of food or drink. (After a day or two, this should be composted, not eaten.)

Create an altar to your friend's memory and spend some time each day mediating there. (M. A. Bovis explains how to erect such an altar on page 276 of Chapter 15.) You might visualize the washing of your friend's body, imagining that pain, injuries, and the marks of violence can flow away. You will need to grieve deeply for someone who has died in some terrible way, but do not dwell or obsess on the details or try to vividly imagine that person's suffering. Doing so will not help your friend. Instead, remember your friend whole, well, and in moments of joy or fulfillment in life. If your friend wrote poems, reread them. If he was a fabulous cook, try out one of his recipes. Do whatever you can to keep alive in memory moments of creativity and vibrancy.

Pay attention to your dreams. In the dream state, we may find ways to help and comfort those whom we can no longer reach in daylight.

At times, our lives are touched by a stranger's death. We witness an accident on the freeway, or stumble across a mugging on the street. Should you encounter such a death, remember to ground yourself and to breathe deeply to release your own fear or anguish. Silently or aloud, say blessings for the dead. Use your intuitive skills and compassion to offer support and comfort to the survivors.

Later, at home, do a cleasing meditation on page on page 28 of Chapter 3 and take a ritual bath. Take time to release the natural emotions of fear, helplessness, guilt, or whatever arises. Light a candle and sing or chant for the spirit of the person who has died. The essay "Always Keep Your Bags Packed," on page 222 of Chapter 13, contains additional suggestions for reintegration after a sudden death.

Be especially good to yourself after an encounter with death, or when you are grieving. Guilt is a natural but not necessarily rational response to death. Death is hard enough; do not add self-blame, especially for things you could not have prevented or changed. Reread the Forgiveness Meditation on page 65 of Chapter 5, and practice forgiving yourself.

Deaths and Hauntings: Practical Work

Diana L. Paxson

Death

The problem of death is a basic issue that must be addressed by any religion. We humans have always had understandable anxiety about our own death, and we have struggled with the death of others because it is a reminder to us of our own mortality.

Death anxiety varies widely from culture to culture and from period to period. The Navajo used to destroy the hogan in which a person died, along with the dead person's possessions. Practitioners of Voudoun, on the other hand, invoke the spirits of their dead as loas and may even keep containers with their ashes on household altars. The Celtic idea of Faeries depicts a mixture of devolved Gods and ghosts, as when the dead are seen riding with the Sidhe in visions. In medieval Europe, death was a major concern; the Black Plague gave rise to the dance of death motif, which appeared on woodcuts and church frescoes as well as actually occurring physically, with frenzied groups of people dancing in graveyards. In some orders, monks slept in the coffins of the dead.

For much of the twentieth century in the United States, the reality of birth and death has been hidden away in hospitals and nursing homes as if both were shameful. Most Americans have never seen either end of the life-cycle. Recently this has begun to change. Birth is happening in the home and at birthing centers in hospitals, where rooms are designed to take family members as well as hospital attendants. With issues such as the right to die being put on local ballots, the same trend may be developing with death.

As might be expected, different religions have very different ideas about what happens after death. Most of Christianity posits a Heaven for the good and a Hell for the evil, both of which last for all of eternity. Buddhists and some Eastern sects believe in reincarnation. Judaism says that good people will be with God but does not talk about the specifics. Our own modern-day neo-Paganism does not have a hard-and-fast position on what happens after death, though many neo-Pagans feel reincarnation to be a strong possibility after the soul has rested in the Summerland.

Hauntings

Though few neo-Pagans would dismiss ghosts or hauntings as fantasy or nonsense, we do not have much thealogy around them. Still, there is sufficient interest in these issues to warrant some discussion.

There are two kinds of hauntings. First, there are the hauntings of place by various discarnate entities so popular in ghost stories. These are actually quite rare. Second, there are the personal hauntings caused by unresolved conflicts in the relationship of the living person to the dead. These are almost universal when we lose someone we have known well.

The dead can haunt us in many ways. Unfinished business: *Now I will never be able to explain.* Abandonment: *How could you leave me?* Resentment: *How could you leave me to deal with this?* Despair: *If there is a God, how could She let my friend die?* Bewilderment after suicide: *If only I had known . . .*

In the Death Transformation Workshop that I facilitate, we have a ritual for dealing with the difficult feelings that engender these kinds of hauntings. We often have anger or resentment when someone close to us dies. But because that person is dead, we feel guilty about our anger or resentment. We can no longer direct it at its object, so it goes inward and causes anxiety, unresolved grief, guilt, and fear. We must remember that our feelings toward the dead person are okay. The fact that someone is dead does not mean she was perfect in life. It is all right to feel anger.

Ritual

Tools: altar, appropriately set up; sheets of paper and pencils; photos of the dead; votive candles in holders; cauldron; copy of prayers and hymns for each person; if possible, statue of Isis.

Participants sit in a circle, with a votive candle in front of each. Everyone should have a photo of the dead person near the votive candle and a piece of paper and pencil nearby. Each person takes a few moments, silently, to remember how the death of someone has haunted her. When people are ready, they go around the circle, each participant briefly describing her problem. The leader then asks, "What would you say to the dead person if you could?" Everyone writes a response down on paper.

Now the leader tells people to use their paper to light a candle in honor of the departed and then let the fire burn their response out of their consciousness and carry the message where it belongs. One by one, the participants twist up the paper and walk to the altar with their individual votive candles. They light the paper from the candle on the altar and use it to light their individual votive candle. They place the paper in the cauldron to burn and put the votive candle on the altar. Then together everyone recites a prayer to the Lady of the Underworld (or one of the prayers in this book).

12

Funerals and Memorials

⟲

The rituals we perform around death have two related but distinct purposes. The first is to help the person who has just died make the transition between life and death. The second is to comfort the living and to aid us in grieving and letting go.

Ideally, these two purposes should support each other. Our grief provides energy the dying person's spirit needs to relinquish its ties to this life and to move on to the realms of renewal. And we take comfort in knowing that we are providing what our beloved one needs.

But in the real world, with many of us coming from families that are not Pagan, these two purposes may be contradictory. The thealogy and liturgy in this book are specifically Pagan—that is, they come from the pre-Christian, earth-based Goddess religions that our tradition derives from Old Europe and the Middle East. Non-Pagan families might be offended or even frightened by the images that work for us. We should take care, in planning death rituals, not to add to the burden of grief a family is already suffering, and not to turn the funeral into a power struggle. You are free to adapt this material and substitute more neutral language as circumstances dictate.

However, neither should we allow a family's prejudices to prevent us from following the wishes of the dead or to deflect us from performing a ritual that reflects our beloved one's life and beliefs. After all, our rituals are not just a selection of pretty songs and poetry; they involve actual magical work, a raising of energy and a calling in of specific spirits that convey a power we do not wish to water down.

If necessary, you might divide the ritual into two parts: one more public part for friends and family, using rather neutral language and focusing on telling stories and honoring the life of your beloved one, and another more private part where the true magical work can be performed to aid the beloved dead in crossing over.

You may also wish to add specific prayers or chants that refer to the particular circumstances of your friend's life and death.

Pagans generally prefer to create our own rituals rather than following scripts or reciting liturgies. But grief is not a state conducive to creativity. When we are grieving, we often take comfort in having a form already set out for us to follow. Following is a script for a funeral service, which you may change, adapt, or use as fits your needs:

Funeral or Memorial Service

The ritual may take place outdoors, in the home, or where the body is to be buried or the ashes scattered. Chairs should be available for those who will need them. Participants gather in a circle around the body, or around an altar if the body is not present.

Play music as people gather. If possible, choose something your friend particularly loved in life. Taped music can be used, or perhaps two or three people might sing. If you like, choose one of the songs included in this book. I would suggest "Lyke-Wake Dirge" or "Set Sail," on page 167. (*Note:* All of the songs suggested in this ritual are printed at its conclusion.)

Make any necessary explanations and introductions, and teach the song or chant that will be used for raising power.

(*Note:* The parts marked LEADER in what follows can be taken by one person or shared among many.)

R ITUAL

Offering to the Land

LEADER steps to the center, holds up a bowl of blessed water or other appropriate offering, and says:

Spirits of this land, of the rocks and trees, of the plants and animals, of those who walked here long before us, we bring you this offering. We come with respect, to ask you to receive the body of our beloved _____. In giving you our beloved dead, we ask to become part of you (though our ancestors did not come from this land). (We know that many painful histories lie between our people and yours.) We ask your compassion, and your teaching, so that we who are living may learn to become strong allies of the land and its peoples. May the body (ashes) of our beloved be a bond between us. Blessed be.

Ground, cast the circle, and call the four directions and center according to the practice of your tradition. Special friends can be asked to ground, cast, and call. If you are unsure of how to do any of these, use the grounding on page 27 (chapter 3) and conduct the casting and invocations as follows:

Casting

LEADER: *Let us all take hands. Breathe deeply, and feel your love for _____. Imagine that your love and all your joyful memories of (her) are colors that you weave into a cord. Now all of our cords weave a circle around this space, marking it as sacred space. By the earth that is Her body, and by the air that is Her breath, and by the fire of Her bright spirit, and by the waters of Her living womb, the circle is cast. Blessed be.*

Calling the Directions

Each person invoking moves to the opposite side of the circle and faces the direction she or he is calling, so that these participants are speaking into the circle and can be heard.

EAST: *Spirits of the East, powers of air, we call you into our circle. Bring us clarity of vision, bright memories of our beloved _____, and the knowledge of sunrise and new beginnings. Blessed be.*

SOUTH: *Spirits of the South, powers of fire, we call you into our circle. Bring us the courage we need to face the reality of death, keep our passion alive even in our sorrow, and bring us the warmth of the hearth and the cleansing power of fire. Blessed be.*

WEST: *Spirits of the West, powers of water, we call you into our circle. Open our hearts, let our tears and love flow, and bring us healing and renewal. Blessed be.*

NORTH: *Spirits of the North, powers of earth, we call you into our circle. From you we come; to you we return. Bring us strength and nurturing, and the knowledge that all that dies becomes part of you again. Blessed be.*

CENTER: *Spirits of the Center, of change and transformation, we call you into our circle. Guide us through this change, help our beloved _____ through the great transformation (she) faces, help us to remember the true core of our lives. Blessed be.*

Invoking the Goddess and God

Special friends can be asked to invoke the Goddess and God by speech or song. Alternatively, the prayer "Goddess of Death, God of Grain," found on page 149 of Chapter 10, can be used.

Giving an Offering to the Ancestors

LEADER steps to the center of the circle and holds up a bowl of spring water, milk, honey, or whatever is most appropriate for the ancestors of your friend.

Ancestors, you have gone before us and given us our lives, you who are ancestors of our blood and you who are ancestors of the spirit, we bring you this offering. May you walk among us now. May you guide _____ to the Isle of Apples, to the realms of renewal. May (she) join your company and there find healing for all the hurts of the body, and may (she) continue to grow in wisdom and power. May (she) meet those among you that (she) has known and loved before; may (she) be embraced and welcomed. Blessed be.

Sharing Music

"The Island of the West" or "All Things Must Pass Away" would be my suggestion.

Telling Stories/Raising Power

This is the heart of the ritual. Depending on time, all the people gathered can be offered a chance to speak. Alternatively, a few special friends might be asked ahead of time. People who are not accustomed to leading ritual or speaking in front of groups will appreciate being given some time to prepare their thoughts. The raising of power should flow gracefully out of the end of the storytelling.

If the body or ashes are present, or if the ritual takes place beside the grave, a basket of flowers, herbs, leaves, or seeds is placed near it before the service continues.

LEADER: _____, *you are dead now. We know that you can take nothing with you but our memories and love. We have gathered to offer them to you. Let these (flowers) stand for the joys and sorrows we have shared together.* (LEADER *turns to the circle.*) *I ask you now to remember* _____ , *to tell us a story about (her). When you are finished speaking, come forward and drop a (flower) into the grave (or coffin).*

One by one, participants speak and make their offerings.

LEADER: _____, *these are but a few of the rich memories you have left us. We can never speak of you enough (and we will continue to tell tales of you as we feast). May the offerings we have made here help you on your journey. May our voices become a river of power to help guide you across the Sunless Sea to the Isle of Apples, the island of rebirth.*

ALL:
May the air carry your spirit gently.
May the fire release your soul.
May the water cleanse you.
May the earth receive you.
May the wheel turn again and bring you to rebirth.

(And/or say "The Blessing of the Dead" found on page 148 (chapter 10).

A cauldron is lit near the body. A mixture of approximately 60 percent rubbing alcohol and 40 percent Epsom salts makes a beautiful clear flame that will not set off smoke alarms. If you are indoors, be sure your cauldron has legs and is sitting on tiles or bricks to prevent marring the floor.

Chanting

"We Are of the Body of the Earth" (see page 170) would be my choice, including the verse "On the Same Wheel We Spin." This chant also works well with "She Changes Everything She Touches."

Depending on space and your own feeling of what is appropriate, you may wish to dance a spiral and raise a cone of power. Otherwise, simply let the chant build to a wordless tone that carries power. Direct it with the image of a river of energy that becomes a current in the Sunless Sea, carrying your friend to the realms of renewal.

Ground the power by touching the earth.

Songs: "Weaver, Weaver" or "All Things Must Pass Away."

Sharing Food and Drink

LEADER steps forward, holding up an offering of food and drink, and says:

Spirits of the land, ancestors, spirits of the elements, Goddess and Gods, we bring you this offering shared among the living and the dead. We give thanks for the sustenance we have received in life and for the promise of renewal after death. May you be fed as we are fed. May _____ be sustained on (her) journey. In the midst of our sorrow, may we also take joy in knowing that the dead are not truly separated from us. May _____ live in our hearts, may (she) come to us with help and comfort and wisdom in times of need, and may (she) be reborn among us that we may know and love one another again. Blessed be.

Food and drink are passed around the circle. While they are passing, you can begin devoking everything you have called in. Whoever invoked should say goodbye.

Devoking What Has Been Invoked

LEADER: *Ancestors, we thank you for guiding the soul of _____. May you continue to be with (her), offering comfort and strength, and may you continue to guide us. Hail and farewell, Blessed be.*

Goddess of life and death, God Who dies and is reborn, we thank You for our lives and for the mystery of death. May You welcome

_____ *with open arms, and may You continue to lend the living Your comfort and grace. Hail and farewell. Blessed be.*

CENTER: *Spirits of the Center, we thank you for change and transformation. Hail and farewell. Blessed be.*

NORTH: *Spirits of earth, we thank you for receiving back the body of _____, and for nurturing us in life. Hail and farewell. Blessed be.*

WEST: *Spirits of water, we thank you for all our emotions—love and sorrow, laughter and tears. Hail and farewell. Blessed be.*

SOUTH: *Spirits of fire, we thank you for passion, for courage, for cleansing. Hail and farewell. Blessed be.*

EAST: *Spirits of air, we thank you for clarity and memory. Hail and farewell. Blessed be.*

LEADER: *Spirits of this land, this place, we thank you for sheltering the body of _____, for allowing us to become part of you. May we learn to become healers of the land. Hail and farewell. Blessed be. By the earth that is Her body, and by the air that is Her breath, and by the fire of Her bright spirit, and by the waters of Her living womb, the circle is open, but unbroken. May the peace of the Goddess go in our hearts. Merry meet and merry part, and merry meet again. Blessed be.*

Song: "When We Are Gone"

Lyke-Wake Dirge

Tune Traditional, Words by Richard Goering

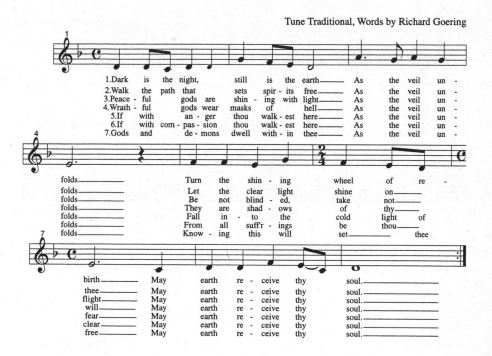

1.Dark is the night, still is the earth___ As the veil un-
2.Walk the path that sets spir-its free___ As the veil un-
3.Peace-ful gods are shin-ing with light___ As the veil un-
4.Wrath-ful gods wear masks of hell___ As the veil un-
5.If with an-ger thou walk-est here___ As the veil un-
6.If with com-pas-sion thou walk-est here___ As the veil un-
7.Gods and de-mons dwell with-in thee___ As the veil un-

folds___ Turn the shin-ing wheel of re-
folds___ Let the clear light shine on___
folds___ Be not blind-ed, take not___
folds___ They are shad-ows of thy___
folds___ Fall in-to the cold light of
folds___ From all suffr-ings be thou___
folds___ Know-ing this will set___ thee

birth___ May earth re-ceive thy soul.___
thee___ May earth re-ceive thy soul.___
flight___ May earth re-ceive thy soul.___
will___ May earth re-ceive thy soul.___
fear___ May earth re-ceive thy soul.___
clear___ May earth re-ceive thy soul.___
free___ May earth re-ceive thy soul.___

Set Sail

Words by Starhawk
Music by Mara June Quicklightning

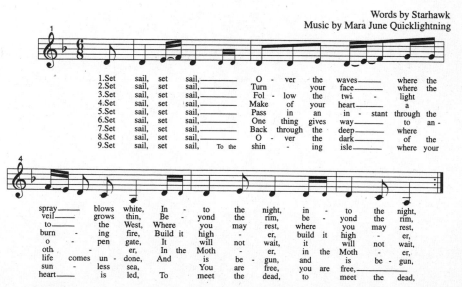

1.Set sail, set sail,___ O-ver the waves___ where the
2.Set sail, set sail,___ Turn your face___ where the
3.Set sail, set sail,___ Fol-low the twi-light
4.Set sail, set sail,___ Make of your heart___ a
5.Set sail, set sail,___ Pass in an in-stant through the
6.Set sail, set sail,___ One thing gives way___ to an-
7.Set sail, set sail,___ Back through the deep___ where
8.Set sail, set sail,___ O-ver the dark___ of the
9.Set sail, set sail, To the shin-ing isle___ where your

spray___ blows white, In-to the night, in-to the night,
veil___ grows thin, Be-yond the rim, be-yond the rim,
to___ the West, Where you may rest, where you may rest,
burn-ing fire, Build it high-er, build it high-er,
o-pen gate, It will not wait, it will not wait,
oth-er is done, And is be-gun, and is be-gun,
life comes un-done, In the Moth-er, in the Moth-er,
sun-less sea, You are free, you are free,___
heart___ is led, To meet the dead, to meet the dead,

fade out, repeating "Set sail, set sail"

When We Are Gone

Words by Starhawk, Music by Anne Hill

When we are gone, they will re-main, Wind and rock, fire and rain. They will re-main, when we re-turn, The wind will blow, and the fire will burn.

The Island of the West

Tune Traditional, Words by Starhawk

She Changes/We Are of the Body of the Earth

The following verses are actually variants of the original "She Changes" chant. There are many more verses in existence. They can be sung on their own, or with "She Changes" as chorus.

Words and music by Starhawk

Weaver, Weaver

Tune Traditional, Words by Starhawk

Chorus

Weav - er, weav - er weave (her) thread, whole and strong in -
to Your web, Heal - er, Heal - er heal (her) pain, in love may (she) re -
turn a - gain.

Fine | Verses

1. We are dark and we are bright
2. No one knows why we are born, a
3. May (she) find the hid - den way be -
4. At that spring may (she) drink deep and

we are formed of earth and light, from joy and pain our
web is made, a web is torn, Like wan - d'ring sea - birds
yond the gates of night and day, to that sweet land where
wake to dream, and die to sleep, and dream - ing spin an -

lives are spun but all too soon the spin- ning's done.
we a - light to rest one mo - ment, then take flight.
ap - ples grow and end - less heal - ing wa - ters flow.
oth - er form, a shin - ing thread of life re - born. *D.C. al Fine*

Gone Beyond

Traditional Buddhist

Gone, gone, gone be - yond——— Gone be - yond be - yond Hail the go - er!

Prayer for Burial

Beloved one,
we give your body to the earth.
Earth Mother, Root Mother,
Father of soil,
we give you this body
of our beloved _____.
These eyes will never greet us again
return to earth.
We will not kiss these lips
return to earth
or touch these hands
return to earth
or hear her voice speak our names
return to earth.
What (she) has been is gone.
What (she) is now has passed the gate,
leaving this body
to become soil,
this flesh to nurture flowers,
these bones to be roots of trees.

Chant: And so return, return, return,
return to the mother.

For Burial at Sea or in River

From water all life arises.
Mother of waters,
Father of rain,
You have taken back your own.
As a stream flows into a river,
as a river flows into the sea,
may (his) spirit flow
to the waters of healing,
to the waters of rebirth.

Chant: We all come from the Goddess

Bo's Cremation

PATRICIA MICHAEL

We cremated Bo because he had killed himself and we needed healing.

When someone kills himself, people almost universally report having had a forewarning of the suicide but not doing anything about it because they did not take it seriously. My forewarning happened around Thanksgiving at a party at our farm in the hill country of Texas, between San Antonio and Austin. Our family had invited a few good friends out for a feast. Among them were Bo and Mangala, and her twin boys.

What stood out so clearly later was a conversation Bo and I had by the fire. He was angry and critical of our community of friends, especially of me as a local "bioregional/Permaculture Queen." He felt that we were not walking our talk in being close with nature and "natural living"; that we were not chopping wood and carrying water; that we were not moving fast enough to the vision we all shared of the "good life," or living directly off the land; that we were all too mainstream, too isolated in our own households, not communal enough, not growing or foraging enough of our own food; that we were not connected enough to be able to rise to the occasion if a crisis did arise.

That memory stands out so vividly because it was only a few months later, that same spring, when Bo himself created just such a crisis that the whole community came together for. One evening, Bo put a gun to his head and shot himself.

Right away his wife, Mangala, called Philip, our physician friend, and he called me.

We all gathered at Mangala's house the next morning. There was a lot of shock and scattered energy. We sat together. Everyone talked and listened in turn as we processed our emotions and feelings, and created at the same time a plan of action. Bo was only forty-four years old, and Mangala was only forty-five. None of us had experienced the death of one of our circle before. As a group, we were untried with death. We knew we wanted the highest good, but did not know what that was. We knew we had to create it because we had never been there before.

At first we expressed grief, shock, and recrimination. Those of us who had been around him and seen signs of his stress but had not acted, who had not taken the action we would have had we thought he might be going to kill himself, felt guilty. Each person had a little piece of the whole picture; if we had put it together, any one of us (all of us) would have taken the situation much more seriously. Our peace and joy were shattered. We worked together to restore the sacred. We all needed it.

We shared our experience (and lack of experience) with caring for the dead, funerals, and short- and long-term action. Bo's body had first been taken to the county morgue; then, two days later, it was transferred to a funeral home. The thought of Bo's body being at the funeral home seemed so cold and uncaring. We just wanted him home with us.

Decisions had to be made, and mostly all we had were questions. Could we take possession of the body ourselves? The funeral home director was called, and he said yes. The state of Texas allows people to care for their own dead.

Bo was a follower of the spiritual teacher Osho. Osho advises cremation as soon after death as possible, because it makes it easier for the spiritual being to accept his or her death. Osho taught that if the body is burned right away, the spirit can see the body totally dispersed and there is no confusion. The body is gone into another kind of energy. If the body is buried, then it is harder for the spirit to get the message.

So many of our death processes—burial among them—are designed by the remaining people as ways to hold on, instead of letting go. We just aren't very good at letting go.

I remembered the deaths I had seen as a young girl. My grandmother had been a kind of folk medicine woman who cared for many friends in her neighborhood in Wichita, Kansas. During World War II she and my grandfather lived near the shops where rail cars were made for the Santa Fe railroad. A large population of immigrants lived and worked there. Many of these people were very poor, living in conditions close to the earth. Most of them, including my grandparents, grew their own food and had chickens and gardens.

My grandmother had been raised on a dairy farm near Tonganoxie, Kansas, where her relatives had immigrated from Denmark. She was a mixture of American Royal horsewoman and Lutheran/Quaker herbal healer, with a lot of what my mom called "superstition"—our great-grandmother's earth-bonded religion of the Old Country. She birthed, healed, celebrated, was helpful in the transition of death, and attended the graves. No one had much money or time or formal education. It was a culture of communal help. Everyone cooperated.

The immigrants were from pre–World War II cultures from all over the world: Russians, Germans, Mexicans, Chinese, Poles, Irish, Spanish Basques, Africans, Appalachian Americans, and more. The railroad was a job—hard, dirty, dangerous work. Many people died, and their community took care of them. Being a part of that experience served me well in the days after Bo's death.

Our community in Austin was well formed. Bo and his family had links with the Waldorf School, the Osho meditators, the Bioregional Congress, and the Austin alternative healing community, and Bo was a Permaculture graduate. We had our Church of the Golden Rule, an earth-bonded church that sponsors Equinox and Solstice celebrations, counseling, education, and rites of passage. But none of us had ever burned a body.

I called my husband, Sid, and asked if we could do it on our seventeen-hundred-acre farm in the hill country. He later told me his first thoughts and feelings. They were typical of many of the thought processes we were all going through: he was hesitant, because of legalities and the knowledge that graveyards reduce the value of land substantially, and concerned that our reputation as nonconformists would be furthered in the area. And yet he saw that caring for our dead was one of the functions that churches traditionally perform and felt that we as a church needed to serve in that way.

Many of us in the community believed that being as animal-like and natural as possible in every way is a worthy goal for the human being. Ideally we would dig a shallow hole, put the body in, and let it decompose, or leave it on the surface and let nature have its way. But flies and animals, especially domesticated dogs and cats, are sometimes a problem. So from a practical standpoint, with as dense a population as there is in our farm area, leaving bodies on top of the ground was not a good solution. In big, less populated areas such as west Texas it would be okay, provided that the body had a steep walled area in which to transform so that the bones would not be scattered too broadly. (Of course, using fuel to burn what could have been compost is not a natural, organic way for humans to live either.)

We did not go into these arguments for natural decomposition at the time, however, because Bo's wishes were for cremation. We felt that we had plenty of fuel out there, and we wanted to do it.

Sid did not know how much fuel it would take, or how long. He worried that we would end up with the fire burning down before the body was fully consumed (with no more fuel readily available). If that happened, the family and others would be nervous or upset and the ceremony would not be a success. Gathering more fuel at that point would interrupt the ritual and take precious daylight time; in short, it would be a mess.

It was amazing how most folks just assumed that caring for your own dead was illegal, that everyone had to be embalmed, and that we in no way could have our own cremation. I checked the law in Lisa Carlsen's great book *Caring for Your Own Dead*.[1] That source said it was legal to conduct a cremation. Many people still did not believe it, so I called our friend John, a lawyer, who called a local mortician and asked who the local licensing authority was. The mortician referred him to the proper state office. After calling the state capitol, John's response was, "Go for it!" His only caution was to involve

[1]Upper Access Publishers, One Upper Access Road, P.O. Box 457, Hinesburg, Vermont 05461; 802/482-2988.

many people from our church and larger community, so that there would be plenty of witnesses to our caring for Bo's body with love and respect. The only charge we would be leaving ourselves open to was "desecrating a body."

The law in Texas is as follows:

1. Obtain a death certificate (the police took care of that).

2. Obtain transporting and disposition permits (which had to be with the body at all times).

3. Wait forty-eight hours to burn the body (twenty-four for burial), unless the person died of a contagious disease. (Hal commented later that suicide is contagious, in a sense: when someone commits suicide, others take that as permission to do it themselves. But he felt that the way we all participated in Bo's burning changed that dynamic in our group.)

4. Conduct the cremation at least five miles from a community of ten thousand people or more.

No additional permit was necessary for cremation, and no law required that people be embalmed. (Check with the authorities in your own area to find out your local laws.)

Within a few hours of receiving this news, we had a plan to burn Bo's body at our family farm. The cremation was to be held as soon as his father and brothers could gather from out of town. Intention and the actual doing of something, however, are two different things; we had a plan but very little practical know-how about cremation. We had many caring, interested, curious, courageous folks giving lots of input, but those contributors had little experience in caring for the ill, let alone the dead.

In my grandparents' time, it was different. It was easier then because there was an existing community culture of cooperation and hands-on experience. When there was an illness or injury among the townsfolk, there was seldom money for a hospital stay and only sometimes money for Dr. Hodson to make a house call. Usually the folks with traditional and folk medicine skills would come forward—a free alternative—and lots of different things were tried.

On Sundays at my grandparents' house, around the dinner table there would be people of many different colors and body types, and many accents of English. The process of keeping the "wellness" of the community together bonded folks in a way that I have seldom known since.

When anyone was seriously ill, a child would alert a neighbor, and the first line of help would come in. Women, children, and men would descend on the house, slowly at first. A friend might appear with a pot of soup, a few eggs, some milk, or a loaf of bread. Soaps, oils, and herbs were used to clean and make the place shine and smell good. Light and fresh air were let in. Extra firewood, kerosene, candles, and oil were brought to warm, dry out, and brighten the place.

Children were separated from the sickroom and given hugs and baths; they were rocked, played with, fed, read to, and sung songs.

The men were given special tasks. They took a worried and exhausted husband out for a smoke or drink and special listening, for example. They stuffed a new mattress cover with fresh straw or wild plants. They washed windows and fixed leaky windows, roofs, or doors. Sometimes they built a new bedframe or rigged support ropes or stacked blocks to get a mattress up into a warmer level of the room. Often an outdoor room was set up for caregivers, in which they could cook over a campfire and sleep. The men who were healers often smelled "special spicy" and wore different clothes.

The women healers usually stayed full-time at the house of the invalid. I remember Grandma's pots of plants and herbs, barks and rocks, clays and soils, meats and oils—things she boiled with clean water or baked to make plasters, casts, salves, tonics, teas, washes, aromas, and nourishments. When she was going to help with death, she would spend a long time in the bath and come out with a newly starched and ironed dress and apron smelling like lilac.

Children were given special tasks at such times too: running with messages, toting stuff, boiling the sheets of cloth for bedding and bandages, and hanging out the wash in the sun to disinfect. My favorite tasks were caring for smaller children, gathering the wild plants that grew along the railroad tracks (where the Chinese had sown healing plants) and roadsides and in vacant lots, and singing songs and chants outside to calm and bless the house and give a sound-tone focus for the healing place and all the worried minds inside. What I remember most from those days, though, was the emphasis on touch-closeness, and the frequent washings.

Any spare hand was asked to help hold a person down, or dip and wash a fever, or soak and clean up the many fluids and substances of the sickroom. The stages of illness were known by all, and there was language for them. When someone was close to death, we all knew by the sounds of the breath, the color of the skin, and the smells. Often organs quit days before a person died, and from that time on no one forced fluids or food; the person was simply kept comfortable and clean. The death rattle could go on for days. It was understood that death took its own time and that some folks die by many stages.

There was a great calm and sense of protection set up around a death house, and that peace was defended and kept by the whole neighborhood. A white cloth was put on the door to tell about the serious illness or injury inside. Black cloth on the door meant a person had died, and a bunch of greenery on the door meant a birth.

At Bo and Mangala's home, help arrived to clean, move furniture, and set up the special meditation room for Bo's body to rest in during the prayer vigil. Paul made a "universal" coffin that his body could be in during that time—a coffin now waiting in some garage, ready for the next one of us who needs it. Special foods and drinks came in abundance. Bo's sixteen-year-old twin stepsons, Dan and Chan, did a great job of taking care of the many telephone calls and messages. They were an incredible family of people whose lives had been woven in and out with each other, and they offered so much. It was wonderful how inclusive Mangala and her family were. Anyone who had a song, a prayer, an offering, a spiritual practice, a sacrament, a charm—whatever, from any religion—was welcome, as long as the offering was respectful and in keeping with the energy of the household.

When it came time for us to pick up Bo's body, we were all a little nervous, because we had to keep him "fresh" for several days until his father could come, and it was June in south Texas. We went downtown in Salila's station wagon, stopping off on the way to buy about fifty pounds of dry ice. The beautiful coffin was not ready yet, so our plan was to wrap him in dry ice and a few blankets and bring him home.

When we got to the funeral home, Bo's brother was there talking to the mortician. He asked me if I would officially identify the body, because he did not feel up to it. The mortician and I went into a chilly room—a walk-in cooler, basically—that had metal file drawers built into the wall. He pulled out a bottom drawer and there, wrapped in lots of clear plastic, was my friend. I identified him and signed the papers. The mortician was very helpful. He sold us the transportation paperwork for about one hundred and fifty dollars and offered an inexpensive coffin that consisted of a fiberboard bottom—no sides—with one-by-two boards around the edges; a cardboard lid would be fitted over it. These coffins are what people are burned in at commercial crematoriums. I bought one for about sixty-five dollars; and Bo was put in his new box, iced down, loaded into the car, and turned toward home.

Mangala rode in the back with him, and I realized that it is just as important for us not to be separated right away from our loved ones at death as it is at birth, especially when the death was sudden. When a person has a lingering illness, then family and friends have time to express their thoughts, say goodbye, get in touch with feelings. But with suicide we had to do all those things after death.

I remember Grandma telling me how important it is to be alert, not drugged, at the time of transition, and to have family and friends present; she said the period at and just after death was crucial because we get information from "the other side." When Grandma died, she was very small and weak from her long illness. She was downstairs, and my mother, who had taken care of her for days, was asleep in an upstairs bedroom. Grandma, who had not walked for ages, went upstairs and spoke to my mother, and then went back downstairs and left her body. Death brings with it an awesome gift of opening to the divine.

We had a room prepared to wash Bo. I had cooked up about a gallon of ointment to slather over his body to keep him sweet-smelling; to diminish the growth of fungi, viruses, bacteria, and other micro- and macro-organisms; and to help him burn quicker when the time came. We also added a little tan-rose color to the ointment, because the death color can be very shocking.

An ointment such as this has to have several properties:

1. *A sticky, fluid, slightly thick consistency.* The ointment needs to stick to the skin without running off. You want lots of it to stay put, especially around wounds, sores, and the genital area. I combine honey and myrrh gum as a thickener because both ingredients have good color—honey, golden; myrrh, tan—and can be added into a hot mixture a little at a time to get the right consistency; furthermore, both are preservatives and work to protect skin.

2. *A good smell.* For a man, I usually go with citrus oil. For Bo I used orange as the base. Then, for "a green spicy direction," I used rosemary, because it is also a preservative and smells good with orange. I added rose for love, lavender for peace, and a local mealy sage for fidelity (which, in death, means each person has clarity of his or her own experience directly with the dead, not stories or anyone else's experience; and can make peace and love with that spirit). For a woman, I use more rose or add vitex flowers, if in season.

3. *Preservative properties.* Our best local source of tannin is mesquite wood, so I boiled up that with a little limestone rock in water. I also added frankincense; and of course the honey, myrrh, and rosemary are classic preservatives. My friend Hal told me that he once put a loaf of rosemary bread in his compost pile; and two weeks later, when he turned the pile, it was still in great shape. That is especially remarkable in our fast-decomposing, subtropical climate.

4. *Pleasing color.* Agarita berries, cranberries, strawberries, and raspberries add a bit of pink. Mesquite, cypress, myrrh, coffee, and cinnamon add a bit of brown. What is important is to lessen the blue and green tones and balance the yellow.

5. *Cleansing properties.* Salt, jasmine, mint, rosemary, honey, lavender, tea-tree oil, pine oil, neem oil, marigold, eucalyptus, and sage are all effective in lessening the development of viruses, bacteria, etc.

To make the ointment, first get water boiling; then add the wood and stones, honey, myrrh gum, frankincense, and berries, and boil the brew for about twenty minutes, stirring all the time. Then turn off the heat, add the leaves, cover the pot, and let the mixture sit for about ten minutes. Strain or squeeze out the solids. Then adjust the liquid by adding the oils and any needed color. Stir the mixture well (you could even blend it) and let it cool. If it is too thick, you can thin it with more oil. You can also add finely ground crystal, gold, or silver to achieve a bit of sparkle.

Other things good to use are clove, garlic, camphor oil, vinegar, clay, aloe vera, lard, meat grease, olive oil, Saint-John's-wort, mullein, mustard, and golden seal (be careful: these last two can be very yellow), mints, comfrey, wisteria, chaparral oak, coffee, ginger, rose hips, rum, lemon balm, or calendula flowers (brown color).

Twenty Mule Team Borax is a good base for a wash. Lanolin is a good thickener, but it smells like sheep. Beeswax can also be used to thicken.

Be sure to wear rubber gloves when you handle the body. If the person died of a contagious disease, get professional help. If he or she has an odor, wear a respiratory mask; an odor means there is something in the air, and the smallest particles go deepest into the lungs. Every time you handle the body, wash well afterward—your skin, your hair, your jewelry, your clothes, everything.

We washed Bo carefully, then anointed all of his body, going lightly on his face. Then we tied him with saffron-colored strips of cloth and wrapped him in a peach-colored sheet. We decided to have his face open for viewing.

Darshana, a friend who had been around a lot of death while serving in Vietnam, had studied *The Tibetan Book of the Dead* to try to make sense of his experience. He contributed the information about tying. I had heard stories of dead people making sounds, moving, even swinging arms and legs or heads, or sitting up and rolling over. When a body is composting, gases build up and tissues and muscles contract and expand, resulting in lots of adjustments. It helps to tie the arms and hands of the body across the chest and bind the legs and feet together, and then wrap the body as if you were swaddling a baby. Sometimes you have to tie the jaw closed and prop the eyes shut for a while until rigor mortis sets in. It is also important to keep a cloth over the various body openings—mouth, ears, nose, eyes, anus, and genitals—because the buildup of gas can shoot material and liquid out at high speed.

Bo looked good when we were finished. We laid him in his coffin, and agreed to keep the top on it except for viewing times, to keep the cold in. By that time, lots of flowers had arrived, and we arranged them around his head.

We put dry ice under Bo so it would not show. None of us had ever used dry ice to keep a dead human before, so we had no sense of how much to use. Like many amateurs, we overdid it. The prayer-vigil room was so cold that the mourners who came to meditate and pray with the body soon were wrapped in blankets. Philip said that it gave a special look to the room to see people huddled together with their heads covered with shawls, only their faces showing. Once during this time Philip changed the flowers, finding them crispy from cold; but the truth that we had frozen Bo solid did not come out until the night before the pyre, when we moved him and discovered that he was way stiffer than rigor mortis could account for. I immediately looked in my cookbooks to see how long was recommended for thawing a 190-pound man. (We kept him off the ice from then on, of course.)

Many people remarked about how unusual it was to have the body so present and close, and what a difference it made. The meditation room where Bo lay became splendid with candles, flowers, and spices. Each person's need for expression was respected: poems were read, music was performed, and many people just sat with his body. Even today, folks report very intimately how they were transformed by the event.

Mangala's first teaching about death from Osho was in India. Osho talked about a woman in the community who was dying. He asked anyone who loved her to go and meditate with her, because her service to us was to help us face our own deaths. He said that she was ready, so there was no need for tears; he explained that if we weep, we weep for ourselves, because the person is gone. When Bo's body was at rest at the prayer vigil, he served us in that way.

I went ahead to our family farm. Robert, Paul, Sid, Ted, and I hauled the wood we had selected for the pyre to the site. We had some fairly heavy old pine pieces that had been cattle pens. They were as long as twelve feet and as short as three. We also had some fenceposts. I stacked an almost solid rectangle about five feet wide, twelve feet long, and four feet tall. The stack looked like a kiln for firing pottery; it was designed for the dominant wind direction to collect air in channels and direct it upward to the body on top. The side away from the wind was built more solidly, and the outside there had the heaviest wood. That way, after the fire burned a while, the body would fall down inside the fire instead of rolling off to the outside. I also laced the center with about fifteen one-pound blocks of candle wax—the sort you buy from a hardware store to make candles or seal fruit. I also made six channels down low on the windy side, and stuffed them with wadded-up newspapers to light the pyre.

There is a beautiful clearing about a mile off the road on top of a hill near the windmill on our farm; our church built a chapel there. The building is six-sided, with a lot of windows and screened openings, painted with designs from the Ndebele women of South Africa. It was near there that we chose to build the pyre.

Hal and his sons picked loads of white yucca blossoms from the roadsides. The blooms were especially beautiful that year, and we covered the pyre with them and with fresh green, aromatic juniper boughs. I made colored prayer flags for the four directions, and we flew them on bamboo poles. All around the large clearing, we placed buckets of water, sand, blankets, shovels, rakes, gloves, and bandannas (to wet for face masks), as a safety measure. We certainly did not want the fire to get out of control.

Bo owned a schoolbus that he had used in driving children to and from the Austin Waldorf School for years. On the morning of the cremation we loaded that bus with people and his coffin and headed out to the hill country. We went over the divide between the Blanco and Pedernales watersheds, where one can look out over the whole Blanco River Valley. It was a special place for Bo, and it seemed appropriate that it was on the route of his body's last trip. The day was bright and windy. The bus went over a low-water crossing on the Blanco. All the elements were involved—earth, air, and water on the way, and of course there would be fire.

There were so many people that they filled the chapel and stood all around the outside. Bo's body was taken out of his coffin and placed on the composition board we had bought at the funeral home. We had drilled small holes in it for the fire to go through.

We took Bo into the chapel and Mangala invited people to say anything they felt was appropriate. There was an outpouring of his humor and who he was; the story of Bo was well told. Philip said it was the kind of talking that was like a mirror, and the mirror was love. It was important for Bo's family to hear and see how deeply people loved this man—their son, brother, husband, stepfather. We decorated his body again in the chapel while the talking went on. He was completely covered with flowers, and he was so cold that the flowers kept quite well.

What we did was bring in something so motherly, so brave, so caring, that it healed; it expressed a love of such courage that it communicated our freedom and dignity as human beings. The pooling of love in the chapel, the taking possession of a man and honoring him in a way that he had not felt in life, was a truly great experience.

When the talking was over, Tomas started playing his saxophone deep in the woods, away from the chapel—a haunting, beautiful melody. He walked slowly toward the chapel, and we were deeply moved. The body was carried by the family—wife, father, brothers, and close friends—from the chapel to the site of the funeral pyre, about sixty steps away. More people had arrived; the pyre was ringed by over a hundred people. We held hands and sang "Step into the Holy Fire, Walk into the Holy Flame, Hallelujah" over and over.

One of the things Mangala had learned in India was how to put wood around Bo's head first, forming a sort of tent, so that there would be respect in the final covering of his face; the skin would not be touched there. His father put wood over the face-frame that Mangala had built; then the rest of the community put wood over him and leaned wood against the sides (so that when the fire collapsed it would do so inside first). We had placed old fenceposts around the clearing for the community to put wood on. The body was completely covered. The pyre was now about sixteen feet long, nine feet wide, and seven feet tall.

Big bundles of incense were handed out and stuck in the pyre by everyone. Lots of people put personal objects on the pyre as well. Philip put his mala on it, and he thinks that action opened growth and transformation for him in the next two years. The Super Natural Family Band played, and the chanting kept up; and the fire was lit by the father, brothers, and wife with torches that had been placed in the vents. It was a huge fire. The flames rose at least twenty feet in the air and burned for many hours. The group grew silent and watched, then began to dance and celebrate. Jim said it was "the best party he attended all year." Most of the celebrants moved across the road to the ranch house and river to swim and feast. Sid, Lee, and Philip stayed on to tend the fire.

A week later, when Mangala, Philip, and Bo's brothers came out to tend the ashes, there were a few small bony fragments. They spread the ashes around a huge oak tree near the chapel.

It is not an easy thing to burn a body that we loved in life. Together we had the courage to stand and honor—and purify with fire—our friend. It was not a few people, or even ten, but many, many people taking a piece of the action in large and small ways. Hal pointed out that it is up to us in our lifetime to develop a circle of friends, to "craft a web" of intimate friendships, for our own well-being. Few of us had experience or training, but our intuition led us. On some level, we all know how to prepare a body and cremate it. It was remarkable that we were in accord throughout the whole process. We had complementary points of view for a process that has been almost lost in our culture. It was a good example for our church community. A large part of the healing came about as everyone joined in with their own work, and took our lives and deaths from "commercial" hands.

Possibly a fraction of what we put out to Bo could have prevented his death. We will never know. But we do know that if Bo can see from the other side, he has seen us walk our talk; and the boy knows that he was loved.

CREMATION PRAYER

Goddess of fire,
sun's fire, lightning,
flame on the hearth,
fire that cleanses and destroys,
fire that purifies,
you have taken our beloved one (name).
(She) has become
flame and ash.
From (her) spirit
a pure flame arises.
We warm our hands
at the hearthfire
of memory and love.

Part Four

Death Has Many Faces

13

AIDS, Children, Violence, and Sudden Death

AIDS

For almost two decades now, AIDS has been a constant presence in our community, bringing us face to face with death on a regular basis. AIDS has cut short the cycle of life for so many of the brightest and most creative of us, made others early widows, (a term we use for either gender) and left us all with someone beloved to mourn.

The response to AIDS in the general culture has been characterized by blame, shame, and fear. Because AIDS can be transmitted by sexual contact, because it has particularly ravaged the gay community, it has been called a punishment for "immoral" acts. But the Pagan tradition affirms sexual expression as sacred, as a way we can connect with the great powers of life and death. Pagans see AIDS as a tragedy, just as breast cancer or heart disease or diabetes can be tragedies. All of these diseases may have some lifestyle component, but none of them is *deserved*. Pagans believe that true spirituality calls us to compassion, not to self-righteousness or judgment of others. To Pagans, people with AIDS should be seen and treated much as Christians might view sufferers from a disease caught at a house of worship. "I am an innocent victim of AIDS," my friend, Leaf said to me once. "I caught it by fucking."

AIDS is also transmitted by shared needles. Again, the larger society seems eager to demonize drug users, making them the lepers of the late twentieth century. The Goddess tradition calls us to compassion instead. Addiction to any substance, legal or illegal, is a disease. Those of us who must have our morning coffee, our cigarette, our diet soda, or our chocolate cake differ more in degree than in kind from the users of crack cocaine or heroin. Drugs relieve pain—physical or emotional— and addiction breeds in conditions of poverty, hopelessness, and despair. Members of the Reclaiming community have been leaders in providing services for drug users with AIDS and establishing needle exchanges to help prevent the spread of the disease. To truly honor the Goddess is to see her face also in those whom society most despises.

No one could call AIDS a gift. Nevertheless, facing AIDS has brought many communities together, taught us the strength that comes at the most painful moments of life, and the love that is evoked when we help each other through the hard times. AIDS has also inspired many of us to organize in order to confront the injustices and inequalities in our health care system. If we are willing to learn, even tragedy can be a teacher.

In the year since the first version of this book was written, medical developments have brought new hope to many who have AIDS or its precursors, though that hope is still far from certainty. If and when it is realized, it may bring with it a special pain at the loss of those who might have lived had they only survived a few more years, months, weeks.

This section is dedicated to all those who have died of AIDS.

Aric Arthur Graf Dies
(or *Rickie Goes to Become an Ancestor*)

DONALD L. ENGSTROM

July 11, 1995
The first night of the first full moon of summer

I had smelled the scent of the power and love of the spirits in the dying room for the last two weeks. This last day was
no different. As I lay there holding Rick, it was as if our bed
were in the middle of a rose garden.

My sweet Rickie, my golden boy, my brave boy, lay in my
arms for the last ten hours of his life. We were able to hold
each other firmly, tightly, in ways that we had missed for so
many months. The last six months and more had found Rick
too frail, too delicate, to be held in my arms; I was afraid of
causing him great pain. The slightest movement could send
shivers of agony through his flesh. Now the morphine gave us
back to each other one last time. AIDS simply would not be
able to steal these moments from us.

Rick was almost ready, but he was still unsure. Would I be
all right? Were all the papers completed (he asked again and
again)? Was the house done? Was everything in order? And
yet, despite these doubts, he was willing to face death head on.
Rick was so brave.

The support of our clan/family gave us the power to
achieve our goals. The two most important of these were (1)
for Rick to die in dignity and grace and (2) for me to be able
to survive the fact that I would have my first morning alone —
that is, that I would live the rest of my life without him. Our
primary desire, though, was to have a successful death, a healing death, a death that would transform not only the two of us
but our whole community. We knew deep within our hearts
that we could pull it off if we all worked together. The prayers,
rituals, and spell-workings that went on before and during

Rick's death—that still continue today—remain a foundation of strength for me. I suspect that they also help to center Rick as he learns the new skills he will need to know as an ancestor.

Together we watched the approach of the Moon Boat of Death. Together we helped each other through the hard parts of the dying. We stayed together up to the last possible second. And our community was there with us. In fact, it has never wavered in its support.

In the middle of that afternoon Rick called out to us, "She's such a fucking bitch." I slipped into a trance and journeyed with him as far as I could go. The person who was coming for him in the Moon Boat (which looked like a translucent golden-amber gondola) was the Bitch Goddess, Matron of Political Activists. She had dark steel-gray hair, which hung loose in long, thin braids that danced in the breezes. The Goddess was dressed in a dark tunic and pants. She seemed to be wearing no jewelry or shoes. The deep, unknowable power that emanated from Her grew stronger as She poled closer to us. The Moon Boat was floating on something—a crystal-clear river, a dense wind, a stream of spirit? A cold clean wind of perfect air filled my nostrils. In the far distance stood mountains (hills, islands?). The light included all the colors of a high summer dusk. The only sounds were the songs of wind and water. The whole vision was supernaturally beautiful.

She slowly and surely brought the gondola to the white stone dock where Rick was expected to board. The Bitch Goddess looked stern but not cold-hearted, intimidating but not hostile. The Goddess was somehow obviously a champion of Justice and Freedom for all. She waved Her hand, signaling Rick to come to Her. He turned and asked me to go with him. I needed to take only one more step and I could have crossed the line between life and death. I could have gone on with my sweet husband. But I had committed not to kill myself because of Rick's death; I had promised Rick earlier not to kill myself. I had also promised the Mysterious Ones that I would live on to fulfill my calling as one of their priestesses.

It was not an option to cross over with my dear Rickie, even though it did indeed break my heart to stay behind. I knew the best choice for me was to remain with the living. Was

Rick's invitation some kind of test question? He seemed to so want me to come along. I am amazed I had the strength to let him go on without me. This bittersweet memory still fills my eyes with tears of wonder and confusion. I would have done almost anything to stay with Rick. But as we all know, a promise is a promise.

The Bitch Goddess got out of the Moon Boat and came over to the white granite bench we were sitting on. Rick got up and walked to Her. They stood facing each other. They began to wrestle and then to box. He would call out to me, "She's such a fucking bitch," and then laugh every so often as the contest continued. She said nothing. Folks who could see Rick's face say that he wore a radiant smile throughout this time. I could see him hitting his hand with his fist repeatedly when I slipped back and forth between the worlds. He still did not want to go. I could not clearly feel why. But I could see that this match had a definite sacred purpose of some kind. Was it something beyond the powers of the living to understand? Whatever it was, they both seemed to be having a hell of a good time.

When the Goddess and Rick took a breather, Moonie, our beautiful golden cat, now dead some sixteen years, jumped out of the bow of the gondola along with many other cat ancestors—domestic cats, wildcats, bobcats, lions, cheetahs, saber-toothed tigers, and others. She came between the Goddess and Rick. The other ancestors formed a wide circle around us all. Without speaking, Moonie told the Bitch Goddess, in no uncertain terms, that no one was going to hurt her Summer Boy. She told Rick that not even a Goddess could take him from her. She would never ever let anyone harm him. When the other cat ancestors signaled their agreement and support, Rickie visibly relaxed. It was clear that he felt—no *knew*—that he was completely safe with Moonie and the other ancestors who had come to escort him to the Apple Lands. Rick agreed to go on. He turned to me and smiled goodbye. He finally knew that everything was ready, done, complete, and that I would be just fine. He became a clear golden light. His body, his soul, his *being* was now made of another flesh. He had left the flesh of Gaia behind and had taken on the flesh of

Mystery. He and the others turned and prepared to board the Moon Boat.

Just before Rick stepped into the boat, I was thrown back into our room, with Rick still lying on top of me. The sky was a deep summer blue. The trees were a vital living green. I was back in the land of life. The living are not allowed to go beyond the point where Rick and I had said goodbye and expect to return. I had gone as far as I could go and still live.

It took three more hours for Rick to die.

Not long after our trance journey together, Rick lost the ability to use his throat and lip muscles. The last things he said, the words he repeated over and over until he could no longer speak, were "I love you. I love you. I love you. I love you. I love you." This was the profound, the mystical, the core message I was waiting for. No other words could have been so sweet, or so meaningful.

The room filled with the heavy scent of night-blooming lilies.

Somehow I knew that Rick wanted to look at the sky. I gently turned his head and we both looked out across our yard into a beautiful blue summer evening framed by the lovely trees that we had planted with our own hands. We gazed contentedly out the window for a timeless season—that is, until Rick's eyes quit working.

Throughout this time I sang Rick some of his favorite songs ("Summertime," "The River Is Flowing," "There Ain't No Mountain High Enough," and others) and chants (including "Hoof and Horn," "There Is No End to the Circle," and "A Dying Song"). I told him over and over how much I loved him. I named him my Brave Boy, my Golden Boy, my Sweet Husband, my Love, my Precious One. I loved him so much. It was terribly hard to let him go. It was the fucking hardest thing I have ever done in my life. But it was clearly time for Rick to go on to the Blessed Lands.

Now the room began to be filled with the scents of a noon perennial garden blooming in high summer. The delicious smells of ripe apples and peaches drifted my way also.

After Rick's eyes stopped working, his head relaxed even more onto my chest. I continued to tell him how much he meant to me, how proud of him I was, how brave he was. I knew that he could still hear and understand me, for at times of deep emotion he would cry without moving face or eyes. Tears streamed down his face to mingle with my own. We knew that our love and bond would certainly survive death, but knowing that we would not be together for so damn long was almost unendurable for both of us.

Throughout Rick's last five or more hours, particularly hard parts of dying came his way—sometimes physical pain, sometimes emotional distress, and sometimes simply not wanting to go. I could feel his body shake when these times came. And they came much more often as the actual death got closer. Rick, true to form, worked his way through each episode. I could not have been prouder. With each hard part he grew clearer. Eventually it seemed as if a visible golden light shone around his face.

The last hard part was deep heart pains. They brought subterranean guttural sounds from deep within Rick's chest—groans that shook his whole body. We gave him more morphine and he was soon able to relax again. But I could tell that we were at the close of this part of Rick's existence. Aric Arthur Graf would soon leave me and become one of the ancestors. Only the reptilian brain kept him tied to earth. Rick's consciousness was just outside of his body. I whispered into his ear, "You can do it, Baby; you can do it, Honey. You can go now, my Brave Boy, my Sweet Love." Over and over again I said these words.

By this time the room was literally filled with the ancestors. Some of them had been hanging out for over a month. And it seemed that during this last part of the dying, many new visitors had arrived from the otherworld. There were so many! I sometimes became confused: Who were the living and who were the dead? But all of us were focused on Rick and his death. That was all that mattered to me.

At the very end I could feel Rick's guts churning and his heart beating wildly. The folks who could see his face say that Rick's eyes were focused and his face came alive. Rick fully entered his beloved body one last time. He clearly focused on the gateway in the northeast corner of the room. Rick then simply shot out of his beautiful blue eyes and on into Summerland. He was gone. Rick did not hang around. There was no confusion on his part. Rick left this world with not one look back . . . only a whisper: "I love you." And as he died it felt as if my still-living heart were being ripped from my chest.

Then a new light fell on us all. I turned toward its source to see that the full moon had just risen above the tree line. It was a beautiful night to die.

I became wild with grief. I could not let the body go. I held it so tightly that I could not breathe. Suddenly I had to get up from under it in order to touch, to pet, and to smell this once lovely and loving body. I tried to memorize every square inch. His eyes were still the blue of summer, but nothing else was the same. Rick had truly left me. I no longer had to be a priestess; I could now be the widow, and I simply became a mammal gone mad. I went out onto our balcony and screamed until the silence stopped me. The bugs had all quit singing, as if in recognition of some great and terrible event. I began to cry, wail, keen, scream even louder, overcome by pain, relief, grief, and joy. When the neighborhood dogs started to bark, I knew that I was done screaming for a while; other jobs needed to be done now.

There were six of us gathered upstairs to tend to Rick's death. There were maybe ten or twelve more folks waiting down below. The six of us became the death priestesses. We washed Rick's body, blessing and remembering aloud the strength and beauty of each part as we washed it. We combed his hair and left his blue eyes open to the world. We put a clean deep-green sheet on his bed and a fresh black cover on his pillow. We dressed Rick's body in his tux and burgundy velvet smoking jacket. His body was now ready to be presented to the folks waiting downstairs. When they came up, I went downstairs into the backyard to give them time alone with the body and to give me a chance to be (for the first time in I do not know how long) alone.

I slept for the last time with Rick's body in our room that night. It was hard to leave its side and go over to my own bed to sleep. But at last, thanks to a sleeping pill and total exhaustion, I fell asleep with moonlight streaming in between the blinds. In the morning I was awakened by a new light. Dawn sunshine illuminated Rick's face. He looked healthier now than he had for the last few weeks of his life. The true gift to the living, though, was the sweet smile that now graced the face of Rick's corpse. The body appeared to be shimmering in a golden light.

Rick had become an ancestor, a resident of the Apple Lands. I had been truly baptized by flame and had become that most dangerous of beings, a Queer Priestess with Nothing Else Left to Lose. We both had passed through the fires of change and had emerged as new creatures.

I sang Rick "The Beauty Song" one last time before the coroner arrived.

The Beauty Song

Words and music by Donald Engstrom

INANNA'S PRAYER[1]

You for whom the house of love
Has become the house of death —
I Who am the Goddess
    of love and death
    open My arms to embrace you.

You are My heras, My heroes,
>My saints, My holy martyrs.
You know Me intimately
>as few have ever known Me.
And whether you come to me joyfully,
>or recklessly, or accidentally,
I welcome you.

Come, enter My house, renew yourself.
Eat from My table,
Sleep in My bed,
Taste unimagined pleasures.

Do you think you paid too high a price
>for pleasure?
I reward those who do not bargain
Who willingly or unwillingly
>give their all

The worst is over
Death is not so terrible
It's the getting there that hurts
Now rest
Now take comfort, now take joy
In the exquisite love
>that you have earned.

The following song expresses the grief we feel for those who have died of AIDS.

---

[1]AIDS is neither just a gay disease nor just a sexually transmitted disease. But two summers, when I (Starhawk) was aspecting Inanna in a ritual, She spoke and said that those who have died from AIDS and *did* catch it through sexual activity—gay or otherwise—are Her holy martyrs. She said that She was very angry at the way they were being treated and wanted shrines erected for them everywhere. While we are working on the shrines, we can begin with this prayer.

Lament for the Queer Dead

Words and music by Sparky T. Rabbit

Gone a-way into the night gone a-way in-to the ground gone a-way in-to the flames, so ma-ny gone. Mm - mm - mm. O, I can see you now, stand-ing with the oth-ers on the deck in the blue and pur-ple twi-light. And we hold each oth-er close on that ship of ma-ny lov-ers and we talk hand in hand be-fore you go.

Lament for the Queer Dead © 1991 from the album *Hand of Desire* by Lunacy

Ashes flying on the air,
ashes scattered on the sea,
burned to ashes in the fire —
so many gone.

Empty house and empty bed,
empty room and empty town,
empty sky and empty arms —
so many gone.

Falling down a well of grief,
drowning in a sea of despair,
how can love begin again?
So many gone.

O I can see the faces there—many ages, many colors—
as they gaze far away into the evening.
There are friends that I know and so many, many others,
and they're eager for the journey to begin.
Some have come there with their loves, some have come alone;
they all embrace in the light and in the shadow.
And we say our farewells, with our arms around each other,
and you tell me I will see you again.
And you tell me I will see you again.

Well, I am happy for you then,
on your journey toward a new home,
but, when I wake, all that I know
is: you are gone.
And I can dream you in that place—
laughing, smiling, healthy, and strong,
but, when I wake, all that I know
is: you are gone.
Well, some days, tears are all I have,
some days, anger and despair,
and, sometimes, dreams are all I have
since you are gone.
You are gone.

So fly away, my love, on that violet ship of beauty,
fly away through the night to the morning.
Fly away, my love, on the silken, purple sails,
fly away through the darkness to the dawn.
Fly away, my love, on the violet ship of beauty,
fly away through the night to the morning.
O fly away, my love, on the silken, purple sails,
fly away through the darkness to the dawn.
Fly away into the night,
fly away into the stars,
fly away into the dawn,
to lovers' arms.
Fly away into the night,
fly away into the stars
fly away into the dawn,
to lovers' arms.

Death and Children

Perhaps death is most painful when it touches the very young. All the aspects of grief are intensified. We expect our children to outlive us; for a child to die seems outrageous, out of the natural order of things. Yet throughout human history, and still today in much of the world, the experience of parenting has been intimately bound up with loss. When we lose a child, when we suffer a miscarriage or stillbirth, we are not cut out of the circle of life-givers. Instead, we join the majority of human beings throughout time, who have known that birth and death are indeed intimately linked.

Six Months

Carol Christmas

His eyes were incredible: dark-brown amber with those long, thick lashes that only children seem to be blessed with. Carl was six. One October day when he was playing baseball, he fell and could not get up. The next day he was hospitalized. Was it a heart ailment, an infection, or something else? Months passed before the doctors named a small gland that wicks away excess moisture in the body—a gland that was malfunctioning. Extremely rare, they said. There was a congenital defect.

I work with Carl's dad at the post office, and I was doing my master's practicum at the hospital in the evenings, so I got to know Carl very well. When I met him, he had ballooned out to twice his normal size. Bedridden, in a room alone, he was very bored. Quite often late in the evening, when his folks would leave, I would visit with him. We would play with puppets or I would read him a story. His favorite book was *The Polar Express*. Once he asked, "Would you hold my hand?" I was very moved as I took his trembling little hand in mine. Sometimes if he was sleeping, I would sit at the foot of his bed with a loving-kindness meditation: "May you be free, may you learn the most from your suffering, may you be at peace."

The doctors were constantly experimenting on Carl, so he was in and out of intensive care. They drained his lungs, putting shunts in here and there; they removed the lining from his heart—and still he continued to inflate with fluid.

I asked his dad if he would take him home to die. Carl had two brothers; he wanted to go home again. His parents feared that they could not meet all his needs at home. In February I asked Carl's mom if she would tell him to "follow the light." She said no. Carl knew when other kids died on the ward. Once he told his dad, "Don't let them take my body away."

The last time I saw Carl alive he was so bloated that he needed his nose wiped with each breath. His skin was stretched and raw. When I tried to carefully blot the discharge, he yelled, "Wipe! Don't dab!" Shortly thereafter, Carl went into a coma. I began to speak silently to him. I know that there is awareness even without consciousness. I told him that it was okay to go, that his parents, his grandmas, and his brothers would all be okay too. I knew he was hanging on for his folks, so I repeated gently several times that all would be okay, that he could leave now. "When you see the light, follow it." Just as I finished saying that, a tear rolled out of the corner of Carl's left eye. He had heard me.

He never came out of the coma, and three days later his folks had the respirator turned off. I went to Carl's funeral, and when everyone else was gone from the cemetery, I covered his grave with tiny crystals to light his way.

Though the death of *any* child is tragic, surely a mother's loss, especially of a very young child, gives greatest cause for pause, reflection, and compassion. Lady Bachu's experience, with its realization of reincarnation, not only moves us, but it reminds us once again of the cyclical nature of life and living.

A Scent of Grace: Surviving the Death of a Child

LADY BACHU

As a young woman I wanted four things from life: to have my own business, to travel, to write, and to have a baby. Alexander Joseph was conceived in January of 1982. You may remember the horrendous, tremendous storm that broke California's drought cycle that year. Hillsides gave way, homes splintered into toothpicks, families were swept away with nothing but carcasses to be found. But on one tree-encircled ridgetop in west Sonoma County, an ambitious sperm swam its way upstream, broke through the walls of my testy little egg, and introduced me to Alexander. It was electrical. I am here to tell you, light is not the only thing that is both wave and particle.

He was pure and simply a gift from the universe. Never was a woman (this is fact) so utterly *woman* as I when I carried Alex. If could spend the rest of my life in just one moment of time, it would be my sixth month of pregnancy with Alex. I glowed; I radiated. Old men touched my belly for luck. Total strangers showered us with gifts. Men begged simply to nestle in the pungent perfume of my fecundity. In the heat of the summer I lay in the cool green water of the Russian River, belly rising above its crest, plum-tipped breasts pointed straight up, winking audaciously at the sun. And when I stood up, canoes would run aground in astonishment at the sight of my body holding forth life. It was almost scandalous, definitely irresistible.

My son Alexander was born on Opeconsiva.[2] So eager to get here, five weeks early, he had to be cut from my belly, for he was a footling breach, jumping out feet first. For years later, at odd moments, I could feel the kick of his feet against my cervix as he tried to step out. Have you ever smelled a new-

---

[2]August 25: a Roman holiday celebrating the bountiful nature of the Goddess Ops. According to Z Budapest in *Grandmother of Time,* Ops is both the planter and the reaper.

born fresh from primordial wake? You would remember if you had. A newborn has a strange fragrance—saltier than an ocean wind and sweeter than night-blooming jasmine, milky clean and absolutely beyond compare to any essence I, or anyone, has ever smelled. Words have not been invented to fully describe the scent.

I nursed him eighteen months. I had so much milk, Rhea could have contracted with me to create Her milky way. When his rosebud lips fell away from me in slumber, milk continued to spray. Family learned not to sit in front of me while I nursed, or they would be covered in a milk bath by the time I was through. I was a veritable font of sustenance. A fountain of cream. Alex grew into a golden child, a magical child, a laughing Buddha with his mother's stubborn streak and his father's charm. He rarely slept (which was hard on me), moving through life with a steady pace. He was quite odd, actually. He was with us but not of us, if you know what I mean. My family, the whole community, was delighted, enchanted with him. I became known in our small town as Alex's mom. And because I was young, it was enough.

One aching autumn day I looked out the kitchen window. Alex sat stock-still on a log, facing west, gazing over the creek and up the hill. He sat perfectly transfixed for perhaps five minutes—a lifetime for a two-year-old. A chill struck the very marrow of my bones at the sight of his stillness. There are things a mother simply does not want to know. I willed him to look at me, at the window, anywhere but at what held him. He did not move a muscle. Finally I could restrain myself no longer, and I went out to him.

"Alex," I prompted, tenderly, quietly. (I was terrified.) "What are you looking at?"

"There!" He gestured grandly, waving his pudgy arm at the hill. As I turned him gently toward me, he looked me straight in the eye and snapped back to the moment. I snatched him up fiercely and rocked him against me, holding him so tight that I would never ever again be able to wholly let him go.

Well, some people may be able to ask Destiny to wait a week or so. I begged/avoided/didn't answer the doorbell for six full months. Finally She sent the ultimate bill collector around to make good the bargain. And in late March 1985, during the Spring Equinox, Alex died in a freak car accident up on the hill he had stared at so intently a few months earlier. He was killed instantly, but his body was strong and his heart kept on beating for an hour or more. I can tell you what I did: I saw it all from a great distance. I can still see myself screaming. I can still see my hands and feet, cuticles stained with his blood days later. I could describe to you the way I looked, lying on a table in the hospital, his broken body held fast in my arms as I rocked and crooned songs that will never be heard from my lips again. I could describe the look on my father's face, his utter pain and helplessness as he held Alex's head with one hand and the small of my back with the other. I can tell you how confused I appeared when my son's quilt was finally drawn over him, how compassionately acquiescent was the face of the nurse when I told her he did not like his face covered and asked her to make sure he stayed unwrapped.

I can even tell you that death smells vastly different than birth.

So what did I, a bereft young mother leaving the hospital without her child, then do? I went home and cut up an entire flat of strawberries as my father watched. Then I stood in the shower and observed the water tinged pink with his blood spiral down the drain. Phone calls were made, arrangements undertaken—and all was possible because shock allows you to do things that you would not otherwise be able to do. On the third night after Alex died, I sat straight up suddenly in bed and howled. I am sure you heard it. I sometimes wonder if everything that ever lived did not hear that mad, frantic wail. I can tell you what Hell is. Hell is nothing at all. The energy that was Alex left in that swirling instant and nothing remained. The void had opened.

The journey I took into the dark labyrinth and back out again lasted three years. At night, past and future lovers came and watched over me as I slept, tormented by bizarre endless nightmares. I awoke to ghosts who sat at the foot of my bed in empathetic commiseration for those caught between worlds. I croned that year, my twenty-second, crazy in Hades' arms. During the worst of it, my web of women friends fed me, bathed me, massaged me, walked me, took care of me.

I began visiting graveyards, sleeping in the earthen hollows of children who had crossed over ten, thirty, a hundred years prior. In return, I left our last name off of Alex's gravestone, committing a certain comfort to future generations of women who will seek similar respite on his grave. I coaxed stories out of my elders, asked them these questions: How did you endure it? Will I survive? I learned that the loss of a child has always offered the worst heartbreak—that it quite literally breaks one in two. I learned that in our society we no longer remember how to die, or how to treat death with dignity.

I traveled to South America, haunted the caves and sacred places where rituals have taken places for thousands of years. It was there that I acknowledged the rubble of my life and made my sacrifices. I drew the proverbial line with my fundamentalist relatives and their stories of Alex sitting at Jesus' knees, and their chastising queries of "Shouldn't you be moving on with your life?" During the hardest afternoons, I played the tape of Cat Stevens songs that I made for Alex's service. As the numbness wore off I wanted to die, but I simply did not have the strength to kill myself. Oh Very Young. I mourned. I mourned bitterly. I mourned softly. I mourned in whatever ways it took for me to heal. What did you leave us this time? I dove deep into the grief spiral and learned to make do with the very smallest of miracles. My senses grew painfully acute.

A bereavement group started at the local hospital. I attended and became friends with a group of other people who had also lost their children. The stories: there are so many stories. I think it was the sharing of stories that saved my life. There were stories of confession, of regrets, of laments, of fury. Each emotion expressed, made tangible, was part of the great healing. We let it all spill out into a collective pool of tears. Compassion filled our hearts. We held each other, remembered other times, and eventually we dared to begin to dream new dreams. We knew our lives were forever divided into two parts—Before and After. I answered the "What if?" question by spending time at a children's hospital in a ward full of severely brain-damaged children. Believe me, there are worse options than death.

In the summer of 1989 I had a dream that was keenly lucid and comforting. In the dream, my new partner and I were at a pool party being given by the children of old friends of his parents. One young couple there had a new baby. I looked at the child, perhaps three months old, and the child stared back at me in delighted recognition. "Mama," the infant chirped to me. The new parents were horrified, but I calmly took the baby in my arms, and his familiar newborn aroma filled me. I looked directly into his eyes and said, "Hello, Alex. Sweetie, you have a new mommy and daddy now." The baby nodded gravely in complete understanding, and in that instant we forgave each other everything. When I awoke to full consciousness, the scent of that child still clung to my arms, and I was filled with a holy peace.

Eleven years later, the sharpest pains have faded. Death still comes to me in the spring. Sometimes, rarely, when I journey, I meet my grandmother. She holds my son in her arms, his hair as golden as the day he died. She whispers to me, her beautiful cheekbones glinting, "I only hold him for you." She reminds me, "I hold the shell; he holds the essence. Darling, you hold only the memory. He has moved on."

In the autumn, at Samhain, she dances with him merrily on the Isle of Apples. My parents, forever dressed in their wedding finery, waltz with considerably more reserve. Eleven years later, I am still filled with the gratitude and the paradoxical grace of having been Alex's mother. The mystery, as he showed it to me, has stood the test of time; there are miracles in each day. Eleven years later, time—the wily trickster—has wrought its magic. But occasionally, even yet, when the light falls on the wheel just so, a moment turns crazily. A small child will leap into the air, and for a moment s/he looks like Alex. Eleven years later, I am the bowl in which the ashes of Alex still reside.

El Dia de los Muertos

ANNE HILL

November 1991

Wrap his little body in black silk,
reach down the damp hole
shoulder deep—place him there,
where the roots of oaks gather
to suck in the cold. The roses,
short-stemmed, go in next, with
stones that sound of the ocean.
Tell the children to get a piece
of candy, a teething toy, and they
do, though he never had teeth at all.
Push the dirt in, first with little hands
then bigger ones, pat it down as acorns
fall onto knuckles and laps. A stone,
gray as the body beneath, marks
the place like a navel, and marigolds
are scattered over earth and rock,
sinking like embers from the sun.
At last, now, in the cold blue air,
a new voice rattles the leaves,
then rises like smoke
through the veil of the day,
into the world's cradle.

Calling Lilith

SOPHIA ROSENBERG

For a friend whose baby died in her womb, October 1991

I light a candle for a friend
in the dark of an anesthetic
and I sing to Lilith.

I call Her: the one who will not be tamed.
          She, who is used to banishment,
          used to the sight of amulets aimed at keeping Her away.

I call Her: COME!
owl talons readied to take the baby from her womb.
COME! Set this spirit as a star in the wilderness of night.

          (She is here!
               sharp smell of the wild,
                    candleflicker.)

She loves to be called and honored, welcomed.
She comes as healer, bringing tools of red flashing rage and a
     living sea of grief.
She comes bat-winged to help navigate the darkness
     blooming all around.
She comes and turns the tender passage through agony
into a dance of strength.

For a Miscarriage or Stillbirth or Infant Death

Mother of life,
Mother of death,
here is a spirit so new
that the gates of life and death
are just an archway in her dancing ground.
She has danced her way back to you.
Her passage is easy
but mine is hard.
I wanted to hold her living flesh
and feel her soft breath and her heartbeat.
(I nurtured her in my body;
I would have fed her from my breasts.)
I would have cared for her
and watched her first steps
and listened for her voice.
No other child that may come to me
will ever be what she would have been.
Nothing, nobody, will ever replace her.
Whatever healing I may find,
this loss will always be a part of me.
(Bless my womb, which has the power
to create life and death.)
Bless my arms
that would have embraced her.
Bless my hands that would have lifted her.
Bless my heart that grieves.

Helping Children Cope with Death

Death is part of life, and even the most sheltered child will encounter death—if only the loss of a pet. We do our best to protect children, but we do not have the power to undo mortality.

The death of an important figure marks a child for life. The loss of a parent or sibling cannot be undone. I (Starhawk) know that the loss of my father when I was five deeply shaped the person I have become. All of my mother's love could not protect me, nor could her training in psychology guide her in making all the right decisions for myself and my brother. Her ongoing grief colored our childhood. Yet with support and love, a person's grief and pain can be transmuted. After many years of healing, ritual work, and therapy, I can see how that early experience of loss and grief became, for me, a powerful sense of urgency in life, an awareness of life's fragility and temporary nature that helped me pursue my own visions and creativity. Loss changes us, but need not destroy us.

I (Macha) lost my baby brother to death when he was only four months old and I three years. He was born with what was at that time an untreatable congenital condition and was not expected to live long. I was told that one day when I came into the room to help my mother care for him, he would not be there. My child's mind could not grasp that such a thing was within the realm of possibility.

Sure enough, one morning I came to where his crib had been and it was gone. Someone in my family—I do not remember who, though it was probably my mother—told me that he had died and gone to Heaven and would never be back. And that was that! No body, no funeral, no overt mourning, nothing.

The loss of my maternal grandfather was treated much the same, although he was a degree or two more remote to me than my newborn baby brother, whom I touched every day of his life. It was not until my Irish Catholic grandmother died when I was eleven that I was able to convince my mother that I should be allowed to go to the viewing and Requiem Mass—and even then I was permitted only because my cousins would be there.

So as Starhawk's loss of her father at a young age gave her a sense of urgency about life, my losses of close family members provoked my concerns with death and dying and how we deal with them.

Pagan tradition encourages the participation of children in funerals, memorials, and all the rituals we do around death. Ritual can be healing for children as well as adults, but kids need support and help to cope with the powerful emotions involved. When other parents and family are themselves grieving, the role of community becomes especially important. The topic of children and death is vast, and many good resources exist. Here we can only offer a few suggestions and examples.

On Children and Death

ELSA DIELÖWIN

Coping with death is always difficult, but helping children deal with loss presents unique problems. Children grieve differently than adults, based on their stages of development. There are stages of grieving that are common in all age groups, though they may be expressed differently. Common steps in grieving are denial, fear, anger, sadness, and acceptance. They do not always follow this order and can sometimes even be concurrent. The grieving process can take a few months or a few years. It can be eased but not rushed. Trying to distract children from the process belittles them and their genuine pain.

Very small children (up to about age three) generally cannot understand their loss. If a child this young loses her primary caregiver, the child's affections will be transferred to another, but she will be fussier and tend to cling and lack trust. The important thing to do with such young children is to give them plenty of loving attention. Though this can be difficult for a grieving adult, it is better that the surviving parent or other person who has a permanent place in the child's life be one to provide a thread of continuity. Specific rituals may be less important to such young children than keeping their lives as normal as possible. The greatest fear they know is of losing yet another person.

From around the age of three to about the age of seven, children are more independent and articulate. A young child's denial may be very strong, with the child asking several times a day where the missing person is. These queries can be given simple answers in keeping with your tradition.

Sometimes the child will not cry. Though this can seem hard-hearted, it is normal. Regressing to acting more dependent is also normal, as are increased temper tantrums, nightmares, and illnesses. An increased likelihood of injury is also common.

This is an age where the child's fear begins to be of the child's own death. If the loss is of another child, that fear can be especially strong.

At this age, simple funeral or memorial rituals may begin to be useful. Planting seedlings, visiting a favorite place imbued with the dead person's energy, and singing have proven helpful. "We All Come from the Goddess" takes on new meaning for the child (and often the rest of us too).

Incorporating stories about loss into the stream of read-aloud books can help the child to understand and cope with death. These should be mixed into a larger group of stories so that death is not the prevailing theme. If possible, these stories should be introduced before the child experiences a loss. For suggested books, see Appendix B.

Older children, from about seven to twelve, respond more as we have been conditioned to expect them to. Often they do not want to hear or speak of the dead person. They may become angry, then burst into tears. They may become withdrawn. Ritual becomes increasingly important. Rather than seedlings, a bush- or tree-planting works better. Involving the child in planning the ritual can be very good for the child.

Sample Rituals

A funeral for a pet rabbit, composed mostly by six-year-old Arthur

The rabbit is placed on a piece of plain white cotton. Near the mouth are placed fresh blackberry leaves, apple pieces, and feed. Some water is poured near the mouth, wetting the cotton.

Arthur casts a circle around the bunny-run. "Goddess and God, my bunny died. Make a circle here."

Mommy silently calls the quarters. The hutch is moved. Daddy starts to dig the hole. Mommy and Arthur take turns; then Daddy finishes.

Arthur says, "Goddess and God, here is my bunny. Please take care of him."

The cloth is tucked around the body, which is placed in the hole. Arthur says, "Goddess, make my bunny be part of the earth again." Arthur begins to fill in the hole. Daddy finishes while Mommy holds Arthur.

*Arthur says, "Thank you, Goddess and God, for helping my bunny.
I miss him." Mommy silently devokes the quarters and opens the circle.
All go inside to wash up and talk about the bunny.*

To help a group of twelve children, ages three to nine, deal
with the death of a teacher, the following memorial for Patricia,
of Parklands Daycare, was conducted. The group was accustomed to following a schedule loosely based on the Waldorf
School's. We stuck to the sequence as well as we could.

*We gathered in a redwood ring in "the Magic Woods," where
Patricia used to take them for nature walks. We checked in, going
around the circle saying our names. We went around again, allowing
those who wanted to talk about Patricia to do so. Each person could
express ideas about where she had gone. "Patricia is an angel," "She's in
Summerland," "Patricia is in our hearts," "She became an ancestor,"
and "She went back to the Goddess" are some of the answers the children
gave. Two of the children were quite angry and refused to speak. Some
wanted to get up and run around, which made the parents uncomfortable.*

*We got up to do stretches, then sang "Sing a Name," ending with
Patricia. During snack, people started talking in smaller groups, and
afterward most of the children got up to play. People left shortly thereafter.*

*While this does not sound like much on paper, the children's "act-
ing out" behavior was noticeably reduced. Some of the children continued to be together as a playgroup for three and a half months.*

*Students at the Waldorf School that Patricia's daughter attended
also had a memorial. They planted a Peace rose at the daycare center so
the children could express their love and distress, and to which they could
later come for solace.*

*We said that the bush would express our love for Patricia and would
give us back some of her love in the scent of the rose blossoms.*

When Death Comes Without Warning:
Violent Death

When someone close to us dies by violence, our basic belief and trust
in the goodness of human beings is shattered. Such a death becomes a
violation of a whole community.

We respond to violence with rage as well as grief, and we quite often desire revenge more than healing. In the Reclaiming tradition, we acknowledge these feelings as normal and human, but we discourage the seeking of revenge, for such actions tend to become obsessive and limiting, keeping us stuck in our pain. We believe in the Rule of Three—that what you send out energetically returns to you three times over—so we discourage hexing or cursing, no matter how well deserved.

On the other hand, we do not urge anyone to forgive the murderer, to send him/her white light or healing. Forgiveness must be earned by repentance. Forgiving someone who has not changed his behavior is condoning violence.

Instead of either revenge or forgiveness, we suggest a focus on justice. In our prayers, meditations, and rituals, we can call for justice to be done, for perpetrators to be stopped from harming others, and for violence to cease. We can commit ourselves to work for justice in the world.

Along with all the work of grieving, when violence strikes we must struggle to restore some sense of meaning, hope, and dignity to life. Private grief is often not enough; only communal action can begin to assuage the pain. So the mother of Sharon Tate, murdered by Charles Manson, works to reeducate criminals. Polly Klaas's father forms an organization to help the families of kidnapped children.

In this section, Salvadoran activist Marta Benevides describes how her community handled years of violent repression and mass deaths. We also include a special prayer for those who have died by violence.

For Those Whose Loved Ones Suffered Violent Death

MARTA BENAVIDES

Life is sacred, my mother has always said. And I know it is. Because of this understanding, I have always chosen to work and participate in life-giving and life-affirming projects and programs. In my country, El Salvador, we have had a history of terrible violence against people and nature since the advent of the colonial period. Indigenous peoples suffered violent death, repression, and oppression in the name of civilization and Christianity. Beginning when I was a young girl, I participated with my parents, especially with my mother, in community efforts to support those who suffered sickness and all types of violence, as well as violent death because of social conditions, repression, or overwhelming pressure (as in the case of people who killed themselves because they could not take the pressure any more).

Whenever death happens, especially when violence is its cause, what is important is to come together and be there for those who have suffered the loss. Listen to them, look at their wants, and provide the needed support, be it accompanying them to make religious and funeral arrangements, offering a cup of tea or a bowl of soup, bringing flowers, or accepting their cry. It is important to be respectful of the religious and/or cultural traditions of the people involved, and the needs of those who have suffered the loss.

In facing violent death, the people of El Salvador follow the same principles of accompaniment and support that we use in our struggle for liberation. A person at risk from the death squads might be "accompanied" by supporters and witnesses when crossing borders or engaging in political work. In death, we accompany the family and friends of the deceased through their grieving.

At home in El Salvador, the wake usually is held at the family home, in a church, or at a community center. The novena—a prayer circle for the dead—involves nine days of coming together, starting right after the funeral day, which enables people to provide support for each other and the family of the deceased. Death is a community concern, and one must make the time to be with those in need. This is one type of accompaniment. It provides emotional sustenance and brings wholeness to a wound.

By the beginning of the 1970s, violence and repression had started to dramatically escalate in El Salvador, as a direct result of world economic pressures. The impoverishment of our people led to protests, which led to further repression by the government, landowners, and factory owners; and the country became militarized. By the late '70s this violence had reached alarming levels. There were at least ten execution-style murders per week. The victims were usually trade union organizers, teachers, students, peasants, community leaders, and anyone who happened to be in the way. I was asked by Monsignor Oscar Romero, archbishop of El Salvador, to join with him in carrying out a national ecumenical ministry for humanitarian aid. Its purpose was to provide various types of support for the victims of death and their families. We set up this program before the bloody conflict in El Salvador became an international issue. Experiences of violence continued to escalate. Communities were bombed, and hundreds of thousands were displaced. Tens of thousands suffered disappearance, imprisonment, and death-squad executions.

Sons, fathers, and brothers could not go search for their loved ones. Though women were also very much at risk, the situation was worse for men, for they were considered suspects by association. They were treated as possible enemies, members of an opposition group. So torture and murder followed their questions and searches. Often we had to hide family members once a loved one disappeared, was taken prisoner, or killed. Every week more and more women, wives, mothers, sisters, and girlfriends, were calling at Monsignor's office asking for help. We accompanied them to search for their loved ones, or to claim the body at the morgue. There were so many tears every day!

Faced with so much loss, so much violence, we learned the importance of support. The committee I coordinated accompanied the people and provided practical, economic, and emotional support, from helping to pay for the casket to bringing flowers to the funeral. In addition, we brought each case to the attention of the authorities and to private human rights groups, who themselves labored under much danger. Many of these workers suffered kidnapping, torture, and death. But stronger than the fear of death was the need to name and account for the dead. We returned dignity to those who had been violated by refusing to be silenced and continuing to demand an end to the killings and the repression.

Church services would be held, with special masses said for those murdered. At memorial services, their names were loudly called. As each name was spoken, the people responded, *"Presente!"* "Here I am!" We proclaimed their presence amongst us, *"Presente"*: "We claim you alive, not dead. We denounce the torture and the rule of terror, and pledge ourselves to bring it to an end."

After weeks of these terrible events, Monsignor Romero asked the women to come together in a committee of Mothers and Relatives of Political Prisoners, of Murdered, and Disappeared. This way they would be able to help each other, and become effective in their demands, as families did in Chile during the time of the Pinochet dictatorship, and as women have also done in Argentina and Palestine.

The internationally known Committee of Mothers — CO-MADRES — was born. The women began by being together, listening to each other, holding one another's hands, wiping each other's tears, offering their shoulders on which to cry. With the support of our committee, they continued to give emotional, economic, and legal support to each family needing it. A unified team approach developed. The women would visit and monitor jails, morgues, hospitals, and the legislature. They were present in church as the members' relatives' names were called, as well as in the public and private human rights national and international offices. They held marches, weekly vigils at the cathedral or at the legislature, and hunger strikes. They offered training sessions on how to carry out this work, and they traveled internationally to denounce the war in El Salvador and to support campaigns to end that war and all wars.

Then, as today, they provided legal, emotional, and psychological support to people in need, people whose loved ones had suffered violence and death. They continue to hold memorial services to honor the memory of those whom we have lost, and whose death reminds us of what should be no more. These memorial services include religious ceremonies, but they are also celebrations of the lives of our people. They include songs, music, clapping, flowers and colors, poetry and art, and the calling of the names for the *presente*! They culminate with the commitment to continue to work for a society that is free and at peace.

From our experience we have learned that three things are vitally important in facing violence: to honor the memory and the living presence of the dead; to support the living who mourn; and to take action to change the conditions that lead to violence.

Only in community can we really carry the pain, transform these situations, and create *our* new world order of justice and peace—one that affirms life. The lives of our loved ones whom we have lost to violent death, regardless of how and why, call on us to be mindful that we must create a different society, for we should suffer those types of deaths no more.

FOR ONE WHO HAS DIED VIOLENTLY OR IN GREAT DISTRESS

Mother of healing,
help us to believe in the
place where wounds can heal.

Mother of weaving,
show us that what has been torn
can there be mended.

The worst has happened.
How can we believe again
in hope, love, kindness?
[Name the loved one three times.]

Boatman, Ferryman,
she has had a rough crossing.
Carry her gently.

Comfort her, Mother,
in your warm arms of
night; rock her to sleep.

And by our rage,
Mother of Justice,
May justice be done.

Even in the most prosaic situations, the most bucolic settings, death can appear in all its finality.

Always Keep Your Bags Packed

MINERVA EARTHSCHILD

When death comes after an illness of some length, the dying person and his or her loved ones and friends are given the gift of time to prepare for that passage. But death often comes without warning, giving no time for preparation, as with a fatal accident, heart attack, or stroke. Even with sudden death, it is possible and even necessary to help the spirit to make the crossing to the other side, to help release the dead.

Early in June 1996, I joined a group of a dozen other parents and teachers to accompany our children on a school backpacking trip to Dawn Lake, a singularly beautiful and relatively isolated wilderness area near Aurora, California. It was to be a three-day trip. Late on the first afternoon after our arrival, the children and several parents were swimming in the mountain lake. Craig, one of the fathers in our group, suddenly plunged into a shallow lagoon where some kids were swimming to help his daughter, Rhea, who he thought was struggling in the water. As he turned around to hand Rhea to a teacher standing nearby, his eyes rolled back and he fell over in the water. My partner, Daniel, who was standing nearby, saw him collapse and pulled him to shore. Instantly he recognized that Craig was not breathing and started CPR. Several other parents, myself included, joined in the "heroic" efforts to resuscitate him.

We realized that Craig had suffered a heart attack. For half an hour we fought to bring him back to life. Then, at a moment when I was resting, having just taken an exhausting turn at chest compressions, I acknowledged to myself that he had died. At that moment, instead of continuing to try to reawaken his heart — instead of resisting death — I wanted to put a halt to those futile efforts at resuscitation and to honor and bless his passing and lovingly release his spirit. Because none of the other parents there shared my Pagan worldview, I knew that this was not an option they would understand or consider. They continued CPR, but I stopped fighting to bring him back to life. I silently held and stroked his hand, grounded and connected with the energy of the granite and earth beneath me. I reached out of my body psychically and went in search of his spirit, which I felt was still present. Looking back on this now, I believe that I wanted to contact him, to find out whether he was really leaving us or wanted to come back. Out on the astral plane, I encountered Craig's spirit at the gate, in a place that was filled with almost blinding light. Wordlessly, I blessed his spirit, told him it was okay to go, and wished him a good journey. What I was not prepared for was the pull that I felt: I was drawn toward the gate myself. I had to consciously pull back and return to my body while Craig went peacefully on his way, through the gate.

Eventually a rescue helicopter arrived. Paramedics literally descended on us, performed various invasive lifesaving procedures, and airlifted Craig to a nearby hospital where he was "pronounced" dead by the medical authorities. Since it had been more than an hour from the time Craig had collapsed until the helicopter arrived, we knew in our hearts and minds that these interventions to revive him were futile. But we did not feel empowered to make that judgment.

Two days later, at the school, we created a ritual for Craig. The entire community of parents, teachers, and children joined in a circle in the schoolyard and spoke of our memories of Craig, our love for him, and our empathy for the grief of his wife and son and daughter. We lit candles, drew pictures, or wrote notes to him and placed them in the center, with flowers and photographs. We sang his favorite Beatles' songs, expressed our sorrow, and comforted one another.

Sudden death may bring vividly to the forefront our own fears of death and the shock and pain of loss. Often we are confronted with the urgent need to make quick medical decisions, such as whether to resuscitate someone or to perform "heroic" life-restoring efforts, and for how long. These questions then arise: When does death really occur? Who decides that a person has died? Many of us may find ourselves caught between different ways of approaching the inevitable. Had Craig, his family, and the other parents at the scene of his death shared a Pagan worldview, we might have handled his passing very differently. We might have attempted resuscitation to a point, and then, sadly acknowledging his death, gently released his spirit and ritually honored his passing with chants, prayers, offerings of food or libation, and lighted candles.

When a sudden death has occurred, we may find ourselves influenced by the energies of others present, or by the dead one's loved ones and family. If an accident or other traumatic event caused the death, these energies may not be consciously perceived or may be jumbled by the shock of the moment. There may be a great deal of anger and confusion among those close to the dead person—emotions that can affect the other survivors. I experienced mixed energies from Craig's family, for example—gratitude for the efforts made to rescue him and anger that not enough was done to save him. Because I had been present at his death, I knew that we had done all we could. I believe also, from a Pagan perspective, that it was his time. Our own personal wills were not really involved in the process of trying to "save" him, as much as we wished at the time that they could be. The Fates were at work, and the ultimate reason for his passing at that moment will remain a mystery.

The most profound teaching from the experience of sudden death, for the survivors, for each one of us, is that it gives us no time for finishing business, for saying goodbyes.

After hearing of Craig's death, one friend of mine attached a note to my front door. It read simply, "Always keep your bags packed!" I kept this note taped to my kitchen cabinet for weeks. It was a reminder that death awaits us all and that the moment is not ours to choose. When we carry with us the awareness that death may come in this way, we become present fully in each moment. The knowledge that a sudden death may await each one of us challenges us to live life so fully and with such awareness that we are always prepared for death to come.

Death makes of life a richer and warm thing. Without death, life is not precious. Death is in all this wind of life. Life is as many-layered as the rocks. It is wonderful, but only because of death. So acquaint yourself with death. Death makes life precious. —A Dogon (Mali) saying

We cannot anticipate whether we will die suddenly or after a gradual decline, but we can be sure of our eventual death. Given that certainty, many people consider donating their corneas so that an unsighted person can see, or donating other organs or tissues for the benefit of sick people who can be helped by having them. The Goddess tradition is a way of viewing the world that inspires people to look deeply at issues of life and death, and the quality of life and death. Dennis Irvine and Beth Elaine Carlson have done just that with regard to organ donations and related scientific use of the bodies of deceased humans.

Organ Donation

DENNIS IRVINE AND BETH ELAINE CARLSON

Organ donation impacts the grieving, funeral, or memorial ritual. It may also affect the afterlife of the donor and the lives of those who remain. If the donor dies at home, generally the body will be available without much more delay than with a hospital death. In the case of a choice to donate one's body to medical science, the body will be extensively embalmed, and the mourners will not have access to it for some time thereafter. When it is returned to the family, it may be only the cremated remains. As Witches, we act "as if," and so the vigil, the washing of the body, and the attendant rituals may be carried out as if the body were present, to assure our beloved's smooth passage and as a vehicle for our grief.

Eight people die each day awaiting organ transplant. The organs of a single donor can heal twenty-five people. These miracles are a result of our modern medical technology. Supporters and activists for organ donation wear folded green ribbons as the symbol of their support,[3] similar to the folded

---

[3]For donor cards and general information, call United Network for Organ Sharing (UNOS): 800/243-6667, 800/24-DONOR.

red ribbons for AIDS support (and other colored ribbons for other causes). Green is the color of healing and the heart.

Yet many of the problems solved by modernity are themselves caused by it. Often organs become available due to the violence of modern technology. Like a monster promulgating and feeding itself, modern medicine is something we all have to embrace or reject to whatever degree we see fit.

Organ donation raises questions about proper burial. Most of the world's major religions support organ donation and have liturgies that accommodate the practical inconveniences of the process. Pagans, on the other hand, are diverse in our views, and we do not have direct access to a body of tradition. What we learn from those elements of the Old Religion that do remain may not be easily applied to the question of organ donation, since we cannot be certain that the ancients faced this dilemma.

There are many rules—cultural, religious, legal—about the afterlife and the preparation of the dead. At their worst the rules judge, control, contain, and disempower. At their best they are the distilled voices of our ancestors. The Egyptians held that the various parts of the body had different fates after death. They had specific deities who watched over the embalmed remains. Babylonian travelers to the underworld were warned to bring no weapons and to wear clean garments. It seems to me that it is important to keep in mind that many of the burial and funeral practices we have evidence of from the past, in addition to often being pieced together from fragments, primarily pertain to royalty: the kings, the queens, the wealthy, and the elite. Given that bias, those of us who cannot pass to the other world with elaborate trappings are not necessarily damned. What does this viewpoint say to us if we arrive in Summerland sewn up like a scarecrow, without heart, lungs, kidneys, liver, pancreas, corneas, most of our tissue, and maybe even some of our bones? I do not know. I *do* know that any potential injunctions against such an arrival are not clear enough to prohibit me from donating a kidney to someone who could live thirty-one more years with it. I am, after all, a part of Artemis, able to choose what to do with my body, what to bring into this world and what to take out.

Apsyrtus's dismembered body was cast overboard to delay Aeëtes's pursuing ship because it was understood that Aeëtes would be compelled to stop, sail about, gather the sundry parts, and give Apsyrtus a proper funeral.

When Antigone "disobeyed" and sprinkled dust on the profaned body of her brother, Polyneices, she probably could not keep the wild dogs from tearing him apart; and even so the birds, the worms, the bugs, and decay herself were sure to dismember him.

What I think emerges from these stories and from the extant fragments of our Pagan tradition is an emphasis on not desecrating the dead body of our beloved, not a prohibition against dismemberment. It is not the act of cutting the body that is unhallowed; it is the intent to desecrate.

With this in mind, I looked to the myths for stories that serve as examples of organ donation. I found that the Goddess divides Herself and makes the world. And the God, Her consort, the Sacred King/Hero, is dismembered, His body and blood cast about the land to feed and renew the earth.

Dionysus, Dumuzi, Tammuz, Bacchus, Zagreus, Sabazius, Adonis, Antheus, Zalmoxis, Pentheus, Pan, Osiris, Orpheus, Attis, JHWH, and Christ are all aspects of the Torn God. Dismembered, their sacred body and blood fed the Goddess, the earth, and its people. The Goddess, and so the God, is immanent. We are them and of them. We can offer our body and our blood as consecrated elements, without hubris, and with the same sacred authority as Dionysus and his descendants.

A mother whose son died met a year later with the young woman who received one of his kidneys. They became friends and decided to meet yearly. The next year the woman brought along her infant son, whom she had named after the donor. The following year she brought a second child. The mother felt like a grandmother-once-removed.

A blind woman who relied on her eldest son—a man who had told her he would always be there to be her eyes—was given back her sight through one of his corneas when he was struck and killed by a car.

The tragic death of a young girl gave her father a perfectly matched heart.

The Goddess is all that is and ever was and ever will be. What She gives life to dies to feed her and replenish those that remain.

Prayer for Those Who Choose to Donate the Organs of Their Beloved Dead

The next of kin who must decide, when asked, whether to donate their loved one's organs face a particularly difficult task. If no consent has been given or withheld by the deceased, medical personnel are required by law to seek permission to procure organs and tissue from all viable candidates. Even people who carry an organ-donor card indicating their consent should clearly inform their next of kin, because those relatives will be required to give final permission.

Beloved _____,
I am of you and you are of me.
You have been within me and I have been within you.
Blood and bone,
I do as you would do.
With the Winnower's hand
I take from you.
What to you is chaff to another is seed.

Love of my bones set sail.
Life from my love's be healed.
Blood on my hands by your will.

Blessed be.

Spell to Comfort and Assure That the Donor Will Have What Is Needed in the Afterlife

Appropriate Gods and Goddesses corresponding to the organs donated can be invoked.

Foods, flowers, herbs, and stones associated with the donated organs are gathered into a cloth and tied with a green ribbon. (You may include a coin for the extra fare if you wish.)

Lady of the Wild,
Dear _____,
That you may have a gentle passage,
A Sweet Summer,
A soon return,
I give you these earthly gifts.
[Name what you have included and why.]
Dark Oarsman, Wounded Healer,
carry these with my beloved _____
to the Isle of Apples.

Bless her/him,
whole and healed.
Hold dear _____,
Lady of the Wild.

Place the offering in the casket before burial or cremation. Alternatively, bury, burn, or cast the offering into moving water.

Ritual to Free a Donor's Essence from Her Organs

When our organs are given to someone else, some of our essence may remain with them. Though they do not appear frequently in medical literature, stories of organ-donor recipients acquiring unusual new tastes, appetites, and even the sensation of a benign presence are commonplace. Some recipients have learned that these appetites and tastes were the donor's. Often this is a source of mystery, hope, and comfort. But in some cases this may be troubling.

Place a picture or drawing of the organ in a small box and label it with the name of the donor and the organ. Tie a silver thread around the box, crossing all four sides as you would tie up a gift, leaving one end long (symbolizing the connection between the body and the essence of the donor).

Say these words: "For you, kind and generous _____ *[donor's name]*, who have brought life from death, as the wheel turns I, _____ *[your name]*, cut the cord that ties _____'s *[donor's name]* essence to _____'s *[donor's name]* heart. I free you from your living heart."

Then cut the cord.

Say these words: "The troublesome bonds fall away into the shining sea. May you continue your journey free and clear of this earthly tie."

Bury the box. (Other versions of this spell call for smashing the vessel that symbolizes the body, but in this case the organ will continue to live on the earth and so should be buried intact.) A biodegradable box is best, so that the whole will decay naturally.

Once the box is buried, say: "May this gift serve as needed. By free will and for the good of all, so mote it be. Blessed be."

Prayer for Those Who Procure Organs or Use Cadavers to Gain Healing Knowledge

Inspired by the story of Inanna and Ninshubur

I walk as servant to the Queen of the Universe.
She awaits me wasting and dying.
I am of the earth, and on the earth.
I petition the Gods, one by one.
Sweet Water and Wisdom, hear my call.
I am a healer.
Show me where to sprinkle the Water of Life.
Show me where to sprinkle the Food of Life.
With my hands I heal and restore to life.
I procure, I harvest, I cut for life.
This scythe of mine brings life from death.
I walk as servant to the Queen of the Universe.
Sweet Water and Wisdom, hear my call.

Torn

A poem as liturgy for the organ donor

What can I say to those who need not board this vessel
that sails the blackened sea?
What last glance, what dockside embrace,
can tell them of my fear
and not leave behind more me than I can spare?

What comfort can I bestow from these my meager doubtful
    stores?
For where I sail who knows what I shall need.
Who portends to tell me, and by what creed?
You, who cannot hear for all the noise of man.
Yet I know no better for having passed the gunnel.

And wait now for the oars to dip,
The gate to slip,
The North Wind to crack your quivered lip.

What comfort can I leave you, dear,
A reddened bean?
A gift so large in your eyes.
And yet what does this gift take from Her stew?
What bite have I denied the White Bitch?
Aren't I a cook as She
For having passed the gunnel?
Who is this Hungry Cunt to deny a sup to me and mine?
Am I not just returning what was given me in kind?

But it is you, Apollo,
To Whom I give no truck,
That cast this act unhallowed.
You, organizer, organ miser, despoiler of the muck.
Do you propose that I must fill Her gut?
That one less morsel is not enough?
Does She measure every grain, and seed, and nut?

I do this thing because I love
Or because I could not love, and grasp at this last chance.
I hardly know what's in my heart,
what's remembered by my blood.
I'm torn from all that we once had.

Doesn't Artemis have province here?
Wild One, Macoun, She has dogs too.

So I go on palsied hind,
On the bough that Cynthia took.
I don't want to go.
I don't want to be cold.
I want you to cry for me.

Death in the Service of Life

Some people die serving others. A firefighter risks her life in a burning building to save a child, and dies of smoke inhalation. A young man leaps into the ocean to save a drowning boy, and is carried away by the tide. A union organizer is killed by company thugs. A student sits down in front of an advancing tank.

Pagans honor those who die with courage, who are unwilling to compromise their values or beliefs in pursuit of safety. We do not glorify martyrdom—life, not death, is the goal of our spirituality. But we know that sometimes the death of the body is the price we pay for preserving the integrity of our spirit.

When we think of heroism, we often think of war and battle. The Reclaiming tradition has a proud history of antiwar activism. Nevertheless, we can respect and honor the courage of those who die for what they believe is right.

Funeral and memorial services can be adapted to honor the values and traditions of the person who has died. Following is a special prayer that can be said.

FOR ONE WHO HAS DIED TO SAVE OTHERS

You who have made your life an offering,
who have laid down your sweet flesh
that others may taste life (freedom),
you have become like the sun
whose radiance sustains us.
You have become like the grain
cut down to feed us.
May you rise
as the buried seed rises.

May the Mother of All
gather you in.
May He who falls and rises
guide your way.
May you return to us
when we are afraid
and teach us to be fearless, generous,
and kind.
May we love our lives the more
for your sacrifice
and may we learn to love
as you have loved
so that the boundaries of self and life
dissolve
and the night sky is filled with stars.

14

Death and Choice

Although death comes whether we choose it or not, facing death may involve many hard choices. In this section, we look at abortion, termination of life support, assisted suicide and suicide.

Abortion is, as we all know, one of the most painful and controversial spiritual issues of our day. The Goddess religion has no hard-and-fast ruling on when a clump of fetal cells becomes a being. In fact, I (Starhawk) was taught that the moment varies greatly with individual pregnancies. Some women have a sense of new life even before conception. Others may not feel that the fetus in their womb has taken on a soul until the time of quickening. This is one of the mysteries. It is in our encounter with the mysteries of birth and death, growth and suffering, pleasure and sorrow, that we meet the Goddess. So to take away our right to have that encounter, to face that often painful and difficult choice, is to deny a woman's deepest spiritual self. For that reason, Pagans on the whole are strongly in favor of choice—although, of course (as with everything), individuals will differ widely in their opinions.

This is not the place for a long thealogical or political argument. Too often the issue must be argued in sound bites and slogans that leave no room for complexity of feeling, for the deep regret and sense of loss that a woman might feel in choosing to have an abortion, even when she knows the decision is right. An abortion is the death of a possibility. Not all possibilities can come into being—that is the nature of life itself—but we can still allow ourselves to mourn and grieve while upholding absolutely our right to make the choice.

For One Ending a Pregnancy

To be said before or during the abortion by the mother, the father, and the one who performs the abortion

PRAYER TO THE GODDESS

Mother of death,
Mother of life,
I stand here as your priestess
knowing that life must be winnowed
to thrive.
You are the Goddess of
all possibilities.
Here is one that cannot come to be.
This is a holy act I perform:
to send back to you
this spark, this might-have-been.
I act as the gardener
that thins the seedlings;
I act as the wolf
that culls the herd.
I act with sorrow.

Plant this seed again, Mother,
in fertile ground
that is ready to receive it,
where it may take root
to grow and flower.

PRAYER TO THE SPIRIT OF THE CHILD

To be said when you want to have the child, but cannot do it now

Spirit, spirit,
I have sent you back
beyond the gate.

How sorry I am
to close my womb to you,
but now is not the time
to bring you to birth.
I light this candle for you
to light your way.
When the time is right,
when the way is open,
I will light it again
to draw you back to me.
Remember the light, spirit.
Remember the smell of this womb.
Someday the right time will come.
May we both be ready.

PRAYER TO THE SPIRIT

To release the spirit to find a new entry into life[1]

Spirit, spirit,
I have sent you back
across the gate.
How sorry I am
to close my womb to you,
but I am not the one
to bring you to birth.
I light this candle for you
to light your way
as you search for the womb
that is meant to bear you.
Here are wombs that are open,
here are women whose arms
ache for a child:
*[Name the women you know
who want to have a child.]*
Each will light a candle for you.

---

[1]The women named in this prayer do not have to be physically present but should be asked beforehand for consent. Each one should light a candle when she is ready to call the child into being.

May you choose wisely.
May you come to birth in joy.

Abortion: A Healing Ritual

MINERVA EARTHSCHILD AND VIBRA WILLOW

Introduction

This ritual is intended to create a healing space for women who have had one or more abortions and to acknowledge and work with the spiritual aspects of the experience. Through our own abortion experiences, we came to reject the dichotomy of abortion politics that would require women to choose between two beliefs: that pregnancy is a miracle, the fetus's life is sacred, and therefore abortion is wrong; or that pregnancy is merely a physical event, the fetus is just a mass of tissue, and therefore abortion is insignificant. As feminists and Pagans, we believe that women are literally a gateway between the worlds and that abortion is a responsible exercise of the sacred power of choice. Using Wiccan practices and feminist process, we have designed this ritual for women wishing to heal from their abortion experiences and to reclaim sacred power in their reproductive choices.

The essential elements of the ritual are these: storytelling, using a cauldron fire to release negative energy and feelings that may have bound us to a sense of powerlessness, taking a trance journey to the Place of the Mothers, and healing and blessing our sacred creative abilities.[2]

[2]This ritual was designed as a four-part workshop, to take place over a weekend or four evenings. We have found the four-part structure essential to the healing component of the ritual. The ritual might be modified to take place in a shorter period of time if only two or three women are working together, provided all four phases of the ritual are incorporated into the working. If the working is to be done over the course of four days or evenings, the circle should be opened after each phase and cast again for the next phase. When the workshop is done during a weekend, or shorter time, the circle is cast for the entire time, not opened after each phase.

Before the ritual begins, have the following tools and materials at hand (in addition to your magical tools): several skeins of yarn, at least two pairs of scissors, a basket filled with marbles or similar-sized stones (about twenty for each woman), a large pouch or "mojo" bag for each woman to wear, thread that can be easily broken, preparations for a cauldron,[3] a pillow and blanket for each woman (for comfort during trance work), sweetly scented massage oil, and materials for necklace-making (string and colorful beads, shells, feathers, and the like).

Begin with a grounding meditation that connects all of the women in the circle with the great source of energy found in the belly of our Mother Earth. Then purify one another: using a branch of fragrant rosemary, sprinkle one another with salt water. Cast a circle and invoke the four directions and the four elements, beginning in the East with the air.

Invoke the Goddess. Kwan Yin, the Healer, brings compassion and deep healing to this working.[4] Sometimes we call the Triple Goddess: the Maiden, the Mother, and the Crone. The Maiden affirms our free will and strength, our ability to make choices about our bodies. The Mother knows not only childbirth but also the other blood mysteries, including choosing when to give birth and when not to bear a child. The Crone is the one who knows the mysteries of the end of life, cutting the cord, taking back the disembodied spirits.

---

[3]If you are working indoors, a satisfying and safe cauldron fire can be created by combining Epsom salts and alcohol in a heavy cauldron with legs or a cast-iron pot with legs (preferably with a lid for snuffing if necessary). Place the cauldron on a tray or mat to protect the floor. Pour the Epsom salts in the cauldron and just cover with alcohol. Light carefully when ready and let the flames burn until they die down. The only drawback to this fire is that generally it does not burn things that are tossed into it.

[4]Again, when this working is done during a weekend, the Goddess is invoked only at the start of each day. For this kind of working, invoke a Goddess (such as Kwan Yin or the Triple Goddess) whose energies will be wanted and needed for the whole ritual. When the four phases of the workshop are done on different days, it may be appropriate to invoke a different Goddess for each phase.

Air

We begin with our stories. Every woman who has made the sacred choice to end a pregnancy through abortion has a story. We ask each woman to tell the simple truth, without fear of any kind. Very often a woman has never told any-one the whole story of how her pregnancy happened, how and why she chose to have an abortion, what the physical experience of abortion involved, and what happened after-ward.

We begin with a bit of background. We ask each woman to tell (1) her religious upbringing (if this is a group of women who are strangers to one another), (2) how many abortions and spontaneous miscarriages she has had, (3) her age now and her age at the time of her abortion(s), and (4) whom she has told about her abortions(s).

Then each women tells her story. It is entirely up to her whether she tells about a single abortion, all of the abortions she has had, or just the abortions from which she has not healed. If other birth or miscarriage experiences are part of her story, she tells about them too. When a woman digresses repeatedly to talk about the man who got her pregnant, or about others in her life, she can be gently reminded that this is the time for *her* story.

Each story begins with the conception, the events that led to the pregnancy. Then comes an explanation about the choice: to bear a child, or not. Then comes the actual abortion narrative. Every woman's story is different. There are stories of illegal back-alley abortions, of the practical decision not to have a child while in college, of a failing marriage or relation-ship, of a new relationship, of a new job, of the decision not to have a child at all, of callous doctors, of walking through gauntlets of antiabortion demonstration at clinics, of lovers or partners who pressured for abortion, of lovers who disap-peared with the pregnancy, of partners who were caring and supportive every step of the way, of varying reactions of rela-tives and friends.

In all of these individual stories, there are threads of simi-larity. Whenever any woman in the group recognizes something in another woman's story that she shares or resonates with, she does not interrupt the narrative to say so; rather, she signals the connection by stretching a piece of yarn between herself and the storyteller. Several women may resonate with the same part of the story, each cutting a piece of yarn to connect to the storyteller. Thus, as the stories are told, we ritually connect with one another, weaving a web of our stories, our experiences, our mysteries.

And there are our feelings. There may be shame and self-judgment, a sense that we have been irresponsible, promiscuous, selfish, that an abortion is just what we deserve. There may be grief, sadness, regret, longing, or just curiosity, for all the children never known, never seen or held in our arms. There may be anger at the government that robs women of the power to make genuinely free reproductive choices, anger at the men or women in our lives who have not supported our choices. As we listen and feel, we weave deeper layers of connection. While some time should be allowed for women to express their deeper feelings, keep in mind that this is still essentially storytelling.

When all of the women have told their stories, place the basket of marbles in the center and ask each woman to take a marble to represent each abortion she has had and each woman she knows who has had an abortion. Each woman should reflect on how many of her friends and relatives do not know about her abortion experiences and on how many women she knows who may have similarly kept their abortions secret. Then each woman places the marbles in the pouch and puts the pouch around her neck (or attaches it to her person in some other way), so that she feels the weight of this burden. This pouch is worn throughout the entire ritual (and in between, if possible, if the ritual does not take place in consecutive sessions), until the very last phase. The pouches remind us of what we share with so many other women and allow us to include others in our healing work.

Chant and raise energy to bless the stories, the web, and the pouches. The women may keep the web intact after storytelling, or take pieces of it to keep in their pouches with their stones.

Fire

After the stories have all been told, it is time to release those deeper feelings of anger, rage, shame, and judgment that have kept us bound and powerless, that have prevented our healing. The content of this phase of the ritual varies, depending on the needs of the women in the group and the common threads among the stories. If many women told of multiple abortions, perhaps this is the pattern or bond that needs to be broken. If women expressed a great deal of rage against the men in their stories, this could be released.

Place the unlit cauldron in the center. Invite the women to speak or shout into the cauldron, at the same time rather than in turns, what it is that they want to release or have transformed. It is often helpful to speak the hurtful words that have been spoken to us about our abortions: "How could you be so careless, so stupid, so irresponsible, so selfish?" "You've had *how* many abortions? Three? Four?" "Abortion isn't a form of birth control, you know!" "Murderer! Baby-killer!" And so on. Just as each of us has our own story, we each have experienced different (but similar) forms of condemnation for our abortions.

When all of the women have completed this speaking, their voices will rise and blend into wailing, keening, moaning, or sounds of fury and rage. Let this build and fall. Be sure to ground this energy, dropping down and touching the floor or earth. Next bind the wrists of each woman snugly with one or two strands of the thread.[5] As you are binding each woman's wrists, talk about the meaning of bonds, both the negative and positive. Bonds can keep us caught in patterns of thinking or behavior that do not serve us, that inhibit our creative energies. Bonds can also connect us to other women who have had the same experiences we have had and who can help us in our healing. Many of us have felt bound in some way to "choose" abortion.

---

[5]If no one in the group has used this tool before, someone should practice ahead of time so she knows how snugly the thread can be tied. The thread should offer resistance but break with determination (and not cut off circulation).

When all of the women have been bound, light the cauldron. When each woman is ready, she can break her bonds and throw them into the cauldron, perhaps shouting what it is that she is releasing. Begin a chant and wild dance around the cauldron, transforming the negative messages, thoughts, and patterns into power. Raise a cone of power over the cauldron. Ground the energy. The women may experience changes in their feelings about their abortion stories, so some time should be allowed for sharing these shifts.

Water

Ideally this part of the ritual should be led by a woman experienced in guiding a trance. If no one in the group has this experience, the women can take turns speaking aloud, imagining the journey described here.

The women make themselves comfortable, using the pillows and blankets. They relax their bodies and clear their minds to prepare for a trance journey to the Place of the Mothers, guardians of the cauldron of life, from which all life emerges and to which we all return. Here the women are greeted by their Mothers—all of the women who came before them, who experienced the women's mysteries of birth, death, life, choice.

Each woman's experiences will be her own. It is possible to greet and communicate with the spirits of unborn children in this place and to ask for help or guidance from the Mothers, Grandmothers, Goddesses, Crones, Midwives, and other wise women of this realm. Some women may meet their unborn child or children here. The soul of the unborn child can be released back into the cauldron, or given into the care of someone who appears to the woman when called. This is an opportunity to communicate with those with whom we may have unfinished business or for whom we have a message, and to speak with those who have messages for us. Take time here to allow all the women in the group to complete their tasks, their healing work in this place.

When the group seems ready, the women must come back by the same path, returning from the Place of the Mothers to the mundane world. Every woman should open her eyes, say her own name aloud, touch her feet, and then touch another woman. The women can then talk about their experiences in the Place of the Mothers.

Earth

In the closing phase of the ritual, we bless our female bodies, our embodied creative energies, and the choices that we make about how to use those energies. We can choose what we create, and we can choose when to create.

Be sure the room is warm. Form a circle. Place a blanket in the center and invite each woman in turn to undress and sit or lie in the center of the circle.[6]

The woman in the center is asked to locate her own creative center in her body. This may or may not be her womb. It may or may not be in one of the traditional chakras, or energy centers, in the body. Each woman will find her creative source in a different place. She may even perceive it to be in a different place now than when she began the ritual. Then the woman in the center tells what she wants to create in her life, what gifts, strengths, choices she wants to affirm. Then softly, repeating back what the woman has said, describing how they envision her creating what she has asked for, the other women anoint the woman in the center, massaging, kneading, stroking, sending healing energies into her body, praising and affirming her creativity and her choices. (Allow lots of time for this. No one will want it to end!)

When each woman has had a turn in the center, begin a soft chant to bless the circle and the working. Bring into the center the beads, shells, feathers, and other necklace-making material. Now the women can surrender their burdensome pouches full of stones, their weighty memories, and exchange them for something beautiful. Each woman exchanges a stone for a bead (or shell or feather), naming what that thing repre-

---

[6]In our tradition, we often work "skyclad." However, not all women feel comfortable with this. Therefore, each woman should be allowed to disrobe only to the extent she feels safe.

sents. Give the women time to create necklaces with their new treasures. Continue to sing and chant softly during this time so that the group's energy stays focused and women remain connected to each other while they create their necklaces. When the necklaces are done, place them in the center and let the chanting rise to charge and bless the women's creations.

When the necklaces are completed, bring out food for feasting. Bless the food and drink and celebrate these gifts of life from the body of our Mother. Thank her for the healing properties of the food, the connection of sharing feast food together, the power and energy for our creative work and for our bodies that comes from food. While feasting, conversation should remain focused on the women's experiences in the ritual and in the trance journey, on changes in their feelings, and so on.

When the women are ready, open the circle, first thanking the Goddess for Her presence and Her assistance in the healing work. Then bid Her farewell, and bid thanks and farewell to each of the four elements and directions.

May the peace of the Goddess go in your hearts. Merry meet, and merry part, and merry meet again! Blessed be.

Mourning Sickness

T. THORN COYLE

A sense of losing something
In the darkness
Before light
Opens your eyes.
        Raspberry. Comfrey. Valerian. Yarrow.
A woman's way
To heal herself.
A woman's way to mourn.
Ways to stop the bleeding.
Blood flows so easily sometimes.
This as Winter sap.
        I sacrificed my son today.

Dark, fertile earth,
too cold to grow
such tender seeds.
Shifting into nether world.
Preparing land to bury
is tilling land for birth.
Dirt black, bloody fingernails.
Powerful hands.
                  Hoe. Break. Carry. Cover.
Walk the knowledge of the Dead.
Feet clutching loam.
Wrap the spiral
shoulders broad
in star-shot mantle.
Softly sinking,
feet walk true.
The labyrinth of womb.
Pivot East to face my task.
                Keeper of the flames of Dawn.

Choosing to Die

In the Pagan tradition, we believe that each of us embodies the sacred. Therefore sacred authority is also embodied in each of us. When we are facing death, and our suffering becomes unbearable, we have the absolute right to say, "I have suffered enough; I'm ready to go now." We also have the right to receive assistance in making an end. Pagans recognize that suffering is sometimes inevitable, but it is certainly not desirable. No one should be forced to continue to suffer unwillingly. Medical "care" that is tortuous should not be inflicted on patients who are near death in a last-ditch effort to preserve a spark of life—unless they want it. To aid a terminally ill person in dying is to act as a priest or priestess of the Reaper, performing a sacred service.

Choosing to die when terminally ill is not the same as committing suicide in a moment of depression or despair. Suicide is not a neutral act: it causes harm to family, partners, and intimate friends. In the Pagan worldview, it is also not much of a solution to problems; it simply transfers them to another plane and intensifies the challenges the soul faces. For these reasons, suicide is strongly discouraged. When someone does commit suicide, however, we attempt to view the act with the same compassion we would accord any other mistake. The person is still considered part of our community, entitled to the same spiritual aid, guidance, and rites as anyone else who has died.

The ancient Maya people worshiped a goddess named Ixtab (pronounced "Eesh-tahb"), Who "is depicted hanging from the sky by a halter looped around Her neck; Her eyes are closed in death, and a black circle, representing decomposition, appears on Her cheek. . . . People who committed suicide by hanging . . . went directly to the Maya paradise. . . . They also said and held it as absolutely certain that those who hanged themselves went to this heaven of theirs, . . . where they said that the Goddess of the Gallows . . . came to fetch them."'[7]

Coup de Grâce: Neo-Pagan Ethics and Assisted Suicide[8]

Judy Harrow

Dying is personal. And it is profound. For many, the thought of an ignoble end, steeped in decay, is abhorrent. A quiet, proud death, bodily integrity intact, is a matter of extreme consequence.

---

[7]Thanks to Sparky T. Rabbit, quoting from Syulvanus G. Morley and George W. Brainerd, *The Ancient Maya*, rev. Robert J. Sherer (Stanford, CA: Stanford University Press, 1983).

[8]This is an expanded version of an article originally published in *Gnosis*, vol. 42 (Winter 1997).

This is the lesson of Samhain: we are all going to die. These days, nearly nine out of ten of us die of chronic conditions. About half of us die of diseases diagnosed two years or more in advance. That means we can all reasonably expect to spend some time knowing that we are in the vestibule of death, or that a loved one waits there. You may even have picked up this book because that is how it is with you right now. In any case, thinking about some of the issues around death ahead of time may make it somewhat easier when death comes close.

Those who work with the dying—doctors, nurses, counselors, and clergy—tell us that people seem to want just a very few simple things at the end. They want to be as free from pain as possible. They want to be as autonomous as possible, in charge of the process if not of the outcome. Most important, they want the comforting presence and support of their loved ones. They do not want to be alone or among strangers at the end. In our time, each of us will probably want the same things.

Our laws against assisted suicide have denied dying people these few bits of final comfort. Instead, they have been offered a series of ugly choices. They can go the full, miserable route. They can choose a quick and clean end, but die alone. Or they can expose their loved ones to severe legal risk and mental anguish.

Two of my friends died during the autumn of 1996. Both were of mature years. Both had illnesses that were painful, debilitating, and incurable. Both had suffered with these illnesses for a long time. Both reached the point where they were no longer willing to suffer without hope of improvement or cure, and so both chose to die. What I write here is dedicated to Bruce and to John.

"One day at a time" has meaning only when a person has a choice. Listening to two cancer patients casually talking about where they hide their little bottles of "insurance," I realized the importance of autonomy. People who are confident that they can quit whenever it gets to be too much, and who still have things they want to do and friends to stand by them, can often keep going far beyond their own expectations.

But there are limits. John, who had been a union shop steward before his amputations, specialized in handicapped access issues after he had returned to work in his wheelchair. Then the stroke took away his ability to use the wheelchair.

No law can force an ambulatory person to live longer than he or she wants to. Bruce could still walk. When the cancer, which had disappeared during chemotherapy, returned bigger than ever, he checked himself out of the hospital against medical advice and went directly to the nearest river.

That is why most antisuicide laws have long since been dropped from the books; they are unenforceable. The only laws that remain are those against helping others to suicide. Assuring people the right to assisted suicide simply means that the choice of a quick death is still theirs even after they are physically incapacitated.

John stopped all medication except painkillers. Steady in his choice for another three weeks, his house filled with friends come to say goodbye. He died in his own home, with those closest to him present to lend support. What would it be like for you, if that were your mate? Could you support his decision, or would you be pleading with him to take his meds?

For Bruce it was much quicker, but he went into the cold waters alone. His friends waited out a long weekend of uncertainty until the police found his body. At his memorial circle, some expressed anger at him for not giving them a chance to say goodbye. Which would be harder for you, as friend or lover of the dying, to deal with? Neither is necessary, except as current law makes them necessary.

Sixty-two-year-old George Delury went to prison in the fall of 1996. His wife of twenty-two years, Myrna Lebov, had long been quadriplegic and was entering dementia. By all medical estimates, her life expectancy was another ten to twenty years. She did not want to experience another decade or two of mindlessness and hopelessness. So, at her request, Delury mixed a lethal potion, steadied it so she could drink it through a straw, then held her as she fell asleep for the last time. Could you do that? What would happen to you if you did? Did anyone benefit from Lebov's agony or Delury's imprisonment?

The existing laws against assisted suicide do not save lives; they cruelly prolong deaths. They hold people in needless physical and emotional anguish. Fortunately, as social consensus is changing, so is the law.

Since the 1990 U.S. Supreme Court ruling in the case of *Cruzan* v. *Director*, it has been legal for a patient to refuse all artificial life support. People can now choose to die of starvation, thirst, or asphyxiation, with their doctor's help. Mind you, this is not legally considered suicide.

Cruzan represented a great improvement over the days when months and years of life support were legally mandated, even in entirely hopeless cases. The next step would be to remove the artificial distinction between life-support withdrawal and assisted suicide. We came close to achieving this during the spring of 1996, when two different circuits of the United States Court of Appeals overturned state laws prohibiting actively assisted suicide. Here's a quote from one of the opinions:

[T]he writing of a prescription to hasten death, after consultation with a patient, involves a far less active role for the physician than is required in bringing about death through asphyxiation, starvation, and/or dehydration. Withdrawal of life support requires physicians or those acting at their direction physically to remove equipment and, often, to administer palliative drugs which may themselves contribute to death. The ending of life by these means is nothing more nor less than assisted suicide. . . .

However, both decisions were appealed to the Supreme Court. In June of 1997, both were overruled, for two reasons.

One was lack of precedent. American law grows out of the English common law tradition, and both are grounded in Biblical religion, which sees suicide under any circumstances as an act of rebellion against God's will. Seven hundred years worth of precedents made it impossible for the Court to discover an already existing right to choose our own time and manner of death. Policy innovations, in our system of government, belong in the legislative branch, and, in this case, with the various States. The Supreme Court opinion made it very clear that they would find it constitutional if any State were to decriminalize assisted suicide.

Even beyond questions of precedent, the Court was being asked to weigh the States' interest in preserving and protecting life against the individuals' "liberty interest" in choosing the time and manner of our own deaths. Several of the concurring opinions pointed out that there is no State law against aggressive pain management. In extreme cases, doctors can resort to techniques of "terminal sedation," in which a patient is drugged into a coma and death is greatly hastened. As long as the declared purpose is pain control, and not death, no law is broken, and no criminal risk taken.

What if the Supreme Court had upheld the Circuit Court decisions? It would have been safer to discuss these questions openly and even publicly. People confronting these terrible decisions would have had better information available to them, the benefit of others' experience. And physician-assisted suicide would have been legal for people who were both mentally competent and terminally ill.

That's another big improvement, but it's still not good enough. Those qualifiers, mentally competent and terminally ill, sound reasonable on first hearing. But imagine yourself as a hopelessly suffering patient who doesn't fit the profile.

That is another big improvement, but it is still not good enough. Those qualifiers, "mentally competent" and "terminally ill," sound reasonable on first hearing. But imagine yourself as a hopelessly suffering patient who does not fit the profile.

People are considered to be terminally ill when they are, by their doctor's best estimate, within six months of death. Myrna Lebov was not terminally ill. If we limit the privilege to people who would soon be dead anyhow, other people who (like Lebov) are facing long periods of restriction, deterioration, and pain are denied relief.

The suicide of Nobel Prize winning physicist Percy Bridgman, recounted in one of the amicus briefs, graphically illustrates the point. Dr. Bridgman, 79, was in the final stages of cancer when he shot himself on August 20, 1961, leaving a suicide note that said: "It is not decent for society to make a man do this to himself. Probably this is the last day I will be able to do it myself. . . ."

What about "mentally competent"? The bitter fact is that some diseases take away our minds. Many of us dread dementia far more than we do death. Whom would we harm by escaping it? Whom would we benefit by enduring it?

The legal argument for freedom of choice at the end of life can be made on the most simple practical and humanitarian terms, without reference to religion. It is wrong to force unnecessary suffering on unwilling people. Ethical and spiritual considerations reinforce the case for choice still further.

The great American tradition of freedom of religion should protect free choice at this liminal and highly charged moment. Many of us are religious, and we seem to become increasingly religious as we approach the great mystery of death. Our religions give us structure and guidance as the lives we have known unravel. No outside pressures should detract from the comfort that can bring.

Different religions have very different teachings about how dying people should conduct themselves, based on their different understandings of this life and the next. Some religions teach their people exactly how to die, prescribing even their last words, and this is their right. Some prohibit suicide under any circumstances. Those who believe in some form of Purgatory, for example, may feel that there is positive merit in suffering. Others simply believe that their deity's will is not to be evaded. We must not tolerate the case managers putting any kind of pressure on such people to shortcut the full course of terminal illness.

But, in a free society, no religion can legitimately bind nonadherents. Tolerance for a wide range of choice at the end of life is essential to living together in a religiously pluralistic community. By necessity, as by principle, we all should be supporting each other's right to choose, even when others' choices differ from our own.

Pagan ethics do not tell us exactly what and what not to do. They are situational on principle. Our core ethical statement, our "golden rule," is the Wiccan Rede: "An it harm none, do what you will." While committed to an interpersonal ethic of harmlessness, we resist any arbitrary restriction on personal autonomy. Pagans are free to do anything they want, including end their lives, unless it is clear that doing so will harm others.

Since my religion requires me to choose and to take responsibility for my choices, whatever arbitrarily constrains my choice prevents me from following the teachings of my religion. So, from religious conviction as well as from political principle, I oppose many kinds of antichoice legislation.

A word of caution here: the absence of legal strictures or governmental enforcement powers does not, by itself, guarantee freedom of choice. While opposing well-meant but ill-considered laws that take away our choices, we need to bear in mind that the law does have a proper role: to protect our right to choose against undue outside influence.

The *Cruzan* decision, which permitted the withdrawal of life-support systems, also allowed states to set strict standards for assuring that the *patient*'s will was being followed, not the will of the family, the institution, or—perish the thought!—the insurance company.

There is a real danger, with the advent of profit-driven "managed care," that case managers will pressure the more vulnerable (poor and/or alone) patients to suicide early in order to save money on their care and to improve the "bottom line." Those of us who claim freedom of choice at the end of life, as at its beginning, need to be very careful that choice is truly free, that it is never economically constrained.

The government exists to defend and develop those interests that we, as a community, hold in common—things like public safety, environmental protection, and the maintenance of as much of a "social safety net" as we decide we want. Although we have no collective interest in prolonging anybody's death, we have a very real interest in assuring that every patient's wishes are honored. Only thus can we make sure that our own wishes will be honored when our time comes.

When there are no more laws about suicide, there will be even more need for conscientious personal decision. Winning the right to do something means gaining permission, not accepting a requirement. Instead of blanket rules, we will face the hard work and great emotional risk of weighing, deciding, and dying by or living with the outcomes of our choices.

The word "right" is ambiguous. It means both something that is "due to a person by law, tradition, or nature" and something that is "fitting, proper, or appropriate." Although we have the right to do something, it may not always be the right thing to do. That is why all rights also involve responsibilities.

Up to now, assisting a suicide has been a criminal act. Beyond even that, in some states people in certain professions have been legally designated as "mandated reporters." This has meant that not only have they not been allowed to help a suicide, they have had to do whatever is necessary to prevent one, including confining a patient to a mental hospital, in physical restraints—even if that person was in pointless and hopeless agony. Such laws have often been reinforced by professional codes of ethics. So to have it be known that you assisted a suicide, or even refrained from preventing one, has been to risk prison or the loss of your career.

Because of these threats, it has been unsafe to talk about when we feel that it may be fitting, proper, or appropriate to commit suicide, to assist in a suicide, or to refrain from blocking somebody's choice to die. We have been effectively prohibited from taking counsel together. We have talked about it, if at all, in tiny groups, in code words. (A dead man's leftover morphine, carried to a dying woman to give her an escape hatch, has become a "hand-me-down.") Or we have made our terrifying decisions all alone.

It is easier and saner to think about such hard issues before we have to actually decide and or act. Without forcing our choices on each other, we can share our thoughts and feelings. Already discussion is beginning in both the medical and counseling professions about the situational ethics of assisted suicide. We need to be talking about it within our respective faith communities as well.

What about neo-Pagans, with our ethic of choice and responsibility based on the Rede? Do our traditions provide us with any guidance? What if you were hopelessly ill? What if a parent, lover, or child of yours was? What if someone asked you, as priest/ess and counselor, to help him or her work through the process of decision? What if that person chose to die, and then asked you to hold the cup? Would you agree?

Would you refuse? How will you know when to agree and when to refuse?

What can neo-Pagans learn from the Rede? Harmlessness comes first. Doing whatever we can to minimize any needless trauma to our loved ones precedes the exercise of personal will. Beyond that, here are few suggestions:

A person considering suicide should take some time over the decision. After all, once done, it cannot be undone. Suicide is not a decision to be made in panic upon first hearing a frightening diagnosis. The cooling-off period can also be used to make some responsible preparations.

Those preparations include tracking down full medical information. People considering suicide can then use that information to answer the following questions: What is their prognosis? What are their treatment options? Is there any realistic hope for a cure? How long can they expect a reasonable quality of life? Can their symptoms be mitigated? Can their pain be controlled by methods that still allow for creative self-expression and loving interaction with their dear ones?

Then they can move on to more mundane issues: Have they taken care of all possible practical business? Have they paid all possible debts, made or updated their will, and made all possible funeral arrangements? Rational and honorable suicide means leaving as little work and worry as possible to one's successors.

Have they come to closure with as many of their emotional issues as possible? Have they made peace in as many of their relationships as they can? Are they clear in conscience that they have made their best effort toward peace and healing?

Have they discussed their decision to suicide with all their close significant others, allowing those people time to adjust to the choice?

Notice that much of this is a matter of taking care of business, both psychological and practical—good practice at any stage of life, whether or not we are ill. I advise working through the nonmedical parts of this checklist between Samhain and Yule of every year, just as a way of keeping in balance, because not all deaths are predictable, let alone self-chosen.

Doing these tasks clears the way for an honorable decision, but the tasks do not by themselves decide the issue. People can update their wills, resolve their grievances, pay their debts, and simply live more comfortably knowing that these things have been done.

So the decision remains. There may still be some purpose in clinging to life, even in a damaged and hurting body. Although Pagans do not value suffering for its own sake, many of us are committed to being "willing to suffer to learn." So the ultimate question for me is, When does learning end?

There is always beauty around us, always something to learn. The Ancient Ones are always among and within us. The Source is infinite, but our receptors are finite. We interact with this glorious world through our bodies, and our bodies wear out. Eventually our abilities to perceive, enjoy, and learn are irretrievably gone. This moment can be recognized only from within a failing body. No one else can ever know; no one else should ever choose.

FOR ONE ASSISTING SOMEONE TO DIE

Goddess of death,
I stand here as your priest/ess
knowing that life must be winnowed
to thrive.
This is a holy act I perform:
to open a gateway
for a willing one
to come to you.
This is an act of healing,
a release from suffering,
an end to pain.
Here is one whose arms are open
to embrace you,

who does not turn (his) head
from the kiss of the Hag.
May (his) passing be easy.
May you enfold (him)
and become beautiful to (him)
and gather (him) in to your orchard
to grow slowly to life again.
Bless my hands, Mother,
that do this work.
Bless my eyes
that are willing to look at your face.
Bless my lips
that speak these words.
Bless my heart
that loves and grieves.

The Releaser

PATRICIA DEVIN

My mother and I sat across from the lawyer who was solemnly checking signatures and dates. Mom had just named me executrix of her will and arranged for me to have durable power of attorney.

"Which means," she announced, with typical Capricornian bluntness, "that if the time comes for the plug to be pulled, it will be your decision to pull it. And if that times comes," she added, "I want that plug pulled."

She went back to initialing pages, while I sat, stunned by the realization that the woman I have honored as the gateway into this life trusted me to act, if necessary, as her gatekeeper into the next one.

As a nurse, Mom was familiar with issues of life and death, but we live in a society where, for many people, death is a taboo subject. We could spare ourselves and our loved ones much confusion and grief with some time spent in serious discussion about and preparation for the inevitability we all face.

In addition, advances in medical technology are presenting us with options and potential ethical questions unknown to previous generations. When is it permissible to terminate the life of a person in a persistent vegetative state? Is it possible that lifesaving medical advances can wrongly prolong death? How much of an emotional, psychological, and financial cost to the family and to society are we willing to accept? What are the limits we can live and die with?

It is certainly preferable to ask these hard questions and to reach the hard answers before the need arises. It requires sensitive interfamily and interpersonal communication. But it is worth the effort. The diagnosis of a terminal illness usually brings with it the gift of at least some time to prepare for the death to come. Sadly, it is very common for the ill person to find herself isolated even by loving family and friends, who are afraid of discussing candidly what is happening. They may be concerned that such talk will seem morbid or depressing, or they may themselves simply be unable to face the reality of impending loss.

Even worse is the sudden stroke, heart attack, or terrible accident that can shatter lives in seconds without warning. People reeling with shock and misery, walking through a living nightmare, can find themselves faced with heartbreaking decisions and choices. I believe that it is far more loving and life-affirming to acknowledge that death is life's close companion. Take the time to discuss with your family and other loved ones the plans, wishes, and ethical decisions that you have reached regarding your transition into whatever lies beyond this life.

It is also important to remember that when dealing with a family member or loved one whose choices, plans, wishes, or beliefs do not agree with yours, the most ethical choice will be to respect her decision. No one can live her life or do her dying for her. You show her the greatest love by supporting her.

On a similar note, do not forget that memorial services, funerals, and other rites of remembrance exist to provide closure and comfort to the living left behind. After all, with any luck the dead are happily engrossed with Life Review 101 or whatever, not hanging around like Tom Sawyer checking out their funeral. Realize that it may be necessary to plan for more than one service to suit the various needs and beliefs of the survivors.

For example, several years ago, when it became obvious that my father's death was imminent, my mother asked me to facilitate his funeral. She knew that I was a Wiccan priestess. I agreed, and knowing that Dad was at least nominally Christian (though I do not believe he had set foot in a church in years), proceeded to plan a service that incorporated a couple of beloved hymns ("Morning Has Broken" and "Amazing Grace"), a couple of poems, a reading from Ecclesiastes ("To every thing there is a season"), the Twenty-third Psalm, and a time for his friends and family to offer their remembrances. I felt comfortable with all of these, and I do not think that anyone noticed that at no time did I offer a prayer "in Jesus' name." (I am not that big a hypocrite.) The readings and the lyrics were printed in the service program so that those in attendance could follow along and join in when appropriate.

Just as the opening organ notes sounded, Mom approached me. Could I please add "Onward Christian Soldiers" to the service? She was sure it was a Salvation Army song, and Dad's mother had been a colonel in the Salvation Army. I stared at Mom in dismay. I *hate* that song. It always makes me think of ravishing Crusaders rampaging through Constantinople. On the other hand, it was not my only lover and husband of thirty-five years lying in the casket. I penciled the song into my service, and when the time came, invited those who knew the first verse to sing it. Mother felt better, and the funeral served and comforted the living, which is its function.

Someday I may stand next to my husband, my mother, or some other beloved friend, knowing that the time to release them has come. I am fortunate in that we have made it clear that we do not want extraordinary medical measures taken in the absence of a likely return to the reasonable enjoyment and function of life. It is still a great responsibility, to be solemnly undertaken, for in that moment I shall be acting as a priestess to the Dark Mother, the honored Crone, and come to know better Her to Whom all must return.

A Ritual for Cutting the Cord

The following suggestions are offered with love and support to those who accept the responsibility of terminating artificial life support for a family member or other loved one. It is assumed that the counsel and recommendations of other family members, loved ones, and the medical staff have been sought and carefully considered. I have tried to maintain flexibility, as individual circumstances will vary.

Purify: Use salt water, much as described elsewhere in this book. In an emergency, plain water will suffice. Be certain to wash face and hands.

Ground and center: There is an excellent grounding exercise in Chapter 3, but if you know and prefer another exercise, use it.

Cast the circle: This can be done silently or aloud, depending upon the circumstances. Call the quarters, the guardians, and the Gods and/or Goddesses, as you are accustomed. Especially remember the Crone and/or the Dark Lord. Envision the space encircled with light.

INVOKE THE GODDESS:

Great Goddess, Dark Mother,
Keeper of the cauldron,
Great womb of promise
From Whom all life goes and then returns.
Great Hunter, Who from each beginning
Tracks the end and knows the time.
All that has ever been, that is, or that will be
Stands before your scythe, awaits your arrow.
I come here as Your priest/ess.
I come here as Your hand.
I come here as the key which opens the gate to You;
And this that I do is sacred,
For this I do for You.
Welcome _____ gently,
That this passage may be easy.
Bless _____ as (she) comes to You,
And bless me, left behind.

Terminate life support: The medical staff may have to handle this.

Conclude the ritual: Stay with your loved one as long as you like, reciting poems or guiding meditations for the spirit.

Follow your heart and intuition. When the time seems right, thank the guardians, Gods and Goddesses, and anyone else you invoked, especially the Crone and/or Dark Lord, and say, "It is done. Blessed be."

The following rite is meant to be performed at some time after the death occurs, away from the death site. Although I have elected to have a priestess portray the Crone, some groups may prefer to have a priest portray the Great Hunter/Lord of Death. The ritual may be adapted to suit the needs of the participants. I suggest that it be performed on a waning or dark moon.

A Ritual for Healing After Cutting the Cord

On the altar have a small bowl of salt, a small bowl of water, a censer, incense or sage (or other cleansing herbs), an apple, a sharp knife, two white candles, and matches.

The circle is cast according to the group's usual manner. The Crone priestess, dressed in black or purple, stands with the Releaser in the West. A second priest or priestess begins with the invocation.

> SECOND: *Great Goddess, Dark Mother.*
> PRIESTESS: *Queen of the Mysteries of Life and Death,*
> *Honored Crone, ancient and ageless,*
> *Known by many names,*
> *Hecate, Cerridwen, Persephone, Ereshkigal,*
> *Kali Ma, Xochiquetzel, Hel:*
> *We call upon You now*
> *To bless us with Your presence.*

The Crone priestess steps into the circle from the West.

> CRONE: *There is one here*
> *Who served Me as My priest/ess,*
> *Who served Me as My hand*
> *And served Me well.*
> *Come forward now.*

The Releaser steps into the circle. She holds a photo of the deceased, which has been fastened to her left wrist with a short piece of black or purple yarn.

> RELEASER:　*Great Goddess, Dark Mother, Honored Crone,*
> *I served You as Your priest/ess.*
> *I served You as Your hand.*
> *What I did was sacred,*
> *and I learned much from my service to You.*
>
> CRONE:　*What did you learn?*

The Releaser shares the experiences, fears, realizations, and emotions she has undergone in the decision to terminate life support. When the Releaser is done, the Crone priestess steps toward her and gently takes the photo from the Releaser's hand, pulling the yarn between them. With a sharp blade, the Crone cuts the yarn.

> CRONE:　*I welcome _____ gently*
> *And blessed her/his coming to Me*
> *And enfolded her/him lovingly*
> *Within My mystery.*

The Crone leads the Releaser to the altar and sets the photo down between the two white candles. The Releaser lights one of the candles.

> RELEASER:　*I light this for _____*
> *For what we have shared together*
> *In life and in death:*
> *The laughter and the tears,*
> *The lessons and the love.*
> *You live on in my heart*
> *And will not be forgotten.*

The Releaser lights the second candle.

> *I light this for myself,*
> *For strength and for courage,*
> *For hope and for healing.*

The Crone priestess puts salt in the water and uses the salt water to anoint the Releaser.

> CRONE: *I bless you by Earth and Water,*
> *for you are My beloved child*
> *And you have served Me well.*

The Crone priestess puts sage or incense in the lit censer and smudges the Releaser.

> CRONE: *I bless you by Fire and Air,*
> *For you are My beloved child*
> *And you have served Me well.*

The Crone priestess cuts the apple crosswise, revealing the pentagram within. She places half of the apple next to the photo.

> CRONE: _____ , *remember the mystery.*

The Crone priestess gives the other half of the apple to the Releaser.

> CRONE: _____ , *remember the mystery.*

The Releaser and the Crone priestess return to the West side of the circle.

The circle is opened in the way usual to the group.

Suicide: One Witch's Perspective

DEBORAH OAK COOPER

I came to the Craft in the process of grieving the death of my father. After a childhood of enduring my mother's repeated suicide attempts, I was shocked at twenty-two when my father finally trumped her by killing himself. Paganism was the spiritual system that called to me and assisted in my healing. As a Witch, I believe that life is sacred, that death exists to remind us just how sacred it is. I have worked in both the magical and mundane worlds for over twenty years to preserve and protect this living earth, believing that we should revere our lives, that we embody deity. As a priestess, I work to build a community where the belief is in worshiping and sustaining the life-force and where we rejoice in our living bodies. As a priestess, I actively fight the forces in popular culture that embody the worst kind of suicidal urge: the urge to not only self-destruct, but to take all living things with you. As a therapist, I work with clients who struggle with their hopelessness and their belief that life is not worth living, that death would be a respite from despair. As Witch, priestess, and therapist, I also believe that we all have the right to make choices that affect our lives, and our deaths. Suicide is a tangled, confusing issue for many of us Pagans. We believe in the sanctity of life, but we also believe in free will.

In most monotheistic theologies, suicide is the ultimate sin. It is an insult to the Supreme Deity, who (it is believed) is the only one who should be able to decide when it is our time to die. Murder is a crime against other humans, but suicide is a crime against God. Some religions do not allow suicides to be buried on hallowed ground or religious services to be held.

This is not the case for Wiccans. We Witches do not condone suicide, but neither do we condemn it. Our approach is complex and contextual. Two of our main tenets are "Do what you will and harm none" and the Rule of Three (meaning that what we do will come back to us three times). Each suicide must be held up against these tenets. But even the suicide that causes great damage to others is not condemned to eternal damnation, in our view. Indeed, we have no such concept.

There are many different kinds of suicides, each with its own issues. Many Pagans support assisted suicide for the terminally ill. To make choices around how you die when death is close and inevitable seems right and potentially healing for all connected to the suicide. Other suicides are less reasoned and deliberate: we use the label "accidental suicide" to describe the demise of a person who engaged in self-destructive behavior that led to death. Many of us have friends or family members who died after overdosing on drugs or in car accidents after taking drugs while in a self-destructive frame of mind. Knowing that they were unhappy and despondent before their death, we are left wondering if they *meant* to take their lives. Other suicides take place to prevent an even worse kind of death, as in those who kill themselves before being captured and tortured. It is part of Craft lore that groups of Witches would do this in the Burning Times, that some would choose to hurl themselves from cliffs into the sea rather than die at the stake. Still other suicides are cult actions: a group of people are led by a charismatic leader into taking their lives. Some suicides are politically or spiritually motivated. Anyone who grew up in the sixties has the image of monks lit on fire etched into her memory—suicides to bring attention to the horror of the war in Vietnam and Cambodia. In the case of heroic suicides, commonly found in war, one person chooses certain death so that others can live. Other suicides are con-voluted aggressive acts, meant to cause pain and suffering for those left behind. The majority of suicides, however, are those due to depression.

When we apply the tenet "Do what you will and harm none" to each of these kinds of suicides, it becomes clear that some suicides are actually in the service of the life-force. These suicides are not problematic for Witches. It is the suicides committed out of despair, anger, or blind obedience that are the most disturbing to us. These are the kind that cause harm to those who are left behind. As a child of suicidal parents, I am statistically more at risk of committing suicide myself. More than twenty years later, the effects are still felt in my family.

This is where the Rule of Three can be examined. Wiccans have diverse ideas and beliefs about what happens after death. Some believe in full-fledged reincarnation and the Eastern concept of karma. In other words, they believe that what is done in this life will affect what happens in the next life. Some remember past lives and lessons learned from them. Others believe that after death we decompose and our souls become part of the life-force by feeding the earth with our flesh. Some believe that there is a place where we can go and be healed, a kind of Pagan Heaven. The one thing you can get agreement on from most Pagans and Wiccans is that there is more to this world than meets the eye and that there is a world of the spirit. Most of us believe that the Rule of Three means that there are consequences to our actions, and we are responsible for them. Since I am bad at Pagan math, I have never been quite sure why it is that things come back at us three times, and not nine or thirteen or seven. In any case, most Wiccans would agree that even after death, we will on some level still be dealing with our actions in this life. This is quite different from the concept of damnation and Hell. While it means that there are consequences to our actions, it also leaves open the possibility of healing.

I have had direct experience of this with my father. Over the years I have worked on my relationship with him between the worlds. For many years after his death it seemed impossible to really communicate with him, for he was consumed by his own suffering and pain. It is very clear to me that suicide done in a moment of despair is no release. Over the years I have sent him healing energy and worked on our relationship at our Samhain rituals, and over the years healing has begun. It is my belief that his healing may take lifetimes, but I truly believe that it has begun. Believing and experiencing this has been part of my own healing. We have a saying in the Reclaiming community: "What is remembered lives." No matter what you believe happens after death, there is always the possibility of healing the relationship with those we have lost, if only in our memory of them.

As a Witch, I believe that the wheel of life is always turning. We move from winter into spring; we move from sadness into joy. Things are always in movement, and things are constantly changing. It is my belief that the most common kind of suicide—the suicide resulting from depression—is a suicide that does not serve the life-force; it is a death that results from the wheel being stuck. When a person is depressed, he is out of balance. He does not believe that life can change, that life was ever good. The thinking of a person in a depression is distorted. Everything is seen through the lens of despair. Pleasure and joy are seen as illusion and discounted. I have sat with many depressed people as a therapist, and I come from a long line of depressives. Quite a few people battling depression have told me of the mythical study that found depressives to be better predictors of the future. In a culture where denial is part of life, I find this not surprising. Even so, I tell them they are not quite in reality either. The best visual picture of depression is the Five of Cups in the most popular Tarot deck, the Rider-Waite. In the Five of Cups, a black-robed figure is fixated on three spilled cups, while at the figure's side are two full cups, unseen by the figure. Choosing to commit suicide while in a state of depression is a choice made without all the facts. As my coven-sister Reya says, "If you are convinced that taking your life is a solution to depression, get a second opinion."

There are many causes of depression, and many ways to heal. As a Witch, I do not ascribe to "one-way" thinking, and I know from therapeutic experience that each person's depression can be lifted in a different way. When a person is depressed, his biochemistry is changed, is out of balance. Some people are born with a genetic predisposition for depression; without treatment, they may battle suicidal thinking all their lives. (Many lose the battle.) Other people fall into depression after a traumatic event. Still others experience depression caused by alienation and loneliness.

I treat a depressed person's urge to kill himself in the same way I would treat a psychotic or drug-induced belief that the person can jump off a tall building and fly. It is distorted thinking and needs to be dealt with as such. I have seen some people transform depression by psychotherapy alone; many others need a physical approach as well as an emotional one. All methods to healing need to be explored, including antidepressants and building a network of support. Physical exercise changes the biochemistry; some herbal remedies are effective at relieving depression for some. I would not hesitate to hospitalize or organize around-the-clock care for a client, friend, or family member in the grips of a suicidal depression.

Depression and despair are part of the human experience, but as the Five of Cups reminds us, the work is to widen the vision to include the full range of what is possible, including pleasure and joy. For some, struggling to increase that vision is a long-term working; for others, healing can be instantaneous. Patience and the belief that the wheel turns, no matter how slowly, are required when dealing with depression.

When someone we love kills himself as a result of depression, the effects can be devastating. Not only are we confronted with grieving the loss, but we are also left knowing that the love we had for that person was not enough to keep him alive.

Our love can feel tossed aside, disregarded. We were not enough. Many of us experience a feeling of guilt: there is something we should have done or said. For many years I went over my last conversation with my father constantly in my head, looking for what I had said wrong, what I had omitted, what could have made a difference. Survivors of loss due to suicide may do this for years before making peace with themselves and the one they lost. I know now that nothing I said in that last conversation caused my father's death, and nothing I could have said would have changed his actions; but it was necessary to imagine the conversation time and time again until I had worked through every possibility, had figured out what I *wish* I had said, no matter the outcome. Survivors of the suicide of a loved one also need to be able to express their anger, and should be encouraged to do so. The stages of grief—denial, anger, bargaining, and acceptance—can be more intense and take longer when you have lost someone close to suicide.

The Wiccan tradition of celebrating the turning of the wheel of the year is one way that survivors of suicide can heal. After many years of celebrating the cycles of nature, I know in my body, mind, and spirit that we can go from dark to light, from ecstasy to deep and profound grief. Every year at Samhain, my father's death is grieved again, and things change and move. The yearly ritual also serves to remind me that grieving the loss of a loved one is a long-term working. There is no quick fix, in this world or between the worlds.

I have seen a bumper sticker that proclaims, "Witches heal." I second that emotion. Our work as Witches includes healing ourselves, healing the damage to this earth, and working between the worlds on healing our relationships with the dead. Nowhere is that more needed than with those we have lost to suicide.

Part Five

Carrying On

15

Making Room for Grief

Grieving

When someone we love dies, we grieve. No matter what we believe about death, no matter how convinced we are that our friend is happily dancing with the Goddess in Avalon, a great gap now separates us from someone we long for. We have suffered a great loss.

Loss can deepen us or diminish us. Grief can intensify our connection to life, or drain our vital energy. To grow from our grief, we need to understand and honor the grieving process.[1]

Our grief is important for the dead. Our sorrow creates a current of energy that helps carry the dead to the Applelands. Honest grief is ultimately a self-healing process, through which we eventually let go of our beloved one and find the strength to move on with life.

---

[1] In writing this section, I am indebted to my mother's professional work on loss and grief, particularly to her book *A Time to Grieve: Loss as a Universal Human Experience*, by Bertha G. Simos. New York: Family Service Association, 1979.

Grief cannot be hurried. But grief is a process, not an end point. We may move through grief quickly or slowly, but we ultimately must move on. We cannot hold on to the dead—nor should we allow them to use our grief as a handle with which to pull us over to join them. We must each live out our own life.

Grief can take many forms. My (Starhawk's) mother, Dr. Bertha Simos, in her book, *A Time to Grieve*, identified many aspects of grief: sorrow, yearning, crying, but also anger, shock, denial, and panic, which can also be aspects of the grieving process. We easily recognize sorrow, yearning, and crying as forms of grief, but we may not realize that anger, shock, and denial, or panic can be part of grieving.

When we are grieving, we may feel helpless and dependent. We cannot function at our usual levels of efficiency or responsibility. A sane culture recognizes that after a loss we need time out from ordinary life, and nurturing care from our community.

We may express our grief by searching—misplacing our wallets or never being able to find our car keys. It is as if we need to heal from the big wound of death by creating smaller losses of things that can be restored. We should be careful, however, because during this period we may create further losses for ourselves. Decisions about money, about the disposal of property or belongings of the dead, should if possible be postponed, or at least talked over with a close friend who is not in grief.

Relief can also be present in grief. When we perceive that death has brought the end of suffering, when the burden of care and worry we have shouldered for a long time is a suddenly gone, when the ordeal is over, we naturally feel a sense of comfort. Relief does not diminish our love nor lessen our loss, but it is a very real aspect of death and one the Pagan tradition honors. The Reaper is also the ultimate healer.

In fact, when we are grieving we may feel a whole range of contradictory emotions at once. We may be crying one minute, laughing the next, hating our beloved one's guts while desperately missing them, wanting company only to decide when they arrive that we would rather be alone.

Grief also spurs us to search for meaning—in the specific life of the person we have lost, in our own lives, in life and death themselves. We may question everything we have ever believed, or embrace it more deeply than before. We may feel a sense of spiritual vacuum.

Nothing may make any sense. Or we may find some new system of thought to believe in. This aspect of grief can sometimes be the most painful, yet in it lies our potential deepening and growth.

What can help us through the painful period of grief is the loving support of others who have also experienced great losses. We need to hear each other's stories, to learn from the variety of ways we encounter the Dark Goddess.

When someone close to us dies, we need to feel that the right things are being done, that the loved one is being treated with honor and respect. The rituals we create should help provide support for the bereaved, offer care both spiritual and practical during a time of vulnerability.

Just as the dead person should not be left alone, those close to her or him should also be offered companionship—even just the silent presence of someone sleeping nearby. The primary mourners should not have to serve as priest/ess of the funeral or organize the memorial—a close supportive friend should take on that task.

When we are grieving, we need most of all to know that our friend's life was of value, so ritual should include a time when people can speak of the dead person, share stories, and sometimes reveal facets that were previously unknown. When my dear friend Stanford died of AIDS, I was asked to priestess part of his wake. I asked the friends and family there to share stories. Among the participants was a sister who had been estranged from him ever since he came out as a gay man. At the end of the afternoon, she said with tears in her eyes, "Now I know what I've missed by cutting myself off from my brother." Painful as that realization was, it was healing for her to know how much Stanford was loved and valued, to recognize that he was a person of courage, humor, and grace.

Grief is work. When we are in acute grief, we should not attempt to do other work. If I could legislate one thing for the Pagan community, it would be to forbid anyone to work for at least six days after suffering a major loss. Nine days would be better: three days for the dead, three days for you, and another three days of gentle transition back to ordinary life. But the demands of modern life create enormous pressure to simply soldier on, meet that deadline, get back to work. Even in the Jewish community, which has a biblically-legislated tradition of sitting Shivah—seven days of mourning—few people still take a full week.

Ritual can help us move through the grieving process. Most traditional cultures have a time line for mourning—things that cannot be done or things that must be done at important intervals. Here is a suggested time line for Pagans:

First Three Days after Death:
The focus is on the dead, on sitting vigil with the body, preparing the funeral, going through the cremation or burial, and activities surrounding them.

Second Three Days:
The focus shifts to the survivors, who need care and nurturing, and should be fed and comforted. Keep a candle burning, continue to use prayers, chants, and songs in this book, do not go back to work!

Third Three Days:
Begin a gentle transition into everyday life, ideally with continued emotional and practical support. If you must go back to work, try to do so on a reduced schedule and postpone any extra commitments. Begin to sort through your friend's possessions and to deal with legal and financial matters, if necessary. Continue to keep a candle burning whenever you are home, (never leave a candle burning unattended!), and to chant, sing, and speak to your friend.

FirstMoon Cycle:
Light a candle every night. Pick one of the prayers, songs, or chants, and use it nightly. Choose one ordinary activity you will not do until the cycle is over—getting a haircut, for example, or wearing red. At the end of the moon cycle, get a new hairdo or a bright red outfit.

First Sun Cycle/A Year and a Day:
Light a candle every dark of the moon, and use the same chants or prayer. Choose something else you will not do for a sun cycle—shaving your beard, for example, or baking bread, and after a year and a day, do it.

The Samhain after the Death:
Create an altar for your friend, with her favorite foods, ritual objects, things that were important to her and call her to mind, and keep a candle burning there whenever you are present. On Samhain night set out a special offering, and either as part of your community's ritual or on your own, take some time to communicate with your friend.

Important Dates:
Especially in the first year after the death, every holiday or special occasion—your friend's birthday, and your own, the birthdays of your

children, happy moments your friend would have loved, even TV shows you used to watch together may bring back sweet and painful memories and reawaken your grief. Use the salt water meditation, light a candle and chant for your friend, and ask for support if you need it.

Offerings to the Dead

At some point, you may feel that your friend's spirit needs some extra help or energy. Many cultures regularly make offerings to the ancestors by burning incense, setting out food or pouring libations. You may wish to do the same. Or you might consider what kind of offering your friend would most have liked. Wine, or coffee? Home-baked bread, or chocolate? A ritual, or a poetry reading, or a night at the bowling alley?

My mother died shortly before her seventy-fifth birthday, and I decided I wanted to make her an offering of a birthday party. I thought about what my mother liked. She was most happy in the midst of a group of intelligent women having an animated discussion. So I invited many of my friends to a salon—an evening party where we shared desserts and stories of our encounters with the great forces of life and death. The evening turned out to be one of the most moving rituals I have experienced, as woman after woman shared some of the hard and intimate moments of their lives. Throughout, I could imagine my mother thoroughly enjoying herself.

Cleaning the Rooms of the Dead

Cleaning out the rooms of a loved one who has died is one of the most painful experiences life has to offer. Too often, circumstances also require that it be done immediately and hastily. Remember that after a loss we have a tendency to create other losses for ourselves. Think carefully about what you want to keep and what you can wholeheartedly give away. Be easy on yourself. You may need to do things that are not practical or efficient. My brother and I, forced to clean out our mother's apartment in three hectic days, ended up renting a storage space for her old furniture, paying hundreds of dollars to truck it up to San Francisco, storing it for several months, and then giving much of it away. However, I never regretted the money or the trouble; it was worth it to allow myself the time to relinquish things one by one, and to decide what I really wanted to keep. What I regretted was giving away her old cotton housedresses, which she wore thin during her last illness. I wished I had kept them, to make into quilts, to use in ritual, to make doll clothes for my children should I ever have any, or to fantasize about making doll clothes for my nonexistent children should I not have any.

The following two prayers may be useful in helping make up your mind about particular objects. They can be said over individual things or generically—for a whole pile of things going to the thrift store, for a bagful of clothes being kept. Obviously the first is for things you are keeping; the second is for things you are giving away.

> Beloved _____,
> I take this in memory of you.
> May something of your spirit remain
> so that as I touch this _____ [book, dress, vase]
> we will touch across the veil.

> Beloved _____,
> this was yours once.
> Now you have no more need of it.
> Withdraw your energy,
> your spirit, your desire.
> We ask your blessing on the one who receives this.

Before taking things to keep or give away, do something to clear the energy: charge a bowl of water and salt and sprinkle the room and objects with it, or cense the room or objects with the smoke from burning herbs—rosemary, sage, cedar, or lavender.

Winter

ROSE MAY DANCE

My mother died on August 18. Cora Naftel May Dietrich. She was eighty. She had been dancing with my dad, and they sat down to rest for a moment, to have a glass of juice. She collapsed and died. I was not prepared for this. I did not know that she was sick, although people who saw her more often thought she was sick. My dad had been the sick one that year, and we had been concentrating on getting him well and getting them moved into a nice place for seniors. I was surprised. My grandmothers had lived into their late nineties.

My present avowed religion was not much of a comfort to me when my mother died. I did not celebrate; I did not dance. It was hard for me to imagine my Christian mother frolicking in Summerland or on the Isle of Apples, ready to reincarnate. My husband, Bill, brought a piece of Wiccan liturgy for the dead to the funeral. It was lovely, something Starhawk had been working on since the death of her own mother in 1993. It was great to hear him read it there in the church, but the most comfort I received at that service came from the hymns and Bible passages that I chose for the service, words and songs my mother knew and loved, words and songs woven into the fabric of my being. Perhaps if my mother had been moving through long illness I would have had time to weave my present beliefs into her dying, into saying goodbye and letting her go. But when she died so suddenly, I was dropped into a basic place of automatic reaction.

I trust it will be different for the children in our community. People like Casey and Shannon—who have been carried to rituals since they were born, who have heard our songs and chants and prayers, who sing them now themselves—will sing them at our death ceremonies and be comforted, even if they have gone off and become Roman Catholics or Zen Buddhists.

But I was not embracing the mystery of death after my mother died. I was sunk in grief and depression. Then, twenty days after she died, I was touched by mystery and miracle. My daughter called me.

Twenty-four years ago I had given up my child for adoption, urged by my parents to take this step since I was unmarried and still dependent on them for survival, unskilled in the ways of the world. They felt that a child born out of wedlock was a disgrace, and they needed to hide my pregnancy and their grandchild. The loss of this child has colored my life, of course. I have had a happy, productive, even fascinating life up until now, but the loss of this child and my continued childless state have been a strong chord of unhappiness, a minor key beneath the other, happier harmonies of my existence. And my mother, with her forceful personality shaping my fate (whether I was near her or far away), molded me as only a mother can do. She was the prime mover in my giving up my child and in a subsequent abortion I had for another pregnancy in the 1980s. I know I had a choice, and I take responsibility for my actions, but if my mother had felt differently or had not been around, I might have acted differently. And if I had acted differently in either pregnancy, the consequences could have been good, bad, fortunate, or disastrous. I certainly cannot tell.

But I feel that after my mother died, when she got onto the astral plane, she saw that she had some unfinished business. I had been registered and searching for my child for seven years. Then, just twenty days after my mother died, my daughter called me. I *talked* to her! I learned of my granddaughter, one year old. Suddenly all of my mystical tendencies popped back to the surface, and I spent days in communication with my mother as I talked daily on the phone to Melissa, my daughter. I felt the power of the Mother as she reached through the wombs of four generations, felt how She stretched back and forward through time, felt how life was a never-ending circle of birth and death and rebirth. I was floating on air. I was all that ever was. I had a future. My joy was boundless.

I am happy to know Melissa and her daughter. Soon we will meet. Melissa is wonderfully loving and accepting of me, very kind to me. It could not be better.

That happiness is one of the balls I juggle in the air. But there are other balls to juggle as well.

For a while my happiness about my daughter softened the edge of my grief for my mother, and I now believe that was my mother's intention. I was drifting in a fog during those first couple of weeks as a motherless child. She sensed my distress, and—by now knowing a thing or two about the nature of death—wanted to comfort me. She sent my daughter and granddaughter, and they *were*—they *are*—a comfort.

But as Samhain approached, I began to put up altars for my mother. My grief reemerged. I am sure such grieving is normal and natural, but now I seem to be stuck in it, tearful all the time. I feel guilty that with so much to be joyful about I sob every morning and cry whenever I have time to relax. Once again the mysterious meaning of death has left me, and I feel only bereft.

So my Craft, my religion, its liturgy and practices—these are not quite enough for me in the instance of a shocking death. Witchcraft is like my house in winter—a wonderful house, beautifully made, old and sound, very strong. But death is strong as well, and it buffets the windows like a gale.

When I encounter people who seem so held up by their faith in God that they can be carried through any crisis, I am often frightened. Such people seem out of touch with reality, inflexible, too brave to be cautious and exploratory. So I guess it is all right that sometimes my faith leaves me to flounder, weep, and question myself and others endlessly. But since I am a teacher of this Craft, an elder of this religion, it seems important that I air my doubts and despair.

I hope we can create traditions and liturgies together that account for the side of death that is madness, as well as the side that is the mysterious gateway. The weather is going to come in under the door from time to time, no matter what we do.

THE HAG PRAYER

Goddess of death,
you are a mystery
and I do not understand you.
You give great gifts
and snatch them away.
You are a cruel joker
with a warped sense of humor
and I hate you.
You give life to those

who don't deserve it and take it from those
who do.
You make no sense, Goddess;
you are not logical,
or if you are, it's a logic we cannot follow.
You are not fair.

Hag, hag,
ugly old hag,
you claim that if we embrace you
you will turn beautiful,
but getting close to you
is like embracing sharp knives —
and I don't believe you,
I don't believe you.

Something has happened here
that is wrong, wrong, wrong,
and there is no way
to pretty it up
and make it be okay.

Mother of lies
Mother of false promises
Mother of tremors and pain
     and the loss of vision as we age
Mother of confusion and memory loss
Mother of stink and decay
Mother of vermin
Mother of viruses
Mother of parasites that eat
     the living bodies of their hosts

You are the Goddess of the bloody face
who eats her own child
in the night.

KALI: The Vampire Time Drinks the Blood of Life
THE PITCH BLACK WITCH

In Your Heart beats the Blood of Death.
Your Pulse drums destruction.
You dance.
Under Your Feet
The cosmos trembles, collapses.
The Gods cry out in dissolution.
You dance.
Panic.
The end of All
We can imagine
And cannot imagine.
You make the Worlds
Want You.

Witch of the Burning Ground,
Your magic bedazzles me with Being.
O Goddess touch me not!
Your Beauty makes me shudder in Your Arms.
My heart becomes Your cremation ground.
I become a corpse.
I bleed for Your Kiss.
I feed Your Hunger.
I burn for You.
I arise like smoke.
I redden Your Eyes with my joy.
You make me
Want You.

An Altar for Death

M. A. BOVIS

Dedicated to Raven Moonshadow

Witches and Pagans often make use of the physical, the visible, the tangible to focus attention on a specific working or set of things they wish to effect or to accomplish. Creating altars is a way to indulge this tendency while at the same time helping us to honor our lost one(s) and to process our grief.

When my brother died in 1989, I was devastated by his death, and I wanted to do something that would help me (and possibly him) with his passing. My friend and teacher Raven suggested that I build an altar. I wanted to create a clear physical message so that, if my brother's spirit stopped by, he would know that I loved him and that I was sad he was dead, but that I understood he had to go and that I had no unfinished business. I wanted it to support him along his way and to support me too. I wanted a place for him and a focus for me.

You can build an altar in the home or any space where it would be helpful, even for a short time. Here are some general guidelines for building an altar. These instructions are as bare-bones as possible, because (1) you can be limited by location (in a hospital room, for example, oxygen may preclude the use of burning candles) and (2) Witches are nothing if not innovative, and what feels right to you to put on your altar probably is! If possible, it is good to meditate on what you are doing. Simply keep silent for a moment and then focus on the thought that you are building this altar to a specific purpose (healing, peaceful passage, rest for the departed). Listed below are some of the most common ingredients for an altar: objects representing the sacred elements and directions and the Goddess and God, personally significant items (photos, gifts).

- Air is the East element. The simplest, easiest tool to represent air is a feather—perhaps from a bird important to you or to the situation. Alternatively, if it is possible to use it, a ritual knife (athame) can represent air. You will want to call the spirits for each altar object. As you place your tool on the altar, say an appropriate invocation: "I invoke air for this altar to provide clarity of mind in a difficult time."

- Fire, the element of the South, can be represented by a lit candle or (if that is not possible due to safety reasons) a wand, a crystal, or even a piece of metal or reddish glass (formed in the heat of the fire). Say, "I invoke fire for this altar for the energy to experience this moment, to strengthen myself and others." (Even if a candle is not the fire/South item on the altar, I feel that it is important to have a candle burning, even if only for a little while. [Of course, for safety, never leave it burning when no one is around.] Because the flame of a candle is perceived from all levels, including the spirit world, I see it as a kind of opening statement: "Ready for business, working here, hey you . . . "—a signpost, a marker for the spirit world that you want to attract for aid and comfort, both to give and receive.)

- Water, the element of the West, is easily available. Put water in an attractive cup or bowl and say, "I invoke water for this altar to channel my emotions into useful paths."

- Earth, the element of the North, can be represented with a pentacle, a rock, or some dirt. Flowers or plants are great too, as their living energy (rather than your own) can be used by both the living and dying. "I call earth, our Mother who forms us and holds us, to join me at this altar."

- The Center is often represented by a cauldron and stands for the Spirit. If nothing else, leave a space and say, "I call the Center, to anchor me in my work with _____."

- Deities honored by yourself and others (Raven was working closely with the Santeria deities at his death) may be honored. For instance, one friend has a Buddha and a Christ figure on his altar.

- The reason there is a tradition of cut flowers, besides the fact that they are cheering, brightly colored, and fragrant, is that the spirits of the sick or dying feed off them rather than you; so it is always good to include some fresh flowers. They also represent regeneration. Because flowers have such a short lifespan in comparison with humans, we can easily perceive the cycle of life in them; this can help us to accept our loss as a natural part of life.

- Finally, you will want to include some things that are personally significant to your beloved dead and you, as well as photos, jewelry, or other mementos. These items can be luxurious or everyday; I like a mix—as in real life.

For the altar I created in honor of my brother's memory, I found some photographs of my brother. I was lucky enough to have photos from throughout his life, so I put up several: childhood, military, fishing, and recent. I put out some foods he liked and Tarot cards—one with fish leaping on it because he liked to fish, and the Sun card to show him he was free from this lifetime and any pain in it.

Next were objects for each direction: a candle burning, dishes with water and salt, earth and crystals, a wand and some flowers.

The altar was very simple and specific. It was important as a marker for a significant time in my life and a way of contact with the Goddess during that time.

A lot has happened in my life since my brother's death. More people close to me have died, and I have experienced many major life changes. I have a deeper understanding of the significance of an altar as a spiritual tool and focal point during a specific event.

I have set up little working altars in my office in the financial district. I have used a space within my home altar as a specific event altar. And when it came time for Raven to die, I was privileged to bring things for both the altar in his hospice room and the one in his hospital room for his dying.

For the dead, the dying, or the living, an altar can be helpful regardless of religion. An altar is a simple concept of creating a space that itself is sacred and that serves as a focus for the Sacred. No matter what is projected as the Sacred, the space can be shared to the benefit of all. In a group setting, the more who participate in creating the altar, the more potent and helpful it is.

A Witch I know performs autopsies in the coroner's office of a big city. Many of the cadavers she examines are of homeless people or indigents found unidentified in alleys or dumpsters, with no one to mourn their passing, no one to honor their lives. She has an inconspicuous altar on her desk, and she lights a candle for each unmourned life.

Just as important as erecting an altar is disassembling it when you are back to "normal." Discard your altar objects with as much respect as you exhibited when placing them on the altar. Water goes into running water; if possible, flowers or food into compost. Purify all the things that you may reuse before you do reuse them.

Every year at Samhain, I make a special altar in the North for my Beloved dead. On it I place photos and mementos of them, along with some of their favorite foods and beverages (lamb for the Greeks, potatoes for the Irish, special bottled water for the gourmets). In fact, I erect the altar on my kitchen table so I can sit and have dinner with those I miss.

An altar can be simple or complex; the intent is what matters most. As a focus for my intent and as a "house away from home" for the sacred, an altar helps me set boundaries instead of having loose sadness all over. An altar is another part of the healing/growing process in death and dying; it is another way we as Witches can profit from our religion for healing and blessed growth. I offer the ideas expressed in this essay to anyone for whom they resonate. May your beloved dead be honored, and may your grief be honored.

With or without an altar, tools such as Tarot cards, whether you are familiar with them or not, can help you find clarity, understanding, and serenity. Reclaiming Witch M. A. Bovis here offers us several ways to work with the Tarot.

Death and Tarot

M. A. BOVIS

I am really fond of the Tarot. I collect cards, I like to hold them, I use them more frequently for introspection than divination, and I am more honest with myself with Tarot cards than I am writing in a journal or speaking with a therapist. In fact, the closest thing I have to a true journal is the little book that I keep records of my readings in. I list the questions that I ask, the date, the deck and spread I use, and the cards that come up.

So it seemed very natural, when I had deaths in my family, to look for a Tarot deck for comfort and a little order in a time of pain and confusion. When my brother and then my father died, I found that putting some cards out on the death altar was important and helpful. The first card I used was the Sun card from the Rider-Waite deck; it shows a child naked and bareback on a horse in a garden. With the help of that card it was easier to visualize my father and brother free of the pain of their earthly existence. My brother really enjoyed fishing, so I found a card that showed fish and put it on his altar.

The first thing I did in preparing to write this essay was to look for the Death card in several decks and to consult books that I have on the Tarot for information on that card. In comparing the similarities and differences, I noticed that while most decks show a skeleton of some sort, the other features of the card differ widely. The Motherpeace Death card has a skeleton arranged in the fetal position on the ground beside a tree circled by a snake shedding its skin, showing rebirth and renewal. The BOTA card shows a grinning standing skeleton holding a scythe against the ground; two heads and various body parts lie around him. This is not as gory as it sounds; the skeleton looks rather like a gardener cultivating his garden. The Wheel of Change Death card features a skeleton in a valley. The skeleton is wrapped in a white cape with a red and green border. There is a body in both the foreground and the background (compare the BOTA card), there is a sunrise (or sunset), and there is a river flowing (on which can be seen a small boat with two figures in it). The Thoth Death card shows a skeleton wielding a scythe as well. In the background are several fetuses, a snake, and other potent symbols of transformation.

The Death card, number thirteen in the Major Arcana, is assigned the Hebrew letter Nun (as a verb, "to sprout or to grow"; as a noun, "a fish") and the astrological sign Scorpio. As shown in the above descriptions, it commonly features a grinning skeleton with a scythe. The positioning of the skeleton's bones can be significant. In Tarot commentaries, the Death card is uniformly referred to as transformative and regenerative; only rarely, they say, does the card allude to someone or something actually dying. In fact, the Death card is considered so transformative that it is mentioned in meanings for many other cards as an allegory of personal transformation (a transformation that makes new rather than rearranges, that starts from scratch).

Dying into a new life is a part of many spiritual confirmations—whether through baptism, confirmation, initiation, or the taking of religious orders (where it sometimes includes a name change). Along with these rituals, a person often has a transforming of the inner landscape, referred to in the Justice card as a (not always pleasant) "overview," and in the Judgment card as a "call" or "revelation."

This is shown in both the Major and Minor Arcana in many decks. The Tower (often known as the hand of God) shows the radical destruction of everything in sight, indicating the ruin of structures real or imagined; the Sun card shows a new beginning after enduring trials; the Four of Swords shows the peace of surrender/retreat; the Three of Swords relates growth through pain; the Six of Swords shows transition through the journey; the Five of Cups depicts disappointment and the possibility of renewal; the Queen of Swords, sometimes called "the widow," reminds me of how I have felt going through a deceased loved one's effects and trying to decide what he would have wanted while feeling deep sorrow.

One of the ways I apply the Tarot in the grieving process is to pull cards that show my feelings and use them for support. This can help me to move beyond a place where I feel stuck. I do not always know which card I will use when I start out, and in fact the choosing is part of the healing process.

Here are some other exercises that work with the Tarot around issues of death and dying.

Exercise 1: Storytelling

Look through your Tarot deck and pick out the cards that you feel relate to death in general, to your beloved dead, or to you the bereaved. Put them in a pile and put away the others. Go through this death pile and separate it into different categories: sadness, release, transformation—whatever categories feel right.

Tell the story of each card within the category. An example: "The Fool card is about my beloved dead going to a new place, watching the Goddess as he changes" (and so on). You may want to write this story down.

Pick one to five cards from all the death cards as a memorial to the beloved dead.

Pick one to five cards as an affirmation of yourself in this experience.

Write this affirmation down and say it to yourself for a week.

Exercise 2: Star of Release

Shuffle the deck while thinking of the beloved dead and lay out seven cards: two in the center and five in a circle around them. The two center ones stand for:

The bereaved
The dead

Put the five remaining cards in a star/circle (each spot corresponding to the points on a pentacle), starting at the top. They stand for:

Your relationship with the beloved dead
The next phase in your life
Your gift to the dead
Your gift from the dead
What you will learn from this experience

Write down the cards you received in the reading and make notes of your interpretations. Review it in a few days (and again in a few weeks), and see what has changed for you.

Exercise 3: Tarot Death Meditation

It is always good to do a meditation/trance exercise in a quiet place, safe from disturbances such as the telephone and doorbell. Close your eyes, breathe deeply, and surround yourself with a circle of protection.

Now imagine yourself riding on a boat at twilight on a river. The boat moves by itself, and gradually comes to rest. You step out of the boat onto the shore, into a quiet, desolate landscape. You follow a pathway.

You move toward some people you see, and a rider approaches them from the opposite direction. As you draw nearer, you can see the rider standing silently, and you observe the people as they face the rider:

A King, robed and crowned
A Bishop, richly gowned (his robes stiff)
A Maiden, dressed in white
A small child, bearing flowers

THE RIDER ASKS THEM:	"What must you give to me?" You notice how the rider is a grinning skeleton in armor, holding a flag as he sits on a prancing white horse.
THE KING REPLIES:	"Never will I give up my status, my riches, my power, my throne!" as he falls lifeless to the ground, his crown rolling off. *How important are these*

things to you? Do they define you? Do they limit you?

THE BISHOP REPLIES: "My position/church will protect me, my robes of office will support me," as he kneels in prayer, eyes closed. *How do you hide behind your position / role? In your relationships? In your community? Does this stop you from growing? Keep you from asking questions? Prevent you from upsetting the applecart?*

THE MAIDEN REPLIES: "Please don't take my beauty. It is precious to me; it is all I have," as she is brought to her knees in fear, turning her face away. *Would the essential you be diminished if you lost your hair? Your teeth? Would you want to live if you became quadra / paraplegic? Would you explore other qualities you were born with?*

THE CHILD ASKS: "Can I ride on your horse? Why is your armor black? Are you from far away?" as she stares in wonder. *What if you were to start over in this moment? How would your life be different? What freedom do you have when you lose everything?*

DEATH, THE RIDER, SAYS: "What I promise you is here." He points to his flag unfurled and says the flag pictures a white rose on a black background. *Look carefully: What is there for you? What is the gift of Death for you?*

After a time, you leave and return to the boat, which is waiting for you at the river's edge. As the boat moves off, you see the sun rising between two towers, and as you contemplate the questions and answers that have been offered, you remember that death is often a new beginning as well as an ending, and that it leaves no one unchanged.

The boat takes you back to the place you started this journey from. Slowly you open your eyes, breathe deeply, pat your body all over, and say your name aloud three times.

After any meditation, it is important to sit in silence for at least a few moments and, if possible, to note your impressions. You may get additional information in dreams or thoughts during the following days or weeks.

These exercises have worked for me, and that I hope they will be helpful to you. Please understand that the Tarot is a tool and you are the tool-user. If you should feel moved to change an element of one of the exercises, then trust your intuition.

Just as working with such tools as the Tarot can help us to actively promote grieving and healing from loss, often just hearing the words of others who address the mysteries of life and death can bring peace, understanding, and perspective. Below are two prayers/poems that we feel do just that.

PRAYER FOR COMFORT

Donald L. Engstrom

May the Mysterious Ones comfort those who still remain.
May the Sandman bring them healing sleep.
May Soma bring them healing dreams.
May She Who Loves Us Beyond All Reason be ever present
    throughout this first year of their grieving.
I am so sorry that this has happened to those whom you have
    loved so dearly.
May we all walk in Beauty and Balance sooner than later.

To the Turkey Buzzard[2]

HAROLD L. OAK SAWYER

Wing tips splayed
    Like fingers spread,
    Soaring birds in search of dead.

        Tilting left
        Tilting right
        Graceful birds
        In glider flight.

                Seven gliders in the sky
            Fourteen wings, circling high
                  and low
                    far and wide
                        to and fro,

Seeming not to care or know
    where they come from
    where they go.

Looking down, always down, down below
      piercing eyes, circling slow,
      What do they know
          of dreadful heights
          and earthly woe?

They are free to fly and gaze,
      in circling flight to spend their days
      in sheer delight on buoyant waves
      of air and light.

---

[2]Turkey buzzards do not fly. They float and glide in their ocean of air. One seldom sees them flapping their wings. They do so only upon takeoff and landing, and then only for a stroke or two.

When my time comes to be their food
and if our God be in the mood
      to give me one more chance to live and die,

I hope my realm shall be the sky
Looking down from on high,
Looking down upon the earth
Giving thanks for so much death,
Giving thanks for such a birth.

The Role Of Community

Death is exhausting! Those who are closest to the dying person may be depleted by sleepless nights and drained by grief. They need the support of community in many ways:

Priest/essing: A grieving person should not have to organize a ritual, be responsible for the energy, or be expected to shepherd the spirit of the dying person. Ideally someone else in the community who is less immediately involved can take a helpful role in guiding rituals.

Practical help: Making phone calls, arranging transportation, dealing with authorities—all these are all concrete acts of love.

Food and companionship: A newly bereaved person needs to be nurtured and cared for. In our community, when a new baby is born, we organize a *doulah:* a period of time in which people take turns coming and cooking a meal or helping to clean house so that the new parents can concentrate on the baby without having to deal with the practical details of life. We should do the same for the bereaved. Companionship should never be burdensome: we do not have to entertain or comfort or make wise remarks; we simply need to be there.

Ongoing help: Death has a way of generating a lot of tasks, from cleaning out the house to years of hassling with lawyers and accountants and sometimes the IRS. Practical support and the expertise of someone who has been through the process can be very helpful.

Remembering the Dead in Community

M. MACHA NIGHTMARE

Over the past many years I have had the honor of calling the names of our beloved dead into the Samhain circle at our large community ritual called the Spiral Dance. Over the years the Spiral Dance has evolved and reinvented parts of itself (and changed emphasis and some techniques), but during at least the last eight or nine years we have invited people to call or write us with the names of their Beloved Dead to be included in the ceremony.

I have collected the names and then spent some time assembling them, arranging them, checking to see if any appear several times (different people often call in the same loved one). And always, of course, people give me additional names just before the start of the ritual, so I add them to my list.

During the Samhain sabbat ceremony, after the purification and the circle has been powerfully sung and drummed and danced into sacred space, and while litanies are being offered, we call the names of our own Beloved Dead, to be with us, to witness our rites in their honor.

For many years there was a special litany that honored political and artistic losses along with events of the past year, while the calling of the Beloved Dead (a separate litany) was for personal Beloved Dead. It was nearly impossible not to overlook some public figure who had died who had significant personal meaning to one or more of the celebrants of Samhain.

Meanwhile, as years passed and we all lost more loved ones to death, I began reading the death notices in the local metropolitan paper every day—and still do. (My Witch sister Val says that when she grew up in San Francisco's Mission District in the fifties and sixties, the obituary column was called "the Irish sporting green.") This task seems to suit me fine; I have always been fascinated by the snippets of someone's life reduced to a few lines in the newspaper in an attempt to convey who that person was.

So, as the Lady would have it, I began to collect names

from the paper—from the obituary column, the death notices, and the news at large. This I still do. Every week or so I add a few more names, and sometimes even bits of information about the people that I feel really should be remembered and honored at this sacred time of year. Sometimes it is a dancer, a labor leader, a 112-year-old Amazonian aboriginal shaman, a murdered child, a distinguished scientist—all people whose lives should not be forgotten. Needless to say, the list grows long.

The Reclaiming Newsletter and the posters and flyers and other announcements for the Spiral Dance always invite people to call my number to leave names for the list. For several weeks immediately prior to each ritual—and off and on during the entire year, at any time of year—people call and leave names on my answering machine. I add these names to my growing list almost every evening.

Then a week or so before the Spiral Dance ritual I go through the list and arrange it. I take great care to intermingle "ordinary folks" with celebrities so that the better-known figures do not get preeminence over anyone else who died. I often include public figures whom I believe to have been a presence in many people's lives.

People have called and asked me if I would take a pet's name. Others have simply left a pet's name on the answering machine. While I do not encourage pet names because the list gets so long, neither do I decline to include them. I feel that if a pet were significant enough in an owner's life for the owner to want to mourn the animal in community, then it is not my place to censor.

Over the years the litanies—political, artistic, or otherwise—that included names of prominent people seemed to change. And as I said earlier, we always missed someone who should have been called. So I gradually came to include those names along with our personal beloved dead. I believe that many of these people are our common loss. Many of them are figures who colored our childhoods or inspired our professional, artistic, or personal pursuits.

As celebrants assemble in the hall for the ritual, I wander around the space. I take notice, when I can, of where people I know who have lost a loved one that year are standing or sitting. I continue to take mental note of this as the ritual progresses. I do not obsess over it, and I certainly do not know everyone (or know of all the losses); but I keep it in a bit of my consciousness for later use.

When the time comes for the beloved dead to be called into the Samhain circle, I take a deep breath and walk into the center. I begin with more general words of honor and invocation, talking about why and how very much we want these souls present. Then I begin to call the names—not too fast, and as carefully and accurately as I can. (Some of the names do not come easily to the tongue of a native American English speaker; they require attention. That attention is important to the honor we wish to give our beloved dead.) Sometimes I need to pause a bit to let the names ring in the air. If I know where someone who has lost a loved one is sitting, I try to direct the focus of my voice toward her quadrant of the room. There are two reasons why I do this: I feel that a Beloved Dead will be more attracted to his living loved one with my voice as guidance, and I believe that the living person's grief is aided/encouraged/loosened by hearing the name so clearly.

People often wail or cry quietly. Graces (priestesses who welcome celebrants, tend to those in need or openly mourning, guide people in the spiral dance, keep aisles clear) throughout the space watch to help mourners with embracing arms, tissues, and sometimes ashes. As the list goes on, grieving builds. Those who have nothing to grieve this year help those who do. We ask those whose loved ones have not been called to name them, to call them to our circle. Our Beloved Dead come among us for a last parting before the final crossing over. We have them with us this night when we are all between the worlds—to tell them one last thing, to ask them one last thing, to give them something or to receive something, or to love them one last time.

People have told me that they *saw* their Beloved Dead one at the Spiral Dance; they have thanked me for calling their loved one's name; they have thanked me for my correct pronunciation; they have even told me that the moment I called their beloved dead was the single most moving part of the ritual for them. Some people, when they call names to my answering machine, weep or choke up speaking the name, others are abrupt and controlled when saying the actual name. And many thank me over and over again. This feedback convinces me that the work I have done in evolving this rite for communal grieving is valuable. I consider it a great honor to be able to summon the Beloved Dead. I take my charge seriously.

I also believe this works from my personal experience of mourning and honoring my own beloved dead at the Spiral Dance. Somehow it seems easier to let go and to reach closure when it is done in community.

I offer this tale of my finding my way to sharing grief with my community in the spirit of a gift. I hope that my experience inspires you to share grief in community with your loved ones at Samhain.

Blessed be.

Opening the Gates

Words by Starhawk and Lauren Liebling
Music by Mara June Quicklightning

These are the gates of youth and age, these are the gates of now and then, these are the gates of mem - o - ry, and de - sire. Pass through them! Step be - tween the worlds, be - yond time, out - side the boun - d'ries of your hu - man life. Pass through them! To dance the spi - ral, the jour - ney of re - new - al.

Repeat through spoken words, as long as desired

(hum... ...)

Here is all that ev - er was, none are for - got - ten, no - thing fades for - ev - er, all that has passed comes a - round a - gain. for

Repeat as round, ad infinitum

here, what is re - mem - bered lives, what is re - mem - bered lives.

The First Grounding of His Bones and Ashes: We Take Rick to the Mounds

Donald L. Engstrom

The day before the Night of the Purple Moon
July 18, 1995

One week after Rick's death. It seems strange to still have no real feeling of linear time. I am still floating somewhere between the worlds. I suspect that I will now live here more than I live in the world many call the mundane. And I must say that the idea does not bother me in the least.

It was time yesterday, the first Purple Moon Eve of summer, to do the first grounding of Rick's bones and ashes. It was time for him to begin to feed the earth, to bless the soils with his rich ashes and loving bones. It was time for us both to become rooted into this new reality—that is to say, that we are now husbands separated by a great distance, with Rick dwelling in the Halls of the Ancestors and I still a living priestess of the Mysterious Ones keeping house in Gaia's Flesh. It was time for me to take that one more step of acceptance. Rick is dead and I will not see him for perhaps many more years to come.

Charles, Patrick, Wild Flower, and I drove up to the Effigy Mounds on a beautiful summer day. It was a leisurely drive. We stopped for doughnuts and treats whenever we wanted to. We stopped at an antique shop and at a concrete art shop. We drove the long way, up through Dubuque on the River Road to Balltown, where we stopped for a nice luncheon.

We arrived at the parking lot for the Mounds in the early afternoon. The weather was beautiful, perfect for a two-mile hike into Sacred Lands. We grounded and named why we were there while standing on the banks of the Mississippi

River. We were ready to begin our journey. We were ready to take Rick's first ashes and bones to the ancestors. I could hardly believe that I was there.

The walk to the Ten Bear, Three Hawk, Two Snake site was a time of quiet talking and singing. The other Radical Faeries asked me questions about the history of the Mounds, magical and otherwise, as we walked through the lovely green wooded entrance halls. When we walked through the prairie section, conversation turned to the wildflowers. The beauty of the earth filled us. I softly sang, "The River Is Flowing" and "White Coral Bells" off and on throughout this part of this walking ritual.

I could feel Rick with me as soon as I got out of the car. I could feel his breath on my neck as we stood by the river. I could hear him following us up the steep wooded path, through the prairie, and into the lane that leads finally to the Mound site. He seemed to be holding my heart and filling me with a comfort, a golden light, a love that would not die. My emotions were a whirlwind. I did not know what I was feeling—joy, sadness, longing, despair, loneliness, unquenchable hope? I was finally doing what Rick and I had talked of so many times before: I was taking my sweetheart's remains to the ancestors. I was spreading the first of his ashes at the Sacred Place that had called us so long ago. I was mingling his bones with those of our beloved Donald. I was taking another step toward healing.

At the gateway to the Mounds, we cast a formal circle and called in the allies of the five directions. We welcomed the old ancestors into our ceremony while we paid homage to our newest ancestor, Aric Arthur Graf. We walked to the Bear Mound, where Donald B's ashes were spread, as I quietly sang "Hoof and Horn." We placed offerings at the Heart of the Bear. I made a spiral of lavender (the Queer herb of purification and protection) around the offerings. I then divided up Rick's ashes among the four of us. We each spread these precious remains with words of blessing and memory. Meanwhile, my heart was feeling the fresh wounds of just a week ago as new ones ripped deeper into my being. It was a hard but beautiful thing.

I feel more at one with the black Iowa soils than I have for many months. My roots are now completely intertwined with the stones and the soils of this place. Actually, I feel closer to the land now than I ever have before. Giving an offering to the Land of Bones and Ashes of your dead husband, lover, best friend, and confidante is more powerfully bonding to that place than I had ever imagined. I am at peace for the first time in I don't know how long around the question of where to live. I will live where I am, where Rick and I have lived these past years. I will live at 628 Second Avenue, Iowa City, Iowa 52245, North America, Gaia, Solar System. It is strange and wonderful to feel so related and committed to a place (a geography) and yet to be so aware of my place in the Multiverse. The Macroverses and Microverse now dwell in my heart and in my home. I now know that wherever I live, it will be a home of blessing.

After the spreading of the remains, we each spent time alone wandering and exploring the Mound site. It was a time of great loneliness for me. I could talk to Rick and expect him to hear me, even to answer me in some way or another, but I would never again in this life taste his sweet lips or feel his strong arms. Fucking damn! I missed him.

I am still missing Rick intensely this next morning. How long will this emptiness last? As long as my deep longings for so many dear ones—Donald, Dicky Lee, Tony . . . ? Even longer, I imagine. Twenty-four years of successful marriage to an adventurous, courageous, and loving faggot will not be filled or replaced by the new times ahead. I am planning for the long haul. Though I expect new delightful journeys and adventures to come my way, the part of me made for Rick will always be vacant until we meet again.

It was soon time to start home. I was told to go by the Mysterious Ones; they gave no reason, just the message, "Leave now." I became very restless; my heart was in turmoil. I asked the others if they were ready to close the circle. They could stay a while, I said, but I needed to leave this place. So we closed the circle, leaving a final offering of lavender and love.

I walked slowly back the two miles to the parking lot. Soon I heard the others following me and then passing me.

Patrick and I quietly talked of plants and animals native to this place, but my heart was not in our conversation. Most of my concentration was on the amazing quality of life that Rick and I had shared together and with our large community of family and companions. What a bittersweet memory!

Our drive home was quicker—only one stop for ice cream. We were too tired to even talk much. I kept dozing off. It was hard for me to think clearly, let alone to analyze what I was feeling.

We unloaded at my house. We said our goodbyes and went our own ways. I was soon in bed sleeping in storms of dream. I floated in and out of long days of blizzard and then into a cold night on a raging sea. I finally awoke to my grief-hives itching so intensely that no dream could keep me in the Land of Sleep.

Rickie, what goddamn adventure have we embarked upon? Can I do this without your strong arms and sweet lips? *Can* I?

As the Widow Engstrom began his healing by taking Rick's ashes to the Mounds, so we recommend that you begin yours in ways that best suit you. These actions and tasks help us to process our grief, and to memorialize our love for someone who has gone. Pagan plant ecologist Anna Korn offers another practical, meaningful, and ecological method for honoring your dear departed—one that continues to honor the life-force and the remembrance of those memorialized by tree planting.

Tree-Planting Memorials

Anna Korn

It is night, after the dinner dishes have been put away. I head to my room, light a candle at my desk, and draw a circle around my workspace. Then I open this month's envelopes:

dedications for tree plantings for loved ones, living and dead. I pick up my pen and begin to carefully scribe the names: a pine seedling in memory of a parent or grandparent, a redwood to mark a wedding or the birth of a child, another pine to celebrate the life and mentoring of a beloved teacher. Each month the envelopes spill out stories of lasting love and human continuity in the face of adversity—triumphs and sorrows, life passages, personal histories, loving memorials, and a deep love for the wounded earth. I was never a very skilled calligrapher, but I hope the memorial parchments I penned and mailed back eased some sorrow or helped in treasuring a moment.

I was working to keep alive the work of Gwydion Pendderwen, the founder of Forever Forests, a volunteer Pagan tree-planting organization. Gwydion sought to inspire people to plant trees to heal the earth. Every New Year's weekend from 1978 to 1991, groups of Pagans, mostly from the San Francisco Bay Area, but some from all over the world, gathered for a weekend of tree-planting, evening feasting, and bardic circles. Hot tubs and shared backrubs eased muscles aching from trudging the Coast Range hills for hours in the mists and cold, a wet burlap sack filled with tree seedlings on one shoulder and a tree-planting tool on the other. A deep bond grew among us tree-planters—it felt good to be bringing in the New Year doing service for the planet, despite aching muscles and chilled fingers and toes. It was also healing to be away from the slick, noisy urban New Year's celebrations, clouded with alcohol and hype.

Gwydion started tree-planting on his own and his neighbors' parcels in Mendocino County with trees from a California State Forestry Department program, but when funds for the woodlot program dried up after the first year, he was determined to continue. For a time he put his own meager funds into buying the seedlings from the State Forestry nursery and invited people up for a New Year's work party. As time went on, the tree-planting developed into an annual festival—always small, about forty-five or fifty hardy souls whom Gwydion chased out of bed early to hit the slopes, armed with tree-planting gear and peanut butter sandwiches. A hair-raising ride in the back of an ancient flatbed truck, bumping along precipitous dirt roads, took planters to the planting sites. Evenings were a time to bring your weary, chilled-to-the-bone body back to the ranch house for hot soup, hot-tubbing, feasting, singing, and the convivial warmth of kicking back with new and old friends. When Starhawk told Gwydion about tree-planting programs in Israel, where, for a donation, people asked for trees to be planted in the name of a loved one, Forever Forests had a means of funding. This was how I came to be a scribe for Forever Forests.

Gwydion died in a car accident in November 1982, but the band of friends that had been coming to the ranch for years kept planting trees, doing erosion-control projects, and pursuing Gwydion's activism on behalf of the earth. The tree-plantings went on for another decade after his death. It was a moment of giddy triumph when some of us walked through a small stand of pines over twice our height and remembered the rainy day we had planted them many years before. We wished we could have shared that moment with Gwydion, who was truly a shepherd of the trees.

Trees link the earth and heavens, forming a universal axis that grants magical entry to other worlds above, below, and between the worlds. Trees are the dwellings of spirits—including plant devas, dryads, yakshas, elves, and ghosts. Among the Celts, each letter was named for a different kind of sacred tree, and the alphabetic series formed a symbolic calendar of seasonal tree magic and lore. The Babylonians decorated or planted a tree whenever they set up an altar to worship. In China, trees were planted on graves to impart their strength to departed souls. In Asia, trees are still protected at temples and sacred sites. (The ginkgo tree, which had become extinct in the Western Hemisphere during the age of dinosaurs, was rediscovered in Asia in the early twentieth century, preserved in a Chinese temple grove.) In Jewish and Buddhist symbol systems, trees represent teaching. Trees are universally seen as sacred: they are the seats of deities, the places of sacrifice, the supports of the heavens, and the bridges between the worlds. The fruits or nuts of certain trees are the emblems of knowledge. Evergreen trees are seen as symbols of everlasting life; deciduous trees, of rebirth after death.

I encourage you to plant trees for friends who have died. Someday in the future, someone will bless you for having done so. It is healing, for yourself and for the earth, to make a living testament of your love and connection—one that can transcend generations. Memorial tree-planting fulfills the Pagan observation that out of death life is born. Trees can offer you comfort, and you may hear voices in the music of their leaves.

On the practical side, do enough research on the kind of tree you hope to plant that you know it is not a pest species (such as acacia or eucalyptus) and that it will survive in the ecosystem in which it will be planted. I strongly suggest using native species of a locally adapted genetic type if you are planting a tree in a wild or rural area. You may need to provide the young tree with protection from deer or cattle by fencing it while it is small. In some climates, young trees may need supplemental water until their roots grow deep enough.

If you are planting a tree or shrub in a developed area, you have much more latitude in your choice, so you may want to plant a species that was a favorite of the person you are memorializing. If you have a green thumb, you might try making a cutting of a plant that was significant to your friend. I have two Angel's Trumpets, one white and one pink; they grew from cuttings given to me by patients I cared for when I worked in an AIDS clinic. (I have *inherited* houseplants from patients too.) One of these men was also an organizer of the AIDS Memorial Redwood Grove in Golden Gate Park, a community tree-planting effort that, like the Names Project AIDS Quilt, memorializes the beloved dead.

Dying people may wish to be involved in planting the chosen tree, depending upon the strength and energy they have. Because the tree will be a gift of continuity to later generations, seeing it planted and present during their lifetime may give them strength. Planting bulbs in the fall expresses a hope of seeing flowers in the spring and may be a tangible magical act for a dying person.

Recently I heard of a woman who planted a "Mr. Lincoln" rose in memory of her mother-in-law, who had loved roses and had supported the Abraham Lincoln Brigade! Such a plant is extra-special; you can share a private moment with your beloved dead whenever you taste its fruit or enjoy the beauty or fragrance of its flowers. As a Pagan, I am certain that such thoughts travel to the spirit for whom they were intended— perhaps with a little help from dryads or plant spirits.

16

Practical Work

Whether you are sick or well, caring for a dying loved one or not, there are many issues to think about and decide upon if you are to leave this life responsibly and with minimal business for your survivors. If you take care of everyday matters now, while you can, you leave them much less to worry about, and you leave them unencumbered by the "mundania" of your life so that they are free to grieve without such distractions. Cancer survivor Deborah Ann Light did just that, and tells us how.

How to Be Prepared to Dance

DEBORAH ANN LIGHT

When the Lord of the Dance extends His hand to you, it is best to be prepared. You *are* going to die. Whether you are fatally injured in an unforeseen accident or die in your bed of terminal illness or old age, the result is the same: death. If you are old enough to be aware that death is inevitable, you are old enough to prepare for its occurrence.

Neo-Pagans annually celebrate the magnificent rite of passage of death. On Samhain, October 31, when the veils between the worlds are thinnest, death's realities are acknowledged. Often symbolized by candle flames, the dead are reverenced; so too are the deities in whose arms they dance. As with all ritual, the participants have prepared themselves for sacred work. Their participation in the ceremony results in transformation.

You came into this world with your mother; you leave alone. Dying is the last act you will perform as a human being. Thoughtful preparation ensures that your death will be as meaningful as possible for you *and* for those for whom you care. Make the last thing you do be your final gift of love. Take responsibility for yourself and your belongings.

What to Do First

If you suddenly become gravely injured and/or unconscious, or if you have a terminal illness, what is done *to* and *for* you in the way of medical procedures may be beyond your control. Under such circumstances, you can be guaranteed the treatment *you* want only if you stipulate that treatment in advance, in documents that (1) state your wishes regarding your care and (2) empower others with the authority to make sure that your desires are carried out. These documents are a *living will* and a *health care proxy*, also known as a *durable power of attorney*.

Living Will

A *living will* is a legal document stating what you want to happen to your *person* BEFORE you die. (See Appendix C for an example of a living will.) It declares what is and is not to be done with you when you are unable to make decisions yourself about your physical and/or mental care. Generally the issues involved are (1) not to prolong your dying unreasonably, (2) to withhold or withdraw life-sustaining procedures if you have so designated, and (3) to limit your treatment to keeping you free from pain. A living will expresses your legal right to refuse health care treatment and releases those involved from liability. A living will *must* conform to the legal requirements of your state of residence. It must be witnessed and then signed by a notary public.

Health Care Proxy

A *health care proxy* or *durable power of attorney* is a legal document that gives another person(s) the legal authority to *insist* that your directions, as expressed in your living will, be carried out. It also releases health care providers from liability, if necessary. You might consider appointing more than one person to serve as "durable attorney," because making life/death decisions for someone can be very hard to do alone. (And if you appoint only your nearest/dearest, s/he may be with you in that hypothetical accident! Or out of town!) A health care proxy/durable power of attorney document *must* conform to the legal requirements of your state of residence, be witnessed by two people *not* named in the document, and signed by a notary public. (See Appendix D for an example.) Make sure that the person(s) you have selected to be your health care proxy/durable power of attorney has a copy of *both* your living will *and* the proxy. Give copies to your primary care physician and/or whatever medical specialists you may be working with for their records. If you have to stay in a hospital, even if only overnight, provide these documents. If you travel, especially out of the country, carry copies with you, just in case.

What to Do Next

Now that you have made arrangements for the care of your person while alive, what about the things you own? You do not want to go out of this world without taking care of your material obligations. Years ago you were taught to pick up your room, to put your things away. To leave a mess for others to attend to is unkind, to say the least; so prepare another legal document: your *last will and testament.*

Last Will and Testament

A *last will and testament* is a legal statement that expresses what you want done with your *possessions* AFTER you die. It should be drawn up by a lawyer, using legal language to record your instructions about the distribution of what you legally own: "your worldly goods" or "estate." It must be witnessed by two persons, not related to you and not mentioned in the will, who swear that you are "of sound mind" and not unduly influenced by anyone or -thing at the time you sign the will.

Be sure that copies of your last will and testament will be readily available at the time of your death. The lawyer who draws it up generally keeps the original. Do *not*, repeat, do NOT, put the only copy in a safe-deposit box. Such receptacles are "frozen" at the time of death, and you want your will to be "done" as soon as possible.

The person who carries out your legal wishes after you die is your *executor*. S/he takes care of your financial affairs and distributes your possessions to the persons you have designated.

After your death, your executor sees that your will and a copy of your death certificate (described below) go to your local probate court and are filed for probate. A probate judge must then rule that your will is valid according to the laws of the state in which it was written. (This process takes time.) The court then gives your executor (in "letters testamentary") the legal authority to list your assets, collect any debts owed you, pay your bills, distribute your cash money and material goods, and close the estate. Depending on which state your legal residence is in and how large your estate is, state and federal estate taxes may have to be paid before anyone else sees money. Usually your executor can distribute your personal items, such as clothes, books, etc., before the will is probated.

It is important to select your executor(s) carefully. Be sure to consult those whom you are considering appointing, to determine if they are willing to serve; sometimes age, infirmity, or other obligations would prevent them from assuming this responsibility. There is a fair amount of paperwork involved in even the simplest of estates, and coping with all the details regarding your literal "things," household bills, and so on is not an easy task. Sometimes it is more efficient to appoint two people: one to deal with the legal details, the other to cope with "hands-on" matters.

The more details you provide for those involved in the legal care and disposition of yourself and your possessions, the easier it will be for your wishes to be carried out. An easy way to determine your preferences about what you *really* want done with what you own—your body and your "stuff"—is to make lists.

Information About You

The following listing of personal information may seem exhaustive. However, even such fine points as your mother's birth name will be needed for either declarations made by you or documents generated after your death, such as your death certificate, death notice, and/or obituary (described below). So take a deep breath and record. You can edit later!

Your name (first, middle, last); sex; race; date of birth (month, day, year) and place of birth (city or town, state, and city/country if not the U.S.); citizenship; Social Security number. Your father's first, middle, and last names and your mother's first and birth names (along with death years if applicable), and names of stepparents if applicable. Your marital status (never married, handfast/married, divorced, widowed); name of present partner/spouse (birth name of wife); names of prior legal partners (and dates of death or divorce). Names and ages of children, including those deceased. Service in the U.S. Armed Forces? If yes, branch and war if applicable. Education: How long, where, what degrees in what subjects? Occupation: What kind of business or industry? Mailing address (street/RFD and number or P.O. box number, town or city, state, zip code); town or city of residence if different from mailing address.

While you are at this, what about your health insurance information? Where do you carry the cards, and where are the policies?

Information About Others

In this "cast list," one person can play multiple roles:

- *Health care proxy holder(s):* who they are and their addresses/phone numbers. Record the contact information for your lawyer and those you have selected as your executor(s).

- *Doctors:* their specialty as related to you (primary care physician, oncologist, etc.), their names, and their addresses/phone numbers.

- *Spiritual advisers:* the names and phone numbers of your High Priest/ess and those coven members, both locally and nationally, that you might wish to "work" with/for you. What are the deities, healing archetypes, angels, spiritual guides, and totem animals that you revere/resonate with and desire others to contact on your behalf?

- *Next of kin and blood relatives:* partner/spouse, children, parents, siblings. Where are they? (Even if you have no personal contact with one, some, or all of them, or if some/all are dead, this information is often needed for an obituary [described below].)

- *Dependents:* minor children, aged parents, and anyone else for whose physical/mental and/or financial well-being you are solely responsible. Appoint caregiver/guardian(s) to guarantee that they will be looked after the way you want. Confer with those selected so that you are sure they are willing and able to take on the responsibility.

- *Pets/familiars:* Who do you want to cherish your cat, canine, ferret, gerbil, snake, and/or plants? Do not abandon them to the "kindness of strangers." What will happen to your garden? Are there any cuttings/plants to go to others?

- *Extended family:* contact information for distant relatives and your "hundred most intimate friends." Where do you keep your address book?

- *Employees:* names, contact information, and the whereabouts of their records.

- *Business partner(s) and/or employer(s):* names and contact information.

- *Partners at the crossing:* names and contact information for those you would like to have with you while you die and those you hope will create and/or supervise your funeral arrangements.

Now you can decide *who* needs to know *what* about *whom!* Make sure your health care proxy holders have *all* the personal details about you listed above. They could be the people who are present at your death, and thus would supply the information for your death certificate. They also should have the contact information for your lawyer (just in case some legal muscle is needed in the line of duty), the names of those involved in your spiritual life, and details about how to get in touch with anyone else you wish to have notified in case of grave emergency or your death. (Do not forget your employer!)

Give your executor(s) the information about yourself, and the contacts for your relatives and others important to you. Make sure that s/he has your lawyer's address (and vice versa).

It is civil to inform your "kin" of the names of those you have appointed to take care of you and your affairs, if they are not the same people. (Civil, yes; necessary, no.) *If* yours is a situation where there might be the possibility of questions raised about your decisions, or attempts made to overrule your wishes, the more prepared your advocates are, the better. That means you must be as clear as you possibly can be, *in writing*, about your wishes.

Lists of Possessions

Compiling lists of your "worldly goods" will help you determine *what* you own, *where* it is, and *who* should get it after your death. When you have finished, you will have more information than you ever believed possible to help you prepare your last will and testament!

Do you have any money? Where is it? List the identification numbers of checking accounts, money market accounts, savings accounts, IRAs, certificates of deposit, savings bonds, stocks, and bonds, along with the names and addresses of the savings and loans, credit unions, or banks where these items are. (Don't forget the sock under the bed!) How about the account numbers of your credit cards? (Make sure your executor knows these; the cards should be canceled immediately after your death.)

Do you have a safe-deposit box in a bank or a lockbox/safe at home? Where is it, what is in it, and where is the key or combination? (Your safe-deposit box will be closed after your death until your will has been probated. Do *not* keep the only copy of your will, or anything else that would be needed immediately, in there.)

Are you the beneficiary of any retirement or pension plans? Do you have any life insurance policies? If so, what are the names and addresses of the beneficiaries? Will you be entitled to any death benefits from Social Security, the Veterans Administration, Social Services, labor and/or credit union(s), and/or fraternal order(s)? If so, list names, addresses, and details about when and how you were connected with the organization.

Do you have any "hidden" obligations, such as a loan from another person, a store charge, or a gambling debt? Put the list with your personal papers so that these obligations can be paid from your estate. Does anyone owe *you* money? Do you want to forgive that person's debt(s) in your will or have the monies claimed for your estate?

Do you, by yourself, own a house, an apartment, or any land, and where is it? Where are the deeds to the properties, surveys, mortgages, leases? To whom should this real estate be given, or should it be sold and the funds designated for a specific purpose or purposes? If you are a landlord, provide the names and addresses of your tenants. If you are a renter, provide the name and address of your landlord.

How about modes of transportation? Where are the titles, leases, licenses, and installment-payment books for your car, truck, motorcycle, RV, boat, airplane, balloon, hang glider? Do not forget your bike, scooter, and rollerblades! Whom do you want to have them?

And how about insurance policies? Homeowner's, automobile, fine arts, office equipment, etc.—list the policies and state where they are.

Do you have special family pieces or antiques (furniture, paintings, china, crystal, silver, jewelry) that you want to give to specific people? Describe these items and designate the recipient: e.g., *Aunt Mazie's 1865 hand-painted tea set for Sally Brown.*

What about your clothes (including all accessories, such as scarves, belts, shoes, purses, hats, jewelry, etc.)? Do you have a buddy (or several) who would enjoy them? Or do you have a favorite nonprofit outlet, such as the homeless shelter, local thrift shop, or Saturday flea market?

Your books, including zine collections, magazine subscriptions, records, cassettes, videos? To individuals, library or school, secondhand book shop?

Basic household goods: sheets, towels, pots, dishes, wastebaskets, beds, lamps, whatever—these can be designated to one or several persons so that recipients can select what they want. The rest of the stuff can be donated to a worthy cause of your determination, or an auction or "tag" sale can be held to benefit either your estate or a charitable organization.

Very personal papers—beribboned letters, scrapbooks, photo albums, journals. To whom should these be given? Should they be destroyed? If so, who should do it, and how?

Magical tools, library, robes, altar cloths—all those things you have "worked" with and regard as sacred—what do you want to happen to these items? List individual recipients, give outright to your coven, donate to the next national Pagan event auction, but whatever you do, make a decision. These items are "charged" and deserve respect. Honor yourself as well as them in their proper disposition.

Now make a separate list of every person (give the mundane names of Pagans) and/or organization you have referred to above, including addresses and telephone numbers. Your executor(s) will thank you on her/his knees.

Composing Your Will

First appoint your executor. Then take care of the people for whom you are responsible. Next distribute your financial assets. (If you own something such as a house or car in common with someone [meaning that both of your names are on the deed/title], s/he will still have title to it after you die. This applies to joint bank accounts also; you die and s/he still has the money. But unless you are legally married, the funds will be subject to inheritance tax.) Designate your cash bequests.

Assign your possessions. You may be descriptive, loving, and/or flowery: *I leave the green tent to Jack in memory of our trip to MerryMeet,* or *I leave my grandmother's cameo brooch to Mary with love and affection because she always admired her.* Last words from you will often have great meaning to the recipient.

You do not have to list *everything* you own in your will. You can leave possessions in a lump (contents of household, wardrobe, library) to your executor. Then you prepare a letter to her/him that catalogues which items in the batches go to whom. (This keeps the will itself from becoming unwieldy and expensive. Lawyers charge by the hour.) In the letter to your executor, as in your will, you may be affectionate or mention those shared experiences of which the designated item is the memento.

At the same time you are working on this letter to your executor, you need to designate someone to "housekeep" the after-death details, such as cleaning your closets, sorting your books, taking out your trash, coping with your pets/plants, watering your garden. Sometimes it is best to assign these tasks to someone other than your executor, because of her/his travel complications, job/family obligations, or age. Make a note or "show and tell" this person where things are, what the cat's dietary program is, which plants need water when.

> *Caution:* You *can* create a *holographic will*—one written entirely *by your hand in ink*—that gives directions for the disposition of your property and names an executor. It must be signed and dated. This is not recommended, but it is better than doing nothing. To do nothing is not only irresponsible, it violates the Wiccan Rede—"Do what you will and harm none"—by thoughtlessness. It is *your* body and *your* "stuff"; *you* take care of them.

The Dying Process

Given your druthers, where do you want to die: home, hospital, hospice, hillside? If at home, where in the house? On/in your bed/resting place, do you want special sheets, blankets, quilts, bed companions (such as live creatures, dolls, or stuffed animals), charms, talismans, amulets?

Do you want anyone with you? If so, who? Is there anyone you want to have telephoned or e-mailed? Who do you *not* want to be present? This is your *last* sacred event and you should not have to put up with the presence of anyone you do not want to be there. A "dragon/guardian" can be appointed to run interference for you by *tactfully* screening phone calls and turning away folks at the door. Those rejected will get over it. However, when you know your death is imminent, if you have some lingering unfinished business with someone, you might want to clear it up. (Your choice.)

What are the concepts of death as taught/indicated by your faith tradition? Do you agree with them? If not, what are *your* ideas about death? Is it personified? If so, by what deities?

What happens when you die? Does that which is *you* continue, and if so in what form? Do you/it go somewhere? What time of year is it there? What do the geography/buildings, if any, look like? What happens? Are there any animals, people, or deities, and what is your interaction with them? Can you/will you return to this world in any form at any time?

If you want ceremony *before* and while you are passing, plan it with your spiritual advisers, coven, support group, and special friends. Create visualizations and/or trance journeys. What about something special to eat/drink? Champagne, whiskey, caviar, Oreos. Smells such as incense, sage, flowers. Videos, music, readings, a death chant/song/spell to be repeated by yourself and by others for you.

Death Itself

The essence of *you* has departed; your body remains. Should quiet time, blessing, and ceremony take place before your body's removal from the place of death? If so, this event must be clearly defined by your caregivers. If you plan to die in a hospice/hospital, those in authority must be informed about your wishes and know who is going to participate in their execution. If you choose to die at home, make sure that those in the house at your death know not to call 911 or other authorities until the special time is complete. (If 911 *is* contacted, those who respond may be legally obligated to perform resuscitation procedures upon the body.)

Do you want your body washed and laid out by friends, family? Do you want your glasses and/or your teeth to go with it? How do you want your body dressed? Skyclad, nightclothes, evening dress, ceremonial robes? How about you and/or your circle designing and making the garment, shroud, or winding sheet?

Do you want anything put over/with your body? A favorite pillow, a quilt made by you and/or friends, flowers, objects that you designate, items/notes that your family/friends want to send with your remains?

What do you want your remains to be put in? Your body *has* to go into something just for transportation purposes. Body bag, cardboard box, plain pine box, handmade or commercial casket/coffin? (A casket is a rectangular box; a coffin is a tapered, hexagonal box—the familiar home of the "Halloween vampire.") How about personally making your own container or fashioning it as a group project?

Death Documents

When you die, your *death certificate* is written up. This is the official document that declares you dead. (Without it your executor cannot get your will probated or obtain any Social Security, Veterans Administration, or life insurance benefits that your survivors might be entitled to. S/he will need at least five *certified* copies, for which there is a charge.) Generally a death certificate gives information about the *decedent* (you), and it utilizes a lot of the personal material you compiled above. It gives the *disposition* of your body (cremation or burial), the statement of the *certifier* (the person who records the time, date, and place of death; if the certifier is *not* the attending physician, her/his signature must be recorded as well), and the signature of the *registrar of deaths* (housed in the town, city, or county clerk's office or Public Health Department in the municipality of the place of death). The death certificate also states the *cause of death:* (1) the immediate cause—e.g., due to, or as a consequence of, a terminal illness—and (2) the details if you were injured in an accident. Usually the death certificate is picked up from the attending physician or the hospice or hospital personnel by a funeral director and taken around to the relevant governmental offices. These local authorities issue a *burial-transit permit* or *certificate of disposition of remains,* which is an authorization to dispose of the body and notes when/where the disposition will take place.

Often the burial-transit permit/certificate of disposition of remains is printed on the bottom of the death certificate. Your name, sex, date of death, race, age, and place of death (city/town, state) are stated. The choice of burial, cremation, removal; cemetery or crematory and location; and funeral director/funeral home and address are given. This permit/certificate must be signed by the attending physician, who (along with certifying natural death) grants permission "to dispose of this body." (The administrative details pertinent to "unnatural" death and its complications are beyond the scope of this chapter.) Next comes the date of the "authorized disposition," and if burial is in a cemetery, the location of the tomb or grave, lot number, and signature of the sexton (if a Christian facility) or person in charge of the cemetery. After the details of the disposition are noted, the permit/certificate must be filed with the appropriate authorities.

Disposition Decisions

Without a burial permit your body *cannot* be transported to its final resting place, nor can it rest in peace. Both it and the death certificate require the names of those who are moving the body and overseeing its disposition.

Therefore, you need to decide a few things:

- Who is going to oversee and/or carry out the disposition of your remains: friends or professionals?

- Do you want your body burned or buried?

- If you opt for burial, where do you have in mind?

- If there is to be a ceremony, where will it take place, and do you want your body there?

Someone has to be chosen to interact with the civic authorities, as indicated above. Funeral directors, as part of their services, often take on that task; they are familiar with all the required paper-shuffling and schlepping involved. A visit to local funeral homes to check out what is offered can be very helpful. Ask your friends what establishments they might recommend and what their experiences have been with them.

In the United States today there are two ways to dispose of a body: cremation and burial. Funeral directors generally offer four rock-bottom procedures: (1) *immediate cremation,* (2) *cremation after viewing,* (3) *immediate burial,* and (4) *burial after viewing.* In all of the above, the professionals remove the body from the local place of death, procure the necessary authorizations and permits, provide a minimum container, and convey the body to the crematory or cemetery. In cases of cremation and burial after viewing, preparation of the body for viewing (embalming/makeup) and use of the funeral home facility/chapel for one day are included in the overall cost. The crematory fees are included in the funeral home's charges; the cemetery fees are billed separately.

If you do not want to use funeral home facilities, make sure that research into the legal requirements pertaining to your choice of body disposition is done well in advance of your death. In order to eliminate unnecessary stress for those responsible for carrying out the procedures, make sure that they are familiar with all the regulations. Theirs is a complex assignment.

Cremation

If you decide to have your body cremated, there is no need for an elaborate container. A plywood box or even cardboard casket is sufficient. Heavy cardboard containers are available from mortuaries; they are used for shipping, paupers' funerals, and cremations. They are *not* displayed on the floor with even the cheapest of caskets, however; you have to ask for them.

Do you want your body to travel in a vehicle other than a funeral home coach (the modern name for a hearse), such as a station wagon, pickup, or van? Do you want anyone personally known to you to accompany your body to the crematory? If so, who; and do you want that person to do any ritual while there?

When your body is burned, the crematory returns your "cremains" (ashes)—in an inconspicuous, sealed, labeled paper bag, cardboard box, or tin—to the funeral home or your designated recipient. Whether the cremains will be buried, scattered, or put on the closet shelf, there are several receptacle choices. The cremains can remain in the crematory container; be moved to a commercial container of wood or metal (often called an *urn*), which can be purchased at a funeral home; or put in a small box (or boxes) of your own choosing—perhaps something you can collect, design, or commission.

Usually there are no legal regulations regarding the scattering of ashes. Cremains are not feathery ash, but are a mixture of very small bone "clinkers" or shards. If they are released from an airplane or boat, someone needs to make sure they are not tossed directly into the wind! This material is completely sterile, having been incinerated at a very high temperature, so digging the ashes into the garden, casting them into a stream, or strewing them along a path are all acceptable procedures. If consumed, they are crunchy and do not dissolve.

Burial

If you wish your remains to be buried, research the regulations that govern *where* you want your body interred. Your township or county probably has specific laws pertaining to burials *not* in an established cemetery. Begin your research by asking your town/city clerk for the local regulations.

If you want to buy a cemetery plot, already own one, or have a share in a family plot, that cemetery will have its own rules. Some cemeteries require concrete grave liners in addition to a casket, to prevent new graves from sinking. (Depressions interfere with contemporary methods of landscape maintenance.) In very high-water-table locations, burial in an above-ground tomb is mandated. Cemeteries have charges for digging graves or opening old ones and for ongoing maintenance.

What is your preference for time of day for burial? Do you want a ceremony to be held at the graveside? Who should lead, who participate? What should happen?

The Ceremony

A ritual held after death and before cremation or burial of the body is called a *celebration, rite of passage,* or *funeral service.* One held at the cemetery is called a *graveside service.* When the ceremony takes place after the disposition of the body, it is called a *memorial service.* When you are deciding what sort of ceremony you would prefer, take into consideration the distance attendees will have to travel. If it would be impossible for someone important to you to be present at a preburial event, a memorial service could take place several weeks after your death (either in addition to or instead of the preburial event).

Do you want people (other than those present when, or *very* soon after, you die) to be able to visit, view, or attend a ceremony featuring your body in an open container before it goes to disposition? If such an occasion is your wish, your body will have to be *embalmed,* a procedure done by professionals.

Tissue disintegrates rapidly when no longer animated. The body's fluids leak, its cavities fill with gas, and its overall appearance is transmogrified. The embalming process removes the body's fluids and replaces them with disinfectant and preservative chemicals.

Generally cosmetics are applied on the face and hands, to give a resemblance to living color. This can be done by friends or family members (who may also dress your body in preparation for the viewing) or by the funeral home at the time of embalming. If you set aside a photograph taken on a "good hair day" and/or note what kinds of makeup you typically use, this information can serve as a guide. Your teeth will be inserted. Do you want your glasses on your nose or in your hands? Do you want your stubble to be shaved?

(Those handling your arrangements are not locked into using a funeral home's other services—chapel, announcements, programs, cremation services, coffins or caskets —just because professionals have embalmed your body. Make sure your representatives understand that they are the customers, the morticians the providers; the funeral home directors are there to satisfy those who purchase their services.)

If you wish a formal occasion, decide on the details now. Where? In a church, in a park or garden, at a beach, at someone's home? What time of day? Who will officiate? What will be the ritual's components, and in what order will they fall? Will the attendees be invited to speak and/or participate in any way? If yours is an open-casket ceremony, do you want people to have the opportunity to put items with your body? What props? Music, flowers, a special altar with photographs and personal items/tools?

Do you want those present to receive a memento, such as a program giving the order of service (but designed as a keepsake, perhaps containing a poem, a short quote with a photograph, biographical sketch, etc.)? If so, select the photograph, quote, and other material now. Do you want the memento sent to those who cannot be present—perhaps all those on your Solstice card list?

If you anticipate that your survivors may orchestrate events in a way not to your liking (perhaps conducting a religious ceremony in a faith tradition not your own or burying your body in a place not of your selection), be sure to record your wishes; often compromises can be worked out between those holding differing viewpoints. An occasion can be publicly arranged by and for others, for example, and then a ceremony held to honor you by "yours" at another time in an appropriate venue. Most people, however, are pleased and relieved to fulfill the wishes of the deceased.

Marker and Memorial

If your body is buried, do you want a stone, plantings, statuary? Do you want anything inscribed on the marker other than full name and dates of birth and death? Some people mention their relationship to others (daughter of _____, father of _____, and so on, as in family cemetery plots), their profession, their military affiliation/rank, or their fraternal order membership. How about any other statement? Sketch out ideas for your epitaph *now*.

Do you want any gifts given in your name to favorite causes? List them. Do you want anything created to memorialize you, such as the founding of a scholarship or an award for artistic, academic, or athletic achievement? How about a costume prize at the annual "tea dance" or Samhain ball, or a fund to supply liturgical tools or defray travel or attendance costs at festivals for those of your faith tradition?

Death Notice and Obituary

Someone familiar with the details of your disposition (or a representative at the selected funeral home) inserts a brief *death notice* into the local newspaper(s). Usually this is printed for no charge, though sometimes there is a fee by word or line. The death notice gives your name, your date and place of death, and your relationship to family members still living (beloved husband of _____, devoted grandmother of _____, adored brother of _____). These familial connections can go as far as cousins. If there is a viewing, its date, time, and location, along with the date, time, and place for the preburial ceremony or memorial service (if any), are listed.

The *obituary* is a longer news article that gives details of your life and accomplishments. It can appear in your local newspaper, your alumni magazine, your professional journal(s), and the Pagan press. Keep these publications in mind when you prepare your material. If *you* record the pertinent details about yourself, rather than the obit writers having to rely on the perhaps faulty memory or just plain ignorance of family members and friends, those writers will be *very* grateful!

An obituary begins with your name, age, date/time of death, place of death, cause of death, and length of illness if applicable. You should also provide the date and place of your birth, your father's full name, your mother's first name and her birth name, those (including stepparents) who are surviving, and their address(es) if relevant.

You may also choose to include your place of residence while growing up; other residences and important dates throughout your life; details about your education (schools and colleges attended, degrees earned, including honorary degrees); career/professional information, including dates and places of employment; local/national civic, academic, religious, or governmental positions held; activities and recognitions/ awards; lifelong interests, hobbies, and passions; and military service (including any awards or honors).

Typically considerable family information is also included. You will want to mention marriage(s), specifying when and to whom and naming the present partner/spouse. If any partners are deceased, give their date(s) of death. The following should also be provided: names and addresses of surviving children (and the ages of minors), names of deceased children, number and names of surviving grandchildren and great-grandchildren, and names and addresses of surviving siblings.

The obituary will also mention the time, date, and place of service (name/address of church/hall/home if relevant), the name of the person officiating, and other events to be held (such as a subsequent memorial service). It will state the disposition of the body (cremation or burial), giving cemetery name and location, and list suggested memorial contributions.

The actual utilization of the above varies. However, if *you* compile the information, *you* can control the obituary contents. Anything you are reluctant to have stated about you, omit. Emphasize what you want to be remembered for, what you feel are your important accomplishments. You can even *lie,* stating something that is almost true or you wish were true. If you do that, however, be sure that your untruth does not affect the realities of others: saying you got a Ph.D. when you did not is okay, but claiming a different birthplace than reality affects your mother's history. Just remember the Rede: "[Say] what you will *and harm none."*

Now you are prepared for your dance in Death's arms. Your mundane matters are taken care of, your worldly responsibilities fulfilled. From this time on, may your life hold joy and may your death be serene.

Appendix A

How to Make a Mask

KATE SLATER

You will need two rolls of plaster gauze (three yards by three inches wide) from an art or surgical supply store for a simple full mask (more if you plan large additions), one and a half rolls for a half mask. You will also need scissors, Vaseline, plastic wrap, a plastic drop cloth, a cloth strip two inches by thirty inches, newspaper, a pan of lukewarm water, and paper and cloth towels. For finishing: an artist's knife or nail scissors, leftover gauze, acrylic paints, one one-inch and two small brushes, white glue, tacky glue, and trim of fur, moss, leaves, bones, jewels, ribbons—whatever fits your image.

Casting the mask will take up to ninety minutes, including cleanup. Painting and modifying the shape will take several more hours. Prepare by cutting the gauze into three-inch by one-inch strips (over paper to catch the dust). Keep these dry until the moment of use. Do not plug drains with plaster-laden water.

This is not a one-person job: it calls for a model and at least one helper. Plan the mask together, make sketches, and prepare any extensions to be incorporated into the mask base (such as a beak cut from a file folder). Some of these details can be decided on later. To shape an open mouth, the model can hold a small cardboard form between her teeth. Plaster sets like cement, so participants should wear old clothes. Read each other's instructions before starting out.

The Model's Job. You must not have sore places on your face. You might protect a small pimple by adhering plastic wrap to it with salve, but anything more sensitive forbids this type of mask-making. You must be able to tolerate lying silent and having your face covered (although your nostrils will be free) for about forty-five minutes while a friend touches your face.

Prepare by lightly coating your face with Vaseline up into the hair roots and tying your hair back. Your helper will help you lie down with your head on a towel-covered plastic sheet and give you a towel so you can wipe away any water that trickles down your neck and ears. Folded towels under your back or knees can make you more comfortable. Play your favorite music. Your helper will describe her progress and frequently ask how you are, watching for hand-signal answers. When your mask is completed and drying, she will wait with you so you will not feel deserted.

Plaster sets very quickly, becoming slightly (and tolerably) warm. Ten or fifteen minutes after the mask is completed, you can remove it. Tap it, and when it seems solid, flex your facial muscles and begin wiggling the edges loose, rocking it away from your forehead and down past your chin. Once free from the mask, you will probably want a shower before admiring the work.

The Helper's Job. Arrange a warm, quiet place for the model to lie, well shielded from plaster drippings. Make her comfortable. Spread a piece of plastic wrap from her cheekbones up over her hair, smoothing it over her forehead and tucking it gently into the hollow of her eyes. Place the piece of cloth above her brows so it extends out on each side. This will reinforce the mask and make simple ties that she can replace more neatly later. Cover her face with three layers of gauze, extending from her hairline (or above it) and curving down to a quarter-inch under her chin. Leave her nostrils free.

Now drop up to four gauze strips at a time into the water. Pick one out and either let it drip onto the newspaper or set it on the newspaper for a moment to drain. Warn your model that you are starting before placing the first strip on her face. Throw away twisted strips. Build quickly, overlapping the strips by a third and smoothing their plaster with your fingers. Make a ring around the outside of her face and fill in with vertical strips, carefully forming them around her features. Keep the mask edges solid. Do not drip water onto the dry strips because they will harden almost immediately. (A second helper can assist with dipping and draining the strips or with building one side of the mask.)

Build the next layer horizontally so you can see where you have been, working as quickly as you can. Then add any special effects by molding gauze or building in cardboard extensions. Finish the third layer with curves and diagonals, which are less noticeable. Hide or trim loose threads and smooth everything as you go. Be sure the nose and mask edges are solid. If you have worked quickly, go on to cover extensions with strips. If you have been slow and your model is tiring, do this after she takes the mask off. Now wipe off your hands, make your model comfortable, and wait with her for the mask to set.

After the mask is off, remove embedded plastic wrap and support the mask inside with crumpled paper towels. Let the mask dry several hours or overnight.

Finishing. Now the model/owner can take over. Hold your mask up to the light and reinforce any thin spots by adding gauze inside. Try it on; study it. Sketch on it with pencil. Support it inside and cut eye-holes with the artist's knife, starting small and trying the mask on to check eye placement as you go. You can cut the mask smaller if that is the look you desire—even down to a half mask. Pierce holes for string ties if you wish. Wherever you cut, paint the edge with white glue to keep it from crumbling and reinforce the edge with bits of gauze. Add any extensions, building them in with gauze, and let these dry. If the surface seems too rough, you can sand it, but consider *using* this roughness, adding more texture as you work. Now coat the mask with a layer of base color. Wash your brushes promptly in water. Keep trying the mask on. Finish painting, letting it dry between layers, and spray with varnish if you wish. Attach trim with tacky glue. Finish when your mask tells you it is done.

Appendix B

Books on Death and Dying for Adults and Children

BOOKS FOR ADULTS
Deborah Ann Light

Concern for Dying. *The Living Will and Other Advance Directives: A Legal Guide to Medical Treatment Decisions.* New York: Concern for Dying, 1986.

Iserson, Kenneth V., M.D. *Death to Dust: What Happens to Dead Bodies?* Tucson, AZ: Galen Press, 1987.

Jones, Constance. *R.I.P.: The Complete Book of Death and Dying.* New York: HarperCollins/Stonesong Press, 1997.

Morgan, Ernest. *Dealing Creatively with Death: A Manual of Death Education and Simple Burial.* Bayside, NY: Barclay House, 1990.

Nuland, Sherwin B. *How We Die: Reflections on Life's Final Chapter.* New York: Knopf, 1994.

Simos, Bertha. *A Time to Grieve: Loss as Universal Human Experience.* New York: Family Service Association, 1979.

Simpson, Michael A. *The Facts of Death: A Complete Guide for Being Prepared.* Englewood Cliffs, NJ: Prentice-Hall, 1979.

BOOKS FOR CHILDREN
Elsa DieLöwin

For ages two and up. *The Witch Who Lost Her Shadow*, by Mary Calhoun, illustrated by Trina Hakes. New York: Harper & Row, 1979. Shadow, the Witch's cat, disappears rather than specifically dying.

For ages three and up. *The Velveteen Rabbit*, by Margery Williams, illustrated by William Nicholson. New York: Doubleday, 1960. Magic, love, and reincarnation.

For ages three and up. *The Tenth Good Thing About Barney*, by Judith Viorst, illustrated by Erik Blegvad. New York: Atheneum, 1987. The tenth good thing about a cat named Barney is that he "is in the ground and he's helping grow flowers."

For ages five and up. *Annie and the Old One*, by Miska Miles, illustrated by Peter Parnall. Boston: Little, Brown, 1971. A Navajo girl unravels a day's weaving on a rug whose completion, she believes, will mean the death of her grandmother.

For ages five and up. *My Grandmother's Cookie Jar*, by Montzalee Miller, illustrated by Katherine Potter. Los Angeles: Price/Stern/Sloan, 1987. Grandma passes on the stories of her Indian people to her grandchild as they eat cookies.

Aimed for about ages five to eight. *I Had a Friend Named Peter: Talking to Children About the Death of a Friend*, by Janice Cohn, illustrated by Gail Owens. New York: William Morrow, 1987. This book is in two sections—one for adults, explaining children's grieving processes, and the other (in the form of a story) for children. It takes an atheistic view that bothers me, especially where the father says, "Wishing or thinking things can never make them happen." When reading aloud, I modify this section or use it as a basis for discussion about how magic works.

For ages seven and up. *The Little Prince*, by Antoine de Saint-Exupery, translated by Katherine Woods. New York: Harcourt Brace & World, 1943. This is the book that kept me alive after my best friend died when we were fourteen.

For ages seven and up. *To Hell with Dying*, by Alice Walker, illustrated by Catherine Deeter. San Diego: Harcourt Brace Jovanovich, 1988. Better read the first time before it is really needed. Mr.

Sweet can always be revived by the loving attention of his neighboring children, including Alice. Finally, when Alice is twenty-four, she visits him and he dies peacefully.

For ages nine and up. *The Secret Garden,* by Frances Hodgson Burnett, illustrated by Tasha Tudor. New York: Lippincott, 1962. Ten-year-old Mary comes to live in a lonely house on the Yorkshire moors and discovers an invalid cousin (with strong fears about dying) and the mysteries of a locked garden.

For ages ten and up. *Bridge to Terabithia,* by Katherine Paterson, illustrated by Donna Diamond. New York: Harper Trophy, 1977. A ten-year-old boy in rural Virginia deals with the feelings raised when his friend meets an untimely death trying to reach their hideaway, Terabithia, during a storm.

For ages two and up. *Cats' Eyes,* by Anthony Taber, Thomas Congdon Books, E. P. Dutton, 1978. The life and death of a cat named Tiger. Beautifully drawn, humorous, and sweet.

Appendix C

Example of a Living Will Declaration

I, _____, residing at _____, in the
county of _____ and state of _____,
being of sound mind, make this statement as a directive to be followed
by my physicians, family, and friends, and by all other persons who
may come to have responsibility for my care.

If the time comes when I am incapacitated to the point that I can
no longer actively take part in decisions for my own life and am unable
to direct my physicians as to my own medical care, I wish this statement to stand as a testament of my wishes. Although at the time of my
execution of this declaration I know that certain states may not recognize such instructions as being legally binding upon those offering
me care, I, _____, request that I be allowed to die
and not be kept alive through life-support systems if my condition is
deemed terminal. I do not intend any direct taking of my life, only that
my dying not be unreasonably prolonged. This directive is made after
careful reflection, while I am of sound mind.

In the event that I should have an illness, disease, or injury, or
experience extreme mental deterioration, such that there is no reasonable expectation of recovering or regaining a meaningful quality of
life, I direct that all life-sustaining procedures should be withheld or
withdrawn. These life-sustaining procedures to be withheld or with-

drawn include, but are not limited to, cardiac resuscitation, respiratory support, surgery, chemotherapy and/or radiation, antibiotics, and artificially administered feeding and fluids. I further direct that treatment be limited to comfort measures and measures intended to relieve pain only, including any pain that might occur by withholding or withdrawing treatment, even if such measures should shorten the term of my life.

These directions express my legal right to refuse treatment. Therefore, I expect my family, physicians, and all those concerned with my care to regard themselves as legally and morally bound to act in accordance with my wishes, and in so doing to be free from any liability for having followed my directions.

In witness whereof I have set my hand on _____ (date).

_____ (signature)

Example of a Health Care Proxy/Durable Power of Attorney

I, _____, residing at _____, in the county of _____ and state of _____, do hereby appoint _____ residing at _____ (and/or _____ residing at _____, and/or _____ residing at _____), as my attorney(s) and agent(s) to make decisions for my health care, including the consent, refusal of consent, or withdrawal of consent to any care, treatment, service, or procedure intended to maintain, diagnose, or treat my physical or mental condition.

My agent(s) shall have authority to inspect and disclose any information relating to my physical or mental health, and is (are) authorized to sign any documents, waivers, or releases necessary for such purposes, including any releases from liability which might be required by a health care provider as a condition of providing or of ceasing to provide any treatment or other services.

This power of attorney shall not be affected by my subsequent disability or incapacity, and the authority granted herein shall continue during such period of disability or incapacity.

In witness whereof I have set my hand on _____ (date).

_____ (signature)

Glossary

This glossary offers a list of words used in this book defined as they would generally be used and understood within the Reclaiming tradition; variations on and additions to these meanings may be found in the lexicon of other Witches and Pagans.

ASPURGE, v.: To purify ritually by sprinkling with salt water. Often this is done by dipping a fragrant branch, such as rosemary, into the water and sprinkling it over the participant in a ritual.

ATHAME (pronounced ah-*thah*-may), n.: A blade or knife used as a ritual tool—usually a knife with two sharp edges; a tool associated with the East, symbolizing and enhancing the power to choose, to analyze, to define, to separate one thing from another. When a Witch chooses not to use a blade because, for example, of its association with weaponry, she or he may substitute a feather, a bone, or a like object.

BELOVED DEAD, n.: People who were known and loved by us when they were alive, and who have crossed over.

CAST, v.: To "cast the circle" is to define the boundaries of the sacred space, usually a circle in which a ritual is about to take place. One member of the group walks the boundary of the circle in a clockwise direction, beginning either in the North or in the East. Using an athame she or he "draws" a pentacle in each of the four cardinal directions and makes a line connecting them, ending at the same point where she or he began, and then walks to the center of the circle and points the athame first toward the sky and then toward the ground. All participants remain attentive and focused, using their psychic vision and imagination to aid this process of encircling the space with a magical cord (or circle of light) on the psychic plane. When the circle is cast, the participants are said to be "between the worlds" and the ritual begins. See also CIRCLE, CUT, and OPEN.

CAULDRON, n.: A pot, often of cast iron and with three or four legs, a handle, and a lid, used in various ways for magical work and rituals. In essence a cooking pot, it is a tool for transformation and a tool of the Spirit or Center.

CENSE, v.: To purify using incense or the smoke of a smudge stick, which is a tightly rolled bundle of dried sage and is a purification tool borrowed from the practice of Native Americans. See also ASPURGE.

CHAKRA, n.: From Hindu beliefs, one of seven centers of psychic energy located along the spine, which can be "opened" through certain physical movements and psychic/mental/spiritual techniques so that the energy can be released and utilized. See the meditation on page 28.

CIRCLE: 1. n. Sacred space in which a ritual or any kind of magical work is done, either by an individual or by a group. Often people stand together in a literal circle to begin a ritual, but during the ritual they may move about in any configuration (and are still said to be "in circle"). 2. n. A concept fundamental to the thealogy of modern Witchcraft, generally referring to the endless cycle of life, death, and rebirth and to the interconnectedness of everything in the universe—thus a sacred symbol. 3. n. Synonym for *coven*. 4. v. To join with others in sacred space.

COVEN, n.: An autonomous group of Witches who meet together regularly to do magic. It is believed that traditionally a coven had thirteen members and met under the full moon. Today the coven may be any size, and members may be women or men. In some traditions there are accepted rules concerning qualification for leadership and membership in a coven. In the Reclaiming tradition covens set their own rules. Often coveners become very close and consider each other family.

CUP, n.: The tool of the West, used to hold salt water, water, or any drink used in a ritual. In some traditions the cup is symbolic of the female. It may be a goblet, chalice, bowl, or other vessel capable of holding liquid.

CUT, n.: 1. Synonym for *cast*. 2. After a circle has been cast or cut, people who must leave (or enter) the circle "cut" themselves out of (or into) the circle, carefully opening a space to pass through and closing it after they have crossed the boundary. This can be done by passing through a "door" (as in a tent), parting curtains, or miming cutting out a door shape. This prevents a "tear" in the circle boundary that would disrupt the focus and dissipate the energy of the circle; furthermore, it is respectful. Circles are permeable, however, to animals and young children, who need not cut the circle to enter or leave.

DEATH, n.: The state of existence that occurs after life—as it is commonly defined according to the definitions of Western biology—ends. Death is understood as part of the circle. Many Witches believe that the "dead" continue to exist on another plane and that it is possible to contact them, especially at Samhain, through a psychic connection. We are all aware of our connections with our ancestors and of the fact that, in some sense, we live on in our descendants. We sing "What is remembered, lives." See also REINCARNATION and the Introduction.

DEITY, n.: Most modern Witches believe in a pantheon of gods and goddesses who are associated with many religious traditions around the world, both modern and ancient. Most commonly, Witches call on the deities of Celtic, Greek, and Roman cultures, but many also use the names of Egyptian, African, Scandinavian, Native American, Chinese, and Indian gods and goddesses.

DIRECTIONS, n.: East, South, West, North (also known as the quarters), and Center. Each direction has an element and particular powers and qualities associated with it; see also ELEMENTS. (The direction "Center" is the center point of the circle.)

DIVINATION, n.: The practice of gaining insight or foretelling the future through magical techniques, such as reading Tarot cards, scrying, reading tea leaves, and so on.

ELEMENTS, n.: 1. The four substances (air, fire, water, and earth) necessary to the creation and sustenance of life. Each element is associated with one of the four directions, a particular tool, certain qualities and powers that exist in the outer, physical world and within each person, and certain colors, life-forms, and natural phenomena. See also SPIRIT.

Air: East; athame; the powers of the mind—the ability to analyze and understand, to breathe, smell, hear; the qualities of the wind—freshness, dawn light, sudden insight, rational thought, perspective; white and pale shades of yellow and pink; birds, insects.

Fire: South; wand; the powers of passion and will—the ability to act effectively, to destroy, purify, change; the qualities of the flame—heat, anger, aggression, affection, sexual desire; red, orange, gold, deep yellow; snakes, scorpions, fire ants, sparkles, the sun, the God.

Water: West; cup; the powers of intuition and emotion—the ability to dream, love, grieve, cleanse, heal, refresh; the qualities of fluid—mutability, purity, depth; blue, turquoise, purple, silver; fish, cetacea, crustacea, waterbirds; shells, seaweed, blood, tears, sweat, the moon.

Earth: North; pentacle; the powers of the body—the ability to create, nurture, nourish, sustain, destroy, heal; the qualities of the planet—strength, endurance, fertility, sustenance, sensuality, abundance, diversity; mountains, rocks, trees, caves; all animals and life-forms, especially bears, deer, cows; the God; fruits and grains, birth and death, the Mother, the Goddess.

GROUND, v.: To consciously become connected to the energy of the earth, usually through a meditation. Grounding is considered essential to the ability to focus and do magical work and to preventing psychic distress.

GOD, n.: 1. All that is born, grows, and dies—that is, all animal and plant life. Sometimes the sun is considered to be the God, because every year it grows bright in summer, fades, dies, and is reborn. The qualities of the God are those of plants (such as growth, vitality, reaching maturity, rising, and falling) and animals (such as wildness, freedom, vulnerability, innocence, ecstasy in nature). 2. A particular deity from any of many religious traditions, ancient and modern. See also DEITY.

GODDESS, n.: 1. The earth, also called the Mother and the Great Goddess, because the earth is literally the source of life, and when people die their bodies return to the earth. Through the earth—the Goddess—people are connected to the mystery and beauty of the cosmos, and Witches consider Her sacred, to be cherished, and worth dedicating their lives to protecting. Qualities of the Goddess are those associated with the earth, such as endurance, fertility, abundance, sustenance, compassion, creativity (birth), destruction (decay), and rebirth. 2. A particular deity from any of many religious traditions and cultures, ancient and modern.

INVOKE, v.: To call a spirit or deity into the circle. A deity is (or deities are) usually invoked to witness and assist magical work, and to empower those who are working the magic, so generally a Witch chooses a deity known for particular powers or qualities.

MIGHTY DEAD, n.: Those who have died and who are widely acknowledged as great priestesses, priests, and/or teachers of the Craft.

OPEN, v. ("to open the circle"): At the end of a ritual, the participants thank all the deities who were invoked, and then all the spirits of the directions, this time going in a counterclockwise direction, inviting them to leave or to stay. Often whoever invoked the directions or deities also thanks and dismisses them and ritually takes down the circle so that it is erased, dissolved, unwrapped.

PENTACLE, n.: Five-pointed star figure, with one point at the top, enclosed in a circle. This tool of the North is used to achieve psychic balance and to enable people to experience various connected energies in a concentrated way. Each of the points is associated with particular powers and qualities. See the essay and meditation on page 110.

PURIFY, v.: To cleanse spiritually and mentally, getting rid especially of any thoughts or feelings that might interfere with participation in the ritual or the ability to focus and do magical work. See ASPURGE, CENSE.

REINCARNATION, n.: Most Witches believe in some kind of reincarnation or rebirth—either in the sense that we all get recycled because everything comes from the earth and our bodies go back into the earth when we die, or in the sense that our individual identity, our spirit, becomes connected to a new person or life-form. See also the Introduction.

RITUAL, n.: An occasion when an individual or a group uses traditional practices in order to focus energy for an identified purpose, such as healing, transformation, empowerment, protection, or celebration. See the sections headed "Ritual Basics" and "Personal Practices of Pagans" in Chapter 2.

SAMHAIN, n. (pronounced *sow*-win [first syllable rhymes with *cow*): October 31 holiday, also known as Halloween. Midway between Fall Equinox and Winter Solstice, this is a major holiday when people honor their ancestors and we contact the spirits of the dead. It is sometimes called the Witches' New Year. See WHEEL OF THE YEAR and the discussion in Chapter 2 (page 16).

SPIRIT, n.: The Spirit is the center of the circle: it is life, which is created by the elements of air, fire, water, and earth; indeed, some Witches consider Spirit itself to be an element.

TAROT, n.: A set of seventy-eight cards with five suits and symbolic pictures, used for divination. There are many different versions and most have a guidebook. Tarot cards are historical precursors to modern playing cards, known to have existed in Europe as early as the fifteenth century.

TOOLS, n.: Objects used for magical purposes. There are particular tools associated with each of the five directions. See also ELEMENTS.

QUARTERS, n.: See DIRECTIONS.

WAND, n.: The tool of the South, usually handcrafted by its owner (and sometimes carved and/or embellished with crystals, feathers, or other objects of significance to that person), consisting of a rod or stick from a few inches long to an arm's length. Used to direct energy.

WHEEL OF THE YEAR, n. The cycle of the seasons. There are eight major holidays, traditionally called "sabbats," celebrating the seasons. A holiday runs from sundown to sundown, so often people celebrate on the "eve."

October 31, Samhain (pronounced *sow*-win [first syllable rhymes with *cow*)—also known as Halloween. Between Fall Equinox and Winter Solstice, this is the major Pagan holiday, a time to honor ancestors and to contact the spirits of the dead. Sometimes called the Witches' New Year, it marks the beginning of the dark half of the solar year. Compare *May 1, Beltane* (below).

December 21, Yule — also known as Winter Solstice, the shortest day and longest night of the year, and the birthday of the sun. Yule is a time of joy and hope as the sun is "reborn."

February 2, Imbolc — also known as Oimelc, Brigid, and Candlemas. Between Yule and Spring Equinox, this is a time to honor Brigid, Goddess of poetry, work, and healing.

March 22, Spring Equinox — also known as Oestar, Eastre, Ostara, or Easter, the Goddess of spring. The days and nights are of equal length, and it is time to start the garden, sow the seeds, and plan and initiate new projects or life changes. On this occasion people celebrate the renewal of life and the endless cycle of rebirth, as symbolized by the egg.

May 1, Beltane — also known as May Day, May Eve, and Walpurgis Night. Between Spring Equinox and Summer Solstice. Traditionally this is a time for lovers to celebrate together, to embrace lying in the fields, sharing in and contributing to the fertile energy of the warming earth. Beltane marks the beginning of the light half of the solar year. Compare *October 31, Samhain,* above.

June 21, Summer Solstice — also known as Midsummer Eve or Litha. The longest day and shortest night of the year. After this night, the days begin to shorten, so this is called the death of the Sun King.

August 2, Lammas (pronounced to rhyme with *Thomas*) — also known as Lughnasad or Lughnassadh (pronounced *loo-noss-sad*). Between Summer Solstice and Fall Equinox. This is the time to rejoice in the first fruits of the season.

September 22, Fall Equinox — also known as Mabon or Harvest Home. This major harvest or thanksgiving festival is again a time when day and night are in balance; that is, they are of equal length. People celebrate by sharing their bounty at feasts and perhaps planting a winter garden. This is a time to slow down and rest, to enjoy all kinds of blessings — especially families and friends.

Contributors

Anna Korn is a Witch, biologist, tree-planter, and former member of the Reclaiming Collective, priestess of a Gardnerian coven in Berkeley, California, as well as an initiate of the Feri tradition of Witchcraft. (page 302)

Anne Hill is a writer, musician, educator, and former member of Reclaiming Collective. She is co-author of the forthcoming book *Circle Round: Raising Children in Goddess Tradition*, and runs Serpentine Music, a Pagan music distribution company. She lives with her extended family in Sonoma County, California. (pages 102, 167, 210)

Beth Elaine Carlson, a Witch in the Reclaiming tradition, lives with her husband and his father, Bill, in the home in western Massachusetts where they were all caregivers for her mother-in-law, Carol, who died of COPD. She cleans houses for a living, leads drumming circles, writes, and creates. Beth was initiated into the mysteries of death by her feline familiars, Isis and Odin. (page 225)

Beverly Frederick, Reclaiming priestess, is a teacher, dancer, drummer, and devoted yogini, and a student of the redwood forest. Her magical practice is nourished by her students and teachers around the world and deepened by her work leading yoga, meditation, and group healing for people with cancer. She offers priestess training at her home in Northern California's Russian River and throughout the U.S. and Canada with Starhawk, The Reclaiming Collective and her partner Douglas. (page 51)

Carol Christmas is a Witch and feminist, animal rights activist, astrologer, Tarot reader, artist, and creative art therapist. Carol lives in Hamden, Connecticut, with her partner of twenty-two years. They have seven cats. (page 203)

Deborah Ann Light, M.A. and Hedgewitch, was diagnosed in 1994 with inoperable large-cell lung cancer caused by cigarette smoking. She researches death in the first person in Sag Harbor, New York. (pages 307, 331, 335, 337)

Deborah Cooper, also known by the magical name Oak, has been a part of the Reclaiming community since the early 1980s. She spent many years exploring the blending of politics and magic in the coven Matrix. She has also worked in a Reclaiming women's coven, Wind Hags, and is currently in the Feri coven Triskits. An initiated priestess of the Reclaiming and Feri traditions, Deborah is a seasoned psychotherapist and artist; she lives in the Mission District of San Francisco with her family. (pages 85, 263)

Dennis Irvine is a Witch and Pirate, an occasional writer, once-in-a-while artist, sometimes poet, near scientist, and healer. He earns his living as a handyman. He would reclaim the terms *dilettante* and *philistine* if he knew more about them. (page 225)

Diana L. Paxson is an author, Witch, and priestess, founder of Fellowship of the Spiral Path, and elder in both the Covenant of the Goddess and Ring of Troth. She is known for her mystical historical novels, the most recent of which are *Sword of Fire and Shadow* (in the Fionn MacCumhail trilogy), and *The Lord of Horses* (in the Wodan's Children trilogy). She is working on a book about the spirituality of menopause, and contributes a regular column on goddesses to *Sagewoman.* (pages 107, 156)

Donald L. Engstrom is an artist, gardener, and Witch priestess living and thriving in the heart of the Ghost Prairie. The Widow Engstrom is also a devotee of the Queer God and is committed to the continuing exploration of the Queer Spirit. Donald has been deeply committed to the growing and nurturance of healthy communities of balance, beauty, and delight for over twenty-five years. Aric Arthur Graf and Donald LaVerne Engstrom were married for twenty-four years and forty-one days. (pages 40, 193, 291, 299)

Douglas Orton is a bard, writer, musician, and facilitator. His articles have appeared in *The Green Egg, Green Man, The Reclaiming Newsletter,* and a forthcoming book on raising Pagan children, *Circle Round.* He and his partner, Beverly, teach magic and ritual with the Reclaiming

Collective through their school, Vela Danza, deep in the cool woods of the Russian River country in Northern California. (page 51)

Elsa DieLöwin is mother of two children and a Witch. She makes herself available to the Santa Cruz, California, community for counseling, rituals, and teaching. She is active with Circle of Fools, The Index, and Covenant of the Goddess. (pages 214, 332)

Harold L. Oak Sawyer spent the sixties trying to make sense of Christianity as the chaplain at Hiram College in Ohio. In 1968 he left the ministry, the church, and Ohio to return to school in Berkeley, where he learned much in the streets and in the classroom. Mainly he learned that while he might not be able to change the world, he could certainly change himself. So with wife and three kids, he moved to the coastal hills of Northern California, where he took up a back-to-the-land lifestyle, earning his way as a carpenter and gardener. Poetry he does for fun. (page 292)

Jenny Sill-Holeman is an initiate and teacher of the Feri tradition and a certified hypnotherapist. She see her clients in an office in a 130-year-old Victorian with the unlikely but appropriate name of Bright Eagle Mansion. She lives and practices magic with her husband and a very witchy black cat in Redwood City, California. (page 91)

Judy Harrow holds a master's degree in counseling. She is High Priestess of Proteus Coven in New York City and is handfast spouse of Mevlannen Beshderen, who also contributed to this book. (page 246)

Kate Slater is a solitary elder working with the Covenant of Gaia Church in Alberta. Her bones grow old in winter cold, and "Harm none" is written on her blade. Death is no stranger. (pages 114, 327)

Lady Bachu writes from a ridgetop in the Sonoma wine region of Northern California. Mystos/priestess/poet/lesbian, Lady Bachu is a co-founder of the MoonWyse coven. Her current projects include a collection of short stories and poetry called "Sparks from the Wheel." Her work appears in *Woman of Spirit, The Green Egg,* and other Pagan and technical publications. (page 205)

Laura Kemp is a member of the Reclaiming Collective. Her primary acts of devotion are creating Goddess-inspired arts (using fabric, ceramic, and other media) and public altar-building. (frontispiece)

Lauren Liebling has realized her girlhood dream and become an expatriate. She works as a neo-Reichian therapist and lives in London with her daughter, husband, and regulation Witch's cat. She writes the occasional poem and is honored to have liturgy still moving through her—and that, for the moment, is that. (page 298)

Lee Henrikson is a priestess and Witch of the Feri tradition. She is active in Covenant of the Goddess and is a former member of the Reclaiming Collective. To remind herself of the cycles of the Earth, she gardens organically and composts. Aikido and computer networking are two other arts that she practices. (page 83)

M. A. Bovis discovered in 1987 that she is a Witch. She is an avid Tarotist. Her magical work is informed by the Twelve Steps. (pages 126, 128, 282, 286)

M. Macha NightMare, in addition to working with the Reclaiming Collective, has served on both local and national boards of CoG (Covenant of the Goddess, a national organization of Witches). She has been a featured presenter at the Harvest Moon Celebration, produced by ESP (Educational Society for Pagans) in Southern California, as well as a panelist, moderator, and workshop-giver at Ancient Ways Festivals and PantheaCons, both in Northern California. She is currently collaborating with Sam Webster, M.Div., Mage, on a series of workshops called "So Many God/desses, So Little Time: Exploring Pagan Deity Yoga." She can sometimes be seen black-winged, viewing the scene from a distance. Her matron is Kali Ma. (pages 135, 294)

Mara June Quicklightning is a voice teacher, composer, improviser, inventor of hums (public participatory vocal events), and member of two jazz ensembles—one in Los Angeles and one in Zurich. She broadcasts avant garde music, with live performances and interviews, on radio. (pages 167, 298)

Mara Lynn Keller, Ph.D. *(Yale, 1991),* is Associate Professor of Women's Spirituality, Philosophy, and Religion at the California Institute of Integral Studies, and a Rosen Method Bodywork practitioner. Her research and writing focus on the Eleusian Mysteries of Demeter and Persephone, Ancient Crete, ecofeminism, and social movements for human rights, social justice, and peace. (page 50)

Marta Benavides is a Salvadoran living and working in her country to implement sustainability for quality of life and durable peace. In that process, rural communities, peasant and indigenous groups, and cooperatives participate in cooperation with concerned urban people and university communities in the construction of El Salvador after the twelve-year civil war. (page 217)

Mary K. Greer is the author of *Women of the Golden Dawn: Rebels and Priestesses*, a biography of four nineteenth-century magicians, and four books on the Tarot. A well-known promoter of Tarot as a tool for conscious living, she has an educational center, Tools and Rites of Transformation, in Nevada City, California, and a website at www.nccn.net/~tarot/. (page 112)

Medicine Story (Manitonquat), Wampanoag elder and ceremonial leader, reevaluation counseling teacher and liberation reference person for native people of eastern North America, is the author of *Return to Creation* and *The Children of the Morning Light*, and editor of *Heritage*, a native liberation journal. (page 68)

Mevlannen Beshderen is a Wiccan priestess intimately acquainted with the ways of sickness, death, and tears, having been quite ill from time to time. She is happily married to Judy Harrow, who also contributed to this book, and makes her home in southwestern Alberta. She is editor of three rather obscure Wiccan journals: *Dayshift*, *Six Roads*, and *The Braidbook*. (page 46)

Minerva Earthschild is a Reclaiming Witch, priestess, poet, and yogini. She has facilitated workshops and rituals for women healing from abortion since 1984. She also teaches magic and yoga, has two daughters and a son with special needs, and works as a mediator, attorney, and children's advocate. (pages 222, 237)

Patricia Devin is an elder priestess of Moon Birch Grove in Los Angeles. She is a former co–national public information officer of the Covenant of the Goddess. (page 256)

Patricia Michael is an experienced social and environmental activist, designer, lecturer, and educator who has produced many educational events in the USA, Europe, Canada, Mexico, and Central America. She has lived, practiced, and taught ecological design that strives to maximize both human and nature's potential. She graduated Magna

Cum Laude from Wichita State University, received her Master of Fine Arts from the University of Oklahoma, is a graduate of the New Alchemy Institute (Ecology and Sustainable Agriculture) and a Vice Chancellor of the International Permaculture Academy in Talguin, Australia. Her studies have been cross disciplinary in art, agriculture, human development, environmental design, health, and social organizing systems. (page 173)

Richard Goering follows an eclectic, intuitive spiritual path that he makes up as he goes along, combining elements of neo-Paganism and Tibetan Buddhism. Walking in the woods is one of his primary spiritual practices. (page 167)

Rose May Dance, Reclaiming Collective member, is a priestess and Witch who teaches and crafts ritual and magic. She works with IV drug users who have HIV. Death and life have been presenting a fugue to Rose lately: she has been caregiver to a friend who was dying of AIDS but is now flourishing; in 1994 Rose's mother died and within three weeks Rose and her birth daughter were reunited; and in 1996 Rose's father died and within three weeks Rose began the process of bringing her new baby daughter into her life, through adoption. Rose wonders what is next. (pages 28, 276)

Sharon Jackson is a familiar name to those who have attended Vancouver, Missouri, or West Virginia Witchcamps (intensive summer workshops) over the last six years. An artist, gardener, and passionate and funny woman, she has also worked as a palliative care volunteer in Vancouver, B.C. (page 123)

Sophia Rosenberg is an artist, writer, and teacher. She teaches Reclaiming tradition magic with the Stone Soup Collective in Victoria, B.C., and at Witchcamps. (page 211)

Sparky T. Rabbit is a Faggot Witch from Illinois. A singer and songwriter (and a big bear-lovin' bear), he was half of the disbanded Pagan *a capella* duo Lunacy, whose passing he mourns. (page 201)

Starhawk is the author of *The Spiral Dance: A Rebirth of the Ancient Religion of the Great Goddess* (Harper & Row, 1979, 1989), *Dreaming the Dark: Magic, Sex, and Politics* (Beacon, 1982), *Truth or Dare: Encounters with Power, Authority, and Mystery* (Harper & Row, 1987), *The Fifth Sacred Thing* (Bantam, 1992), and *Walking to Mercury* (Bantam, 1997).

Her works have been translated into German, Danish, Italian, Portuguese, and Japanese. A feminist and peace activist, she is one of the foremost voices of ecofeminism, and travels widely in North America and Europe giving lectures and workshops, drawing on her twenty-five years of research and experience in the Goddess movement. She consulted on the films *Goddess Remembered*, *The Burning Times*, and *Full Circle*, directed by Donna Read and produced by the National Film Board of Canada, and is presently at work with Read on a biographical film about archaeologist Marija Gimbutas. Together with Anne Hill and Diane Baker, she is co-writing *Circle Round: Raising Children in the Goddess Tradition*, forthcoming from Bantam. A part-time San Franciscan, she lives primarily in the hills of Cazadero among the wild boar people and works and teaches with the Reclaiming Collective.

T. Thorn Coyle is a Reclaiming tradition priestess and Feri initiate. She is a poet, writer, dancer, teacher, warrior, student, and master dishwasher. Thorn leads workshops in devotional dance and Witchcraft throughout the United States and Canada. She lives in San Francisco in an eclectic Catholic Worker community that runs a soup kitchen and hospice. (pages 16, 19, 22, 54, 75, 135, 150, 244)

Timothy Wallace, also known as the Pitch Black Witch, is a poet, essayist, calligrapher, and practicing Witch who has been involved with spirituality and magic since he was a stammering teenager. He has experienced several brushes with death; once, as a child in a coma, he had Roman Catholic Last Rites said over him. He lives in Northern California with his cat Chutney. (pages 93, 124, 281)

Vibra Willow, priestess of the Labyrinth, also known as Irene Kiebert, is a Reclaiming Witch who works with women in all sorts of ritual settings, including abortion healing. She also teaches magic, has worked with the deaf, has four daughters and two grandchildren, and works as a death penalty defense lawyer. (pages 93, 237, 339)